Revenge in A.

Revenge in Athenian Culture

Fiona McHardy

B L O O M S B U R Y
LONDON · NEW DELHI · NEW YORK · SYDNEY

Bloomsbury Academic
An imprint of Bloomsbury Publishing Plc

50 Bedford Square   1385 Broadway
London   New York
WC1B 3DP   NY 10018
UK   USA

www.bloomsbury.com

Bloomsbury is a registered trade mark of Bloomsbury Publishing Plc

First published in 2008 by Gerald Duckworth & Co. Ltd.
Reprinted by Bloomsbury Academic 2012
Paperback Edition first published 2013

British Library Cataloguing-in-Publication Data
A catalogue record for this book is available from the British Library.

ISBN: HB: 978-0-7156-3569-8
       PB: 978-1-4725-2434-8

Library of Congress Cataloging-in-Publication Data
A catalog record for this book is available from the Library of Congress.
Reconceiving medical ethics/edited by Christopher Cowley.
p. cm. – (Continuum studies in philosophy)
Includes bibliographical references and index.
ISBN 978-1-4411-2338-1 (hardcover: alk. paper) –
ISBN 978-1-4411-2127-1 (ebook pdf : alk. paper) –
ISBN 978-1-4411-0397-0 (ebook epub : alk. paper)   1. Medical ethics.
I. Cowley, Christopher, 1967– II. Title. III. Series.
R724.R426 2012
174.2–dc23   2011031713

Typeset by Deanta Global Publishing Services, Chennai, India
Printed and bound in Great Britain

Contents

Acknowledgements

This book has been many years in the making and I would like to thank all those who have taken the time to discuss revenge with me and commented on papers I have given on the subject. I would particularly like to thank Richard Seaford for his support and encouragement over the years and for his helpful comments and advice. Tom Harrison, Helen King and Charlotte Behr all gave me valuable guidance in developing the outline of this project for which I am very grateful. I would also like to thank Trevor Dean, David Harvey and Nancy Sorkin Rabinowitz for taking the time to read and comment on drafts of this book. Their help and support during the final stages of writing the book was very much appreciated. Finally I would like to thank Judith Owen for reading through the proofs so carefully.

Introduction

Vengeance has been a hot topic of debate among classical scholars for several years now. Particular attention has been given in recent works to how revenge is represented in various literary genres and whether revenge was suppressed in Athenian society or whether it openly flourished.[1] This book takes a new approach, focusing on motivations for revenge across a range of Greek sources and attempting to explain why revenge is taken in one situation, but not in another. A close examination of the circumstances in which revenge is taken or avoided suggests that reactions vary substantially according to the situation, the individuals involved, the literary genre or author and the particular offence depicted. It is not possible to generalise about revenge saying that it was a popular ethic applauded by all or an evil force in society which was universally rejected.[2] Instead it is necessary to scrutinise each example carefully.[3] It has been argued that a cross-genre approach is problematic,[4] and this is certainly the case if the different genres are treated uncritically. Tragedy in particular delights in exceptional and problematic revenge acts among *philoi*,[5] and this needs to be considered when using the plays as evidence for Athenian thoughts about revenge.[6] Indeed, none of the sources is entirely straightforward and none can tell us completely reliably about revenge in everyday life at Athens. However, it becomes clear that ancient authors, and apparently Athenian citizens in general, were inspired by mythical examples and earlier literary representations of revenge, in particular those found in the Homeric epics.[7] Because of this connection, these sources offer valuable evidence for gaining a better understanding of revenge in Athenian society and should not be excluded from consideration.

The book is divided into chapters looking at four key areas: the different responses to homicide (Chapter 1), to sexual offences against women (Chapter 2), to raiding, theft and attacks on property (Chapter 3) and to insults and threats to power (Chapter 4).[8] In the final chapter, Orestes' multiple motives for his attack on Clytemnestra and Aegisthus are examined in detail. The aim of the study is to determine where violent responses are most prominent, where other types of responses occur and where responses are averted or there is said to be no response at all. Although commentators most frequently associate revenge with violent responses, other types of response are also categorised here as 'revenge' where they can be shown to be vengeful in spirit.[9] The vexed problem of defining what

1

constitutes revenge is discussed in the next section of this introduction. Throughout, the insights of anthropologists and evolutionary psychologists are utilised to inform our understanding of vengeance in ancient society and to suggest reasons for the patterns depicted in the sources.

What constitutes revenge?

Difficulties in determining what constitutes revenge are at the heart of many of the recent scholarly debates and disagreements. In particular the putative distinction between (private) revenge and (civic) punishment, advocated by philosophers ancient and modern, is central to this debate, leading some scholars to conclude that in a legal context men can inflict only punishment, not revenge.[10] As Allen notes: 'Our intuition says that punishment resembles but finally differs from revenge; punishment is legitimate, but revenge is not.'[11] This 'intuition', based in part on the negative connotations of the word 'revenge' in modern English,[12] has led Allen in her book to assign the term 'revenge' only to those acts which are portrayed in a negative light, and to use the word 'punishment' instead.[13] However, as Allen herself has convincingly argued, an examination of the ancient evidence shows that this clear-cut distinction between revenge and punishment cannot be sustained.[14] In particular, the involvement of private individuals in the detection and prosecution of public and private cases at Athens means that prosecutions were not necessarily dispassionate and that the motivations of individuals bringing actions were not always aimed at civic justice, but were often self-interested.[15] The context of the law court is not in itself sufficient to make calls for retribution by prosecutors the type of 'punishment' outlined by philosophers.[16] Nor is the fact that a prosecutor does not attack his opponents violently an indication that his actions constitute 'punishment' not 'revenge'.[17] Instead the attitudes of the participants, their emotions and their motivations frequently indicate that their prosecutions are vengeful in spirit and therefore not proper civic punishment.[18] That revenge does not need to be a violent act and that prosecution can be conceived of as vengeful in spirit is evidenced in the New Testament passage in which Christ teaches that it is better to 'turn the other cheek' rather than take revenge. Immediately after this famous comment, he goes on to say that it is better not to take a man to court over the loss of a cloak (Matthew 5:38-40). This passage suggests that it was commonly perceived that a man suing another in court for a piece of property was motivated by ideas of vengeance when he did so.

Authors can express that a reaction is conceived of as 'vengeful in spirit' in their texts through a combination of some or all of the following indicative elements: (i) vocabulary and metaphors referring to the transfer of honour, payment or just deserts, (ii) reference to emotions (especially anger) driving a response, (iii) participants making assessments and valuations of the response in comparison with the original offence, (iv) creation of causal links between act and response, (v) speeches given by participants explaining the motivations for their actions.[19]

The first of these elements is perhaps the most controversial as the translation of the pertinent Greek terminology into English is notoriously difficult.[20] There is also the added difficulty of perceiving where Greek words shift in meaning according to time, place and genre.[21] In particular there is disagreement over whether the words τιμωρία (and cognates) and δίκη shift in meaning from 'vengeance' where a violent retribution is described, to 'punishment' when they are used in the Attic law courts.[22] However, the use of the word τιμωρία in Demosthenes 21 (*Against Midias*)[23] to describe both Eueon's violent retaliatory attack following an insult (21.75), and Demosthenes' own idea that men should retaliate through the laws, not violently (21.76) indicates that a clear-cut distinction of this nature does not work well.[24] Elsewhere Demosthenes uses the same word in maintaining that there is a difference between legal and private reactions (πλεῖστον δὲ δήπου διαφέρει τὸν νόμον κύριον τῆς τιμωρίας ἢ τὸν ἐχθρὸν γίγνεσθαι, 23.32). Here τιμωρία occurs in both cases, but Demosthenes argues that only when it is legal is it done properly.[25] It is clear from these examples that Demosthenes distinguishes violent from legal reactions, but it is not clear that he intends to say that legal reactions are not vengeful in spirit. Rather than assigning precise meanings to the Greek vocabulary, then, it is perhaps better to be aware of each word's nexus of possible meanings and of the application of certain common metaphors with reference to revenge. Because of these difficulties with the exact interpretation of the Greek terminology, a specific piece of vocabulary alone cannot be used to determine whether an act should be considered vengeful or not. As such the focus of this volume is not on the ancient Greek vocabulary, but on patterns and themes associated with revenge acts in ancient texts.

Some of these themes and patterns are alluded to in the metaphorical significance of the relevant Greek terms and in their etymologies.[26] Τιμωρία and cognates are connected etymologically to τιμή, a term usually translated as 'honour'.[27] Saïd notes that the word group (seen first in Aeschylus *Persians* 473) is derived from a combination of τιμή and ὄρομαι, meaning that an avenger is a man who 'watches over honour'.[28] Scholars have suggested that 'watching over' τιμή was of great importance not only in the Homeric epics, in which, as van Wees has argued, heroes engaged in a struggle for prestige,[29] but also in Athenian society, where it was a prize which Athenians could win (or risk losing) through public competition and recognition.[30] Any perceived loss of honour, then, through insult (ὕβρις) or slight (ὀλιγωρία) might lead to an angry counterattack by a man keen to restore what he had lost.[31] Anger (ὀργή) is the driving force behind τιμωρία following loss of honour, as noted by Aristotle (*Rhet.* 1378a30-2, cf. 1369b11-12) among others.[32] By retaliating against the culprit with like insult or attack, the avenger attempted to make the man who had attacked him suffer matching humiliation and loss of honour in turn.[33] Τιμωρία, therefore, be it violent or legal, aimed at rebalancing the levels of honour which an original attack or insult had left unbalanced.[34]

This idea of 'achieving a balance', which is apparent in the imagery of payment and exchange frequently associated with revenge, can be detected in the Greek terminology. Τίσις and cognates are connected to ideas of payment ranging from the metaphor of payment akin to the English expression 'to pay the price' in authors such as Homer and Herodotus, to the payment of fines.[35] The metaphorical sense of this word implies that a wrongdoer is thought to owe a debt to his victim which he must pay for in kind or in compensation.[36] Orestes, for example, is said to have wanted 'payment' (τίσις) for the murder of Agamemnon and the loss of his patrimony, and Aegisthus is said to have 'paid' in full for everything he did (νῦν δ' ἀθρόα· πάντ' ἀπέτισεν) (*Odyssey* 1.29-43). Here the inflicting of a harm is the inflicting of a loss which the perpetrator has to repay,[37] or, as Miller suggests, the insults of a wrongdoer are like gifts that must be repaid.[38] By attacking the wrongdoer in revenge, the victim or his kin seek to equalise the exchange.[39] The idea of 'getting even' is that the perpetrator will suffer what he inflicted at the hands of the victim. Lloyd notes the 'essentially imitative quality of revenge, which leads avengers to replicate the brutality of their enemies'.[40] Ideas of balance and equivalence are also associated with justice, especially through the image of the scales.[41] Some of these ideas are implicit in the Greek term δίκη (seen first in Hesiod *Works and Days* 238-9), which has a basic meaning of 'settlement' in early texts.[42] It is later connected with the concept of 'exchange of justice' between the original attacker and the avenger in phrases such as λαμβάνειν δίκην (take justice) and διδόναι δίκην (give justice).[43] These terms are used equally of violent and of legal responses.

However, difficulties exist with determining what constitutes a fair balance and authors depict participants making calculations of what they believe to be fair according to the circumstances. Needless to say, though, their calculations do not always match. Miller has stressed how opponents will place different values on their losses and it is unlikely that they will agree on their assessment of what is fair.[44] The problem of making an accurate assessment to balance the wrong committed is made clear by Demosthenes' story of the one-eyed man who suggests a change in the Locrian law of 'an eye for an eye' (24.139-41). He argues that if his one eye were knocked out, the person who did it should lose both his eyes in return. The Locrians accept his arguments, judging them to be just.[45] This story demonstrates a keen interest in questions of equality and balance in retributive justice in ancient Greece. While the simple equation of 'an eye for an eye' appears at first glance to be fair, the circumstances of the particular case must be considered before conclusions can be drawn.[46]

Images in a text of an angry individual desiring to get even, obtain just deserts, receive payment in kind and regain lost honour all go some way

4

to suggesting that a reaction is conceived of as vengeful. However, authors often go further than this to suggest that an act should be conceived of as revenge. Authorial connection of events to create a tale in which action is followed by reaction is one key method. A second is having characters express their motivations for action linking their current attack with some previous offence or perceived wrong on the part of the target (or the target's *philoi*). In this way authors can build a picture of revenge by linking events in a chain of causality.

Herodotus is particularly prone to representing events in this way, as de Romilly has noted.[47] Herodotus frequently describes ancient disputes in terms of vengeance of a personal, individual nature, even when an explanation of a more abstract, political nature might be expected.[48] The linking of two possibly unrelated events to suggest vengeful motives can be seen clearly in his account of Demaratus, king of Sparta. Herodotus maintains that Demaratus made an enemy of Leotychides when he carried off his fiancée by force. Leotychides is later said to prosecute Demaratus, swearing in court that he was not the true son of Ariston, thereby showing that Demaratus had no right to the throne (Herodotus 6.65). Placing these two stories side by side suggests a link between them – that Leotychides acted out of anger at Demaratus' theft of his fiancée when he decided to depose him. However, it is possible to explain these events in a very different way. Herodotus suggests that Leotychides was motivated to speak against Demaratus because of the encouragement of Cleomenes (who desired a more co-operative co-ruler in order to push forward his political intrigues) and because he would rule in Demaratus' place. Following the deposition of Demaratus, Leotychides does indeed succeed to his throne (6.67.2). His political motivations to act could therefore have formed the core of a different telling of this story which did not mention the theft of the woman at all.[49]

This story reveals several things about the nature of revenge in ancient Greek texts. First, the passage presents an idea of revenge taken against an enemy through a non-violent, non-conventional method: the public announcement of illegitimacy ensures the demise of Demaratus' political career. Christ has suggested that Athenian politicians employed similar methods of revenge: 'A harmed party could wait for an opportunity to take vengeance on his foe by bringing a suit against him alleging a direct harm to the city.'[50]

Second, it is not necessary to use specific 'revenge' vocabulary to suggest that a reaction is vengeful. By implying that Demaratus' original action led to Leotychides' hostile reaction, Herodotus provides a vengeful motive for Leotychides. Indeed the story only becomes a tale of revenge (rather than a tale of political wrangles over power) because of the way the acts are interpreted by the author and presented in the text. In Herodotus' story, the theft is seen as the starting point of the enmity between the two men and the cause of Leotychides' later hostility towards Demaratus, perhaps giving Leotychides a publicly acceptable justification for his actions, rather than purely selfish motivations. Elsewhere establishing the starting point of a dispute (who threw the first punch) is important for Greeks in that a man who responds to an attack on him gains greater sympathy than a man who attacks for no reason.[51] Naturally enough, though, participants do not always agree on the starting point for a dispute and there is also a tendency to recall past grievances or to dredge up long-forgotten disagreements in order to provide justification for an attack.[52]

Third, although this tale may not tell us about the real-life motivations of the characters involved, it does provide insight into the kind of actions which might be thought to provoke a vengeful reaction. In this story, Demaratus is said to have stolen Leotychides' fiancée – a crime of the type which often elicits very strong reactions, according to the sources.[53] It is therefore unsurprising to the reader that Leotychides would decide to attack Demaratus in turn. His decision to aim at Demaratus' status and power in Herodotus' tale is also a notable one in that the evidence suggests that status and power are very highly prized assets which are rigorously defended by Greek men, both for their own sake and because of the additional benefits they bring with them, such as greater access to women and wealth.[54]

Why take revenge?

Herodotus' story points to the kind of offence thought to make a man angry and vengeful. Desire to take revenge in these circumstances is natural enough and readily understood, but not everyone decides to act on their anger and take revenge.[55] Usually it is argued that people can suppress this desire according to cultural or other constraints.[56] I want to place a slightly different slant on the issue, suggesting that men are most likely to act in revenge in support of their own interests and that the individual circumstances of each case are important in determining whether someone takes revenge. Certainly the views of others are of significance. If support is not forthcoming from others, this can make taking revenge more difficult and risky. In his story, Herodotus suggests that Leotychides did not strike Demaratus physically, but found another way to get back at him. It is possible to speculate that without public support for a physical attack or public acceptance that physical revenge in such circumstances is acceptable, attacking a king of Sparta might be unduly dangerous.[57] Instead Leotychides manages to promote himself at the same time as attacking his enemy in Herodotus' version of events.[58]

Anthropologists have stressed that individual actors make decisions based on calculations of benefits and risks. Boehm writing on Montenegro, Herzfeld writing on Crete, Peters writing on the Bedouin and Wilson writing on Corsica have all emphasised the importance of rational decision making by individuals involved in taking revenge.[59] Milovan Djilas, whose

6

autobiography contains many examples of individuals going against the norms of Montenegrin society, contrasts the simplistic ideals of folk-songs with the many-sided reality of life, commenting: 'Man is not simple, even when he is of one piece. That piece has many corners and sides.'[60] People do not blindly follow cultural rules as if by habit, but are involved in what Boehm terms 'social engineering'.[61] This means that when scholars of antiquity remark that revenge was obligatory or prescribed, they are oversimplifying matters.[62] According to the individual circumstances, actions can be interpreted benignly or aggression can follow. For example, if you are touched by a lover this could be erotic, if touched by a friend this could mean nothing, and if touched by a stranger this could make you angry or repelled.[63] Miller stresses that men can get out of difficult situations by offering up a benign reading of events (e.g. they can maintain that the act was accidental).[64] Such readings are based on the perceived costs and benefits of acting in any given circumstance.[65]

The evidence suggests that men often decide to take the largest risks in order to protect valuable possessions and assets, in particular women, livestock and other valuable property. Achieving higher status than others and fighting over power are also important reasons for acting aggressively and hence, revenge is frequently associated with disputes over status and power. Revenge in these circumstances is the tool with which a man protects the possessions he owns and with which he threatens all who desire to attack his belongings. Oatley and Jenkins say:

> Fighting fuelled by anger, in our species as in certain other mammalian species, functions at least in part as the lever of individual power to control resources, including the resources of access to females.[66]

Revenge here has a deterrent quality in that it aims to show others that a man is not weak and that any attacks on him or his family will not benefit the attacker. By reacting to threats a man might make others think twice before attacking him or trying to take his belongings.[67] When seen like this, revenge is a survival technique which helps men to survive and prosper. Scholars have suggested that the 'tit-for-tat' approach is a very successful social strategy, because competitors will avoid you and co-operators will seek you out.[68] Greek evidence suggests that reciprocity of this nature (doing good to friends and harm to enemies) was felt to be a useful guiding principle.[69]

This analysis has been influenced by the ideas of both anthropologists and evolutionary psychologists. The former tend towards culturally specific explanations of revenge behaviour, while the latter prefer more universal explanations. At first glance it might appear, then, that these two methods are mutually exclusive and that it is not possible to combine them. However, this absolute dichotomy between cultural and universal explanations cannot be maintained. Instead, it is clear that a combination of 'natural' and 'cultural' factors is important in understanding revenge.[70] My account has been much influenced by the work of the historian Brian Ferguson who argues well that material self-interest is a strong motivating factor underlying disputes.[71] Certainly the Greek evidence presented here suggests that men are very likely to run risks and to attempt revenge when there are material gains to be made. However, it is not sufficient to say that men fight to get more land or money without then asking why they require this additional wealth. This is where the evolutionary-psychological perspective enters the picture. Superior technology in weapons or tools can allow a man to acquire greater wealth through fighting or farming and this in turn can enhance his status and mean that he is able to attract better marriage partners.[72] Here wealth and status are desired not just for their own sakes (although this is also relevant), but also because of the better reproductive prospects they bring with them. The all-important interest of Greek men in having children to continue in their bloodlines is certainly attested in the sources. Indeed the importance of securing and protecting female reproductive resources and the significance of offspring and the male bloodline are central themes in some of the most well-known Greek myths (e.g. the story of the Trojan war, Odysseus and the suitors, the Oresteia story and the tale of Jason and Medea).[73]

The patterns for revenge suggested in the following chapters support these theories. The sources make it clear that revenge is not an automatic response, but that calculations are made and that the individual participants evaluate the situation to decide whether revenge is in their own interests or not. Sexual attacks on another man's women appear to drive some of the most violent and aggressive responses both in myth and in historical accounts. Attacks on property, status and power also prompt violent revenge at times, although there is also some tendency to reconciliation in these cases, especially where men feel too weak to act or they do not believe they can benefit from taking revenge. Notably, though, cases of homicide are the least readily associated with revenge attacks by Greek men across all the sources. Without other compelling motives, the evidence suggests that men are more willing to settle and compromise in cases of homicide than in any other cases. Detailed discussion of this subject follows now in Chapter 1.

1

A Life for a Life

Blood revenge for a homicide, where a killer is killed in turn by relatives of his victim, is often thought to be a natural response following the death of a loved one.[1] Revenge in these circumstances aims at re-establishing a balance following the loss of a life, and avengers pay careful attention to notions of equality and to assessments of their victims' worth. Such assessments of worth are carried through into laws relating to homicide and wounding. Blood revenge of this type is often conceived of as part of an endless cycle of reciprocal killings forming a blood feud or vendetta between two families. However, there is little evidence to suggest that blood feuds were rife in ancient Greece; there is instead a tendency in the extant texts to show attempts at settlements and compromises following a homicide. A close examination of the Greek textual evidence suggests that although an ideal of revenge on behalf of kin is frequently expressed, family members might not act without other compelling motivations such as financial or political gains and men are depicted making careful calculations before leaping into action. Most frequently, the exile of the killer is deemed a suitable exchange for the loss of life of a family member. Alternatively monetary compensation might be accepted or another form of settlement brokered. In particular in peacetime situations blood revenge tends to be eschewed, although in war opponents are free to avenge their comrades by killing their enemies on the battlefield. While men are often portrayed preferring expediency to the demands of blood revenge, women are closely associated in the texts with desiring blood revenge whatever the risks and with rejecting attempts to settle or compromise. This accounts for some of the most notable instances of blood revenge in Greek literature, as will be discussed towards the end of this chapter.

Achieving a balance

When exacting blood revenge anthropologists note that the usual exchange to achieve fairness following a homicide is a life for a life.[2] This is expressed in modern proverbs such as 'There should be one grave opposite the other grave.'[3] That balance in reciprocity lies at the heart of ancient blood revenge too is made clear by Aeschylus' chorus in *Choephori* who proclaim that it is traditional for further blood to be shed in exchange for blood spilt in murder (ἀλλὰ νόμος μὲν φονίας σταγόνας / χυμένας ἐς πέδον ἄλλο προαιτεῖν / αἷμα, 400-2).[4] Blood here is an important symbol: for the taking of enemy blood through a vengeance killing restores the blood lost by blood relatives. 'Blood for blood' is the clear equivalent of 'life for life' or 'death for death'. The biblical law of 'an eye for an eye', otherwise known as the *lex talionis*,[5] appears to be an encoding of this principle of fairness and balance (Deuteronomy 19:21; Exodus 21:22-7; Leviticus 24:19-20; cf. Matthew 5:38-40).[6] Similarly, Antiphon says that Athenian homicide law decrees that a murderer must pay with his own life in requital, the Greek term expressing 'a death for a death' (ἀνταποθανεῖν, 5.10). In this respect, the law enshrines a principle which is familiar to those who react violently to murder.[7] Although it was possible to avoid death by going into exile (and potentially to avoid losing an eye by paying a fine),[8] these laws testify to the underlying desire to achieve balance and equality in legal reciprocity.[9]

As explained by the scholars of talionic law, this drive towards equality and balance can be seen as an attempt to limit excessive responses.[10] The prevention of escalation is cited by Demosthenes (54.18-19) as the reasoning behind Attic laws regulating insults, punches, wounding and murder.[11] However, the effectiveness of these codes and laws at preventing such escalation is somewhat doubtful. It might be felt that the balance can only be met by a stronger response. For example, participants might perceive that the death of a chief requires double revenge to restore the balance.[12] Alternatively, what is deemed fair recompense for an accident might not be thought fair in a case of deliberate harm. Demosthenes stresses that the level of resentment felt against someone who deliberately set out to hurt you will not be the same as against someone who hurt you by accident (21.43). Differences between modes of attack can also cause problems in assessing what response will create a fair balance. Lysias claims that Polemarchus was put to death without a trial although he had not done any private or public wrong (12.17-20).[13] Because of this, he claims, sufficient revenge (δίκην λάβοιμεν) against Eratosthenes is not possible, even if he is put to death along with his children, since he has been tried justly (12.83), while Lysias' brothers and father were killed untried.[14] This is a very important example as it demonstrates how participants assess the losses they have made and how they desire to have them paid. Lysias does not believe that he can achieve equal balance for the loss of his relatives through the courts even if all of Eratosthenes' relatives were put to death with him. However the example also shows the value put on due process by Lysias. Justice can only properly be achieved through the laws. Lysias makes a comparable argument in *Against Agoratus* (13.78) where General Anytus argues that the democrats should not kill Agoratus outright, but should wait to be returned to power then seek revenge (τιμωρήσοιντο) through the laws.[15] The contradiction between the demands of due process and the desire for equality in revenge causes difficulties here for the Athenians.

1. A Life for a Life

Kin-help

It is frequently said that in the absence of civic authorities and legal institutions blood revenge by relatives is the normal reaction (or even the necessary reaction) to a homicide. Where there is no alternative legal system, participants must resort to self-help.[16] 'If aggrieved parties did not take the initiative in redressing their grievances, nobody else would.'[17] Their natural helpers are the members of their own family group. Daly and Wilson explain that ties of blood will lead people to take risks to ensure future gains for their descendants.[18] Siblings each have a stake in each other's survival and reproductive success, since nieces and nephews are vehicles of fitness although they are less valuable than one's own children.[19] When you must defend yourself, brute strength is the most important quality, measured by the number of men and weapons a group can produce.[20] The cultural preference for male offspring is explained by the desire for family groups to feel strong and able to defend themselves (cf. Herodotus 1.136).[21] This means that kin are very supportive of one another and the killing of blood kin is very rare. Relatives are far more likely to collaborate with one another in violence than to commit violence against each other.[22] According to statistical analyses, kinship in general mitigates conflict, especially among close agnatic kin.[23] The commonality of interest between genetic relatives makes killing one another especially anomalous and, in fact, murder in the family is not as frequent as is often believed. In modern statistical analyses from North America and Europe, most homicides are committed by acquaintances, then strangers, then spouses.[24] Murder of blood kin is also less common than is generally believed in Greek literature, even in a genre like Attic tragedy where harm to *philoi* lies at the heart of almost every plot.[25] Obviously if the battle is within a family, the two sides will only be further weakened by attacking each other and taking revenge at all may be seen as counterproductive.[26] Isaeus points out that revenge on kin brings no consolation, only double the misfortune (1.6). In such instances it may be considered more prudent to do nothing rather than pursuing revenge.

Anthropologists note that close agnatic male kin are the most likely avengers,[27] although in the Greek sources comrades at war, guest-friends and the gods (through acts of divine anger) are also conceived of as possible avengers of homicide. Many scholars of the ancient world have discussed the idea of blood revenge as 'kin-help'.[28] These ideas are based primarily on proverbs and sayings about the justice and honour of avenging a dead kinsman. For example, in the *Odyssey* it is said to be a good thing to have a son who can avenge you (ἐτίσατο), just as Orestes avenged his father (3.196-8). Similarly, in the *Rhetoric* (1401a38-b1) Aristotle mentions that it is considered just (δίκαιόν ἐστιν) for a son to avenge his father (τῷ πατρί γε τιμωρεῖν τὸν υἱόν).[29] Another commonly expressed sentiment which follows on from this line of thought is: νήπιος ὃς πατέρα κτείνας παῖδας

11

καταλείπει 'Foolish to kill the father and spare the sons' from the lost *Cypria*.[30] The logic of this saying is that sons are expected to desire and seek revenge for their murdered fathers. Therefore it can be dangerous for a killer to allow them the opportunity to do so. These proverbial statements demonstrate the oft-cited link between 'blood' vengeance and blood kinship.[31]

Male kin also act as avengers in Athens by prosecuting in cases of homicide (Demosthenes 43.57 = *IG* 1³.104.20-1; cf. Antiphon 1.1-5). The spear which was carried by relatives at the funeral of a murdered person in Athens symbolised their desire for revenge (Demosthenes 47.69).[32] Kin were morally obliged to act in these cases,[33] and it is possible that it was their exclusive duty to prosecute in cases of homicide.[34] The obligation to avenge a death was occasionally placed upon kin by the dying man himself.[35] A clear example of this appears in Lysias 13 (*Against Agoratus*). Dionysodorus, imprisoned and put to death under the Thirty, instructs his kin to avenge his death. When visited by his wife in jail, he tells her that Agoratus is responsible and charges the speaker (his wife's brother who is also his cousin), his brother and other relatives to avenge him (τιμωρεῖν).[36] He also instructs her to tell their as yet unborn child (if male) to avenge his father (Lysias 13.41-2).[37] His cousin/ brother-in-law brings the case to court, saying that it is his particular responsibility as a relative (13.1).[38]

While it might be maintained that this case calls for punishment not revenge because it is prosecuted through a court, the role of the family discussed in this case is clearly the direct descendant of a system in which family pursue a killer to kill or exile him.[39] In addition, the victim died after being condemned in a trial and so retaliation through prosecution and execution corresponds well with what the victim suffered. Moreover the stress placed on the importance of fulfilling the wishes of the dead man, along with the mention of the personal feelings of the speaker in connection with the prosecution of the alleged killer (13.1-2), show that the desire for personal revenge underlies this case. The speaker further extends the appeal to revenge through his emotional pleas on the part of all the weak family members who have allegedly lost the male relatives who supported them because of the deeds of Agoratus (13.45-6). However, the responsibility and risk of revenge are lightened by the court system since the relatives of the victim are able to share the difficulties of achieving revenge with the citizens of Athens. This is made clear at the outset by the speaker who maintains that the jurors too have a duty to avenge (τιμωρεῖν) those who were put to death as democrats under the Thirty (13.1; cf. 13.48). He further argues that the dying injunctions of the executed men to avenge their murders extend to the jurors too as their friends, not only to their blood relatives (13.92, 94). Later he appeals to the jurors not to support the enemy (the Thirty), but to avenge (τετιμωρηκότες) their friends (13.96-7) because of what they have suffered both as individuals and as citizens of Athens. That the jurors are asked to reflect on the suffering of the victims, of the victims' relatives and on their own suffering when contemplating the fate of Agoratus suggests that personal satisfaction commensurate with revenge is the aim rather than impersonal, objective punishment of a man for his crimes.

Greek sources often portray kin as keen to exact revenge for dead relatives. However, although kin routinely express grief and anger at the death of a relative, leading to a desire for revenge, they also make calculations about the risks of action and are driven by considerations of expediency.[40] This means that revenge is not always an automatic response, but depends upon an individual's circumstances. Blood revenge can be a difficult thing to achieve and many examples reveal that individuals or families felt unable to act on their own without seeking help from more powerful allies.[41] Lack of close male relatives can prove problematic for those who wish to take revenge. Although Telemachus would have liked to settle matters (τίσασθαι) with the suitors earlier (3.205-7), he felt that alone he was too weak. His lack of brothers and cousins and other male relatives (for Odysseus and Laertes are also only sons) puts him at a disadvantage (16.114-21).[42] Here it is stated explicitly that brothers are of help in such a fight as this. Notably Odysseus states that he will treat the cowherd and swineherd as Telemachus' brothers when he recruits them to help him fight against the suitors (21.215-16). Fathers without sons are represented as weak in their old age, unable to defend themselves against enemies (11.494-503; cf. Hesiod *Theog.* 603-7). In Athens, if someone without enfranchised relatives were killed, the murderer could escape prosecution.[43] In the case of the nurse who is killed while preventing the seizure of a drinking cup, her former master is advised against prosecuting the killers for homicide because he is not a relative or her current master (Demosthenes 47.70). This evidence suggests that, even if non-relatives could prosecute for murder, they might not do so unless other strong motives were present because of the risks to themselves.[44] Slaves attacked by their own master were also in a particularly weak position, as there was no one to avenge them (μὴ ἔστιν ὁ τιμωρήσων), as Antiphon points out (6.4).

Because women were deemed too weak to kill a grown man on their own, they were not usually thought of as blood avengers. To overcome this problem, women are frequently shown soliciting help from others to achieve their ends.[45] In Athens their powers to achieve revenge were very limited as they could not take cases to court themselves, but had to persuade men to act for them.[46] Even those women who reached the highest positions in the social hierarchy in places other than Athens are generally represented as too weak to act against men without the aid of other men: their power is restricted to the power of speech by which they can persuade or deceive.[47] Women are also depicted using curses, including suicide curses, to achieve revenge.[48] The fascination of Greek men with the female association with desiring and exhorting blood revenge is reflected in many literary texts, especially Attic tragedies.[49] This subject will be discussed in detail below.[50]

Guests in a foreign land suffer especially from the deprivation of kin and this influences their portrayal. The experiences of Odysseus and his men in the cave of the Cyclops are symbolic of the terrible peril faced by guests in antiquity and the story depicts the fears of travellers. Although Zeus ostensibly protects guests from such danger when visiting overseas, there is no hint in the text that he intervenes in any way to help Odysseus' murdered companions.[51] In theory, a host should protect a guest who is attacked in his house and avenge him, just as Telemachus threatens to kill Ctesippus for physically abusing his guest (*Od.* 20.304-10; cf. Euripides *Hec.* 799-805).[52] Isocrates mentions the killing of guest-friends as unAthenian, barbarian behaviour (12.122; cf. Euripides *Hec.* 1247-8) and Aeschines tells us that on one occasion all the citizens in the assembly and foreigners standing around gave out a cry of protest on hearing of the impious crime of killing a host (3.224). This reaction displays the significance of the guest-friend relationship in the eyes of both Athenians and others.[53] However, in practice it is clear that guests were exceptionally vulnerable to attacks and it is only these feelings of morality and justice which protect them.[54]

Subjects who desire revenge against their rulers are also in a difficult position. Gobryas (with Gadatas) ultimately succeeds in taking revenge against the Assyrian king who murdered his son (τετιμωρημένοι ἦσαν τὸν ἀνόσιον βασιλέα), but he only achieves this with the help of Cyrus and his army (Xenophon *Cyr.* 4.6.2-7, 7.5.26-32).[55] The situation is doubly difficult for Smerdis who is killed by his brother Cambyses after a dream tells Cambyses that Smerdis will sit on the throne of Persia (Herodotus 3.30). Not only is Cambyses a powerful man, he is also the most appropriate avenger of his brother, as Herodotus points out in the following tale. Cambyses' sister-wife is said to have burst into tears after watching a puppy go to help its brother against a lion cub (τὸν σκύλακα τῷ ἀδελφεῷ τιμωρήσαντα). When questioned she explains that her brother, Smerdis, has no one to avenge him (ὡς ἐκείνῳ οὐκ εἴη ὁ τιμωρήσων) (3.32). Later Cambyses realises his error: it is Smerdis the Magus who has seized power in Susa and he has killed the very man who would have avenged him (τιμωρέειν) (3.65; cf. Xenophon *Cyr.* 8.7.14-16). Although this story is clearly invented, it is informative about ancient notions of the behaviour of absolute rulers. They are associated with brutal acts of kin-killing (cf. Isocrates 8.113) and there is not thought to be any appropriate person to intervene or take revenge (cf. also Herodotus 1.92, 3.39).

In a similar way, it is impossible for a mortal to take revenge against the gods or to escape from their revenge (Sophocles *Ajax* 401-4; Xenophon *Anab.* 2.5.7).[56] While gods can attack mortals as they please, mortals cannot take revenge against them (Homer *Il.* 22.18-20). Those who are foolish enough to attempt revenge against the gods do not survive. Amphion is killed attempting to take revenge against the gods for killing his children (Sophocles *Niobe* P.Oxy. 3653 fr. 2) and Neoptolemus is killed demanding restitution from Apollo for the death of his father (Euripides *Andr.* 1002-9; *Or.* 1655-7). A sensible man will avoid such a battle.

Even a strong man supported by many relatives does not necessarily react violently and insist on blood revenge on every occasion, but instead considers the circumstances carefully before acting. This means that individuals will not necessarily take violent revenge following a homicide in their family, even if proverbs or traditions suggest that this is an 'automatic' response. Instead, decisions are made according to perceived costs and benefits.[57] Taking revenge can be a scary and difficult business and many want to avoid the dangers.[58] In addition, the costs of fighting can be too high, since ongoing violence can have a great impact on farming and other activities needed for survival.[59] Individuals and groups make decisions based on self-interest; sometimes no revenge is taken or sometimes a threatened group will move closer to allies to prevent retaliation. Instead of automatically launching a bloody attack, family members need to consider whether it is better for them to accept compensation, to allow the killer to flee the community or (given the appropriate mechanisms) to take the killer to court. It is often when the desire for blood revenge is combined with other compelling motives that action is taken.[60]

Although the choice of prosecution might seem to be the most straight-forward and obvious to us, trials were deemed risky and difficult for the prosecutors as well as the defendants in antiquity. That kin sometimes felt reluctant to act in Athens can be inferred from the custom where a dying man instructs his family to avenge his death discussed above. This custom might be seen as a way of obliging his relatives to prosecute. Plato also implies that relatives might be reluctant to prosecute for murder and suggests that the laws should encourage that they do so with threats of pollution (*Leg.* 871b). Although MacDowell uses Demosthenes 22.2 as evidence that failure to prosecute a homicide was seen as impiety, this particular case refers to patricide and is therefore conceptually different.[61] Instead it seems that those who failed to prosecute for homicide might be deemed cowardly, but could not be forced to bring the case.[62]

Responses to homicide

Evidence across a broad range of ancient Greek sources suggests that taking blood revenge was only one of a range of possible responses to a homicide. In our extant texts the killer is most likely to flee into exile thereby avoiding blood revenge or other penalties. Although Lintott has suggested that exile is a particular response of kin-killers and the weak,[63] exile is the usual response for all killers outside of warfare.[64] Fleeing into exile ensures that the killer is out of the sight of the relatives of the dead man protecting him from their wrath and protecting the community from the horrors of feuding.[65] This point is made clearly by Tyndareus in Euripides' *Orestes* (494-517), who also maintains that exile rather than blood revenge had been established as the norm in the distant past (φυγαῖσι δ' ὁσιοῦν, ἀνταποκτείνειν δὲ μή, 515). The credibility of this claim seems questionable appearing as it does in a play concerning the story of Orestes. However, the prominence of exile as a response to homicide in other texts, concerning both mythical and historical events, appears to support Tyndareus' claims and suggests that Orestes' reactions were not the norm and did not necessarily reflect historical practice as is often assumed.[66]

Grieving relatives might readily accept the exile of the killer, since exile can be seen as a living death. A man who is driven into exile is no longer able to offer assistance to his family by labouring to sustain them or fighting to protect them. In this way, exile (like 'a life for a life') achieves a form of balance and equivalence: just as the dead man's kin have lost their son, the son of their enemy's family is also lost to them. Although he is not dead, to that community he is like a dead man. Moreover, exile was not considered an easy option for the ancients. In Euripides' *Hippolytus* Theseus maintains that exile is a worse punishment than death and that many exiles long to die (1045-50; cf. *Med.* 650-2).[67] The vivid depiction of the horrors and suffering of exile in the *Odyssey* includes reference to the fact that Odysseus craves death during his lengthy exile from Ithaca (1.57-9). Poseidon's attempts to keep Odysseus in exile for as long as possible rather than killing him ensure the maximum amount of suffering.[68] A man in exile lost much of his status with the loss of his homeland and frequently had to rely on others to survive. In myth exiles in a foreign land could expect to undertake servile tasks (Patroclus is appointed to be Achilles' attendant and Phoenix to be his tutor),[69] or to fall on hard times and be reduced to penury (Odysseus in his beggar disguise is supposedly a killer-in-exile fallen on hard times). Athenians also spoke of exile in these terms. In the *Tetralogies* Antiphon focuses on the loss of city (and political rights that go with being a citizen) and loss of property, stressing that exile would reduce him to being a beggar in a foreign land (2.2.9).[70] This conjures up the image of the blind and impoverished exile Oedipus in Sophocles' *OC*. Notably, Achilles thinks that Agamemnon's lack of respect for him and his poor treatment of him is similar to the treatment afforded to an honourless fugitive (ἀτίμητον μετανάστην). This comparison highlights the expected lack of honour and status associated with being in exile (*Il.* 9.648).[71] The difficulties of losing civic status, avoiding public places and remaining apart from the city are suggested in the example cited by Demosthenes of a man arrested in the assembly when he was supposed to be in exile (23.31). This man apparently chose to risk death in order to participate in political decisions.[72]

In Homer exile is the norm following a killing outside warfare.[73] Beye has noted that migration to avoid blood revenge is a typical theme in the catalogues of the slain in the *Iliad*, along with such everyday subjects as the man's birth, place of origin, marriage, status and wealth.[74] The pedestrian nature of these topics might imply that exile following a homicide was a relatively regular event. Reference to a fugitive killer is also contained in the simile of the suppliant-exile in *Iliad* 24 (480-3).[75] The use of the image of the suppliant-exile in a simile might also imply that this was a concept that Homer's audience could readily imagine rather than a rare event. The simile describes how a killer-in-exile seeks refuge in the home of a wealthy man. In most of the Homeric examples the killer is said to have been taken in by an influential man elsewhere after fleeing from his homeland.[76] Prominent in taking in these killers-in-exile is Peleus, the father of Achilles. He accepts the boy Patroclus, who has killed another boy by accident in a quarrel over a game of knucklebones (23.85-90). Epeigeus, who has killed his cousin and escaped into exile, is also received by Peleus (16.571-4). Phoenix too finds a home with Peleus and Achilles when he goes into self-imposed exile after contemplating patricide (9.458-61), although he does not actually go through with the act.[77] Notably his relatives beg him to stay even keeping watch over him, since they do not wish to lose him, but Phoenix is determined to leave (9.464-77). In other sources Peleus himself is said to have been exiled for killing his step-brother Phocus (Euripides *Andr.* 687 and schol. ad loc.) in collaboration with his brother Telamon (Apollodorus 3.12.6; cf. Pausanias 2.29.2).[78] In Apollodorus' version the brothers are said to have been jealous of Phocus' athletic ability.[79] Peleus is then said to have gone into exile again for killing his father-in-law Eurytion during the hunt for the Calydonian boar (Pindar fr. 48 SM). Although there is no mention of Peleus' experiences as a killer-in-exile in Homer, it is possible that early versions of these tales influenced his portrayal as a man who frequently received fugitive killers.[80]

Telamon's house too is said to have received a killer-in-exile named Lycophron who killed a man in Cythera (*Il.* 15.431-9). Distressed at his death, Ajax calls on his brother Teucer to help him achieve revenge for the killing. The nature of Lycophron's relationship with Ajax and Teucer is comparable to Achilles' relationship with Patroclus.[81] Just as Patroclus is assigned to be Achilles' attendant and is much loved by him, Lycophron is the attendant of Ajax and is said by him to have been like a parent to himself and his brother. The relationships between the exiles and their hosts revealed in these examples demonstrates that while exiles who go to the house of a man who has sons might not achieve the status and standing of these sons, they are still regarded as quasi-kin who are respected and loved to the extent that in the cases of Patroclus and Lycophron revenge is sought following their deaths.[82] Exiles who arrive at the house of a man with daughters might even hope to marry and inherit, as in the cases of Peleus and Telamon who regain their lost power and status in this way. In these mythical tales there appears to be little or no stigma attached to

17

being a murderer and little fear is manifested that a man who has killed before might kill again.[83] Rather the killers are accepted and go on to attain positions of trust in their new household.[84]

Not every killer goes directly into exile in Homer. Aegisthus elects to remain with Clytemnestra and rule in Mycenae instead of going into exile. Tellingly, he is the only killer in the Homeric texts to die at the hands of an avenger outside warfare.[85] Neither Hercules (who kills his guest, *Od.* 21.24-30) nor Oedipus (who kills his father, *Od.* 11.273) goes into exile. Gagarin has suggested that they are able to do this because there are no relatives present to take revenge.[86] Hercules kills a man who is not from that region and is therefore without avengers, while Oedipus kills his own father and is therefore the most likely avenger himself. Similarly, it seems that in the *Aethiopis* Achilles avoided exile after killing Thersites because Thersites had no one to avenge him (Proclus *Chrest.* 2).[87] The notion that exile is motivated by fear of vengeful relatives is supported by examples from the Homeric epics. The prophet Theoclymenus states explicitly that he left his home after killing a man of the same tribe in order to avoid revenge at the hands of the dead man's kin (*Od.* 15.272ff.). Similarly, Tlepolemus, the son of Hercules, is said to have gone into exile after killing his father's uncle to avoid conflict with his brothers and nephews over the death (*Il.* 2.661-70). Eumaeus tells of an exile from Aetolia who claimed that he was being pursued all over the world because he killed a man (*Od.* 14.380-1). Such thinking also influences Eupeithes' urgency in recruiting a posse to pursue Odysseus and his party. His fear is that the killers will escape into exile overseas before they can be stopped (24.430-8). The suggestion in these examples is that the relatives are eager for revenge, but that it will be difficult for them to pursue the killers once they have gone into exile overseas. A killer who does not go into exile, but remains where he is, faces revenge from the relatives of the dead man. If the lure is strong enough (as in the case of Aegisthus who desires to attain and keep the throne and wife of Agamemnon), then a man might elect to take his chances, even when advised of the risks (1.32-43).

The Homeric examples indicate that the threat of revenge was a decisive factor in motivating killers to escape into exile. A similar idea is current in Athens where killers could avoid prosecution at the hands of angry relatives by escaping into exile. The rules of the Attic court, where an accused murderer could apparently choose to flee either before his case began or half way through it (Antiphon 5.13; Demosthenes 23.69), suggest that here too exile is, in a way, a method of avoiding the retribution of the victim's family who take the role of prosecutor (ὁ διώκων) in the law court and demand that the defendant (ὁ φεύγων) pays with his life for what he has done.[88] Although MacDowell has suggested that the exiling of a killer should be seen as revenge, as well as being a deterrent and a means of removing pollution from the state,[89] it is perhaps better to view the prominence of exile in the laws on homicide as the enshrining of norms and customary actions in law. The sources imply that men would have taken advantage of going into exile to avoid the death penalty (Antiphon 5.13), even after the verdict had been passed, it is suggested in Plato's *Crito* (44b-c).[90] It is certainly notable that the extant cases of homicide are not straightforward, and it can perhaps be conjectured from this that guilty men tended to flee into exile without even waiting for a trial (Aeschines 2.6; Andocides 1.3; Lysias 20.21). In particular it can be postulated from what is said in Antiphon 5 (*On the Murder of Herodes*) that the relatives of Herodes acted as they did in an attempt to prevent the defendant Euxitheus from escaping into exile. Instead of being tried for homicide (by δίκη φόνου), Euxitheus maintains that he is being tried improperly as a malefactor (κακοῦργος, 5.9). This means that he is held in prison rather than being allowed the option of exile (5.13).[91] The law cited in Demosthenes (23.53; cf. 21.43) states that a man who kills in circumstances deemed to be justifiable does not have to go into exile, highlighting once again that fleeing into exile was the natural response following a homicide in Athens.[92]

Other possible responses to homicide are the payment of material compensation and the arrangement of a marriage alliance between opposing families. In settlements material goods come to the fore. An adequate payment can compensate the bereaved family sufficiently for loss of labour and, at the same time, ensure that the killer's family do not have to suffer from loss of manpower. That compensation aimed at avoiding exile following a homicide is made clear from Ajax's statement to Achilles in the *Iliad* (9.632-6) that a killer is able to remain in his community, if his victim's brother or son accepts his offer of blood money. It follows from this that without threatening blood revenge, the victim's family could not hope to get compensation from the killer or his family.[93] A family that agrees to accept monetary compensation or other goods in exchange for the death of a loved one must agree with the killer on the value of that person's life.[94] Potentially this is the difficulty raised in the famous trial scene on the shield of Achilles (18.497-508).[95] Gagarin suggests that there is some bargaining about the amount of compensation where the killer has offered a certain amount (which is considered the norm in such circumstances), but that the victim's family claim more and therefore refuse to accept anything until they feel adequately compensated.[96]

Examples where blood money is accepted are not plentiful in the ancient texts and it is difficult to assess the extent to which monetary compensation was used in reality. Although Gagarin takes Ajax's statement to mean that accepting blood money for a murder was normal behaviour,[97] in fact what Ajax says is necessary for the logic of his argument and is therefore unhelpful in determining whether payment of blood money was ever the norm. Ajax particularly stresses the importance of the acceptance of material rewards because he hopes to persuade Achilles to accept the gifts offered by Agamemnon and to reach a settlement with him. Difficulties exist with later evidence too. Because blood money was not deemed acceptable in Athens, as Demosthenes tells us (23.33),[98] accusing someone of accepting monetary compensation for the murder of a relative was a useful way of slurring his character in court. The following example shows this clearly: 'When his brother died a violent death, the attitude of Theocrines towards him was so callous that, after seeking out those responsible and discovering who they were, he accepted money and took no further action' (Demosthenes 58.28).[99] Given that relatives had the power to pardon a killer and allow him to go free, the accusation that a man accepted money could easily be an empty one. On the other hand, a man might calculate that he would be better off accepting money from the killers rather than attempting to prosecute them. Either way, the example is interesting, as the slur implies that taking appropriate revenge for a relative by prosecuting the killers in court was deemed morally correct in Athens and brokering other forms of settlement was deemed unacceptable. The implication is that some people must have accepted blood money, but because receiving money in such circumstances was deemed ignoble (and perhaps also weak), there is a lack of examples in our texts.[100]

Another possible way of bringing a peaceful end to fighting is through a marriage alliance, by offering a very valuable piece of 'property': a woman.[101] Here the idea is to cement relations between the two sides and prevent further fighting (Isocrates 7.12).[102] A girl who can bear male children is offered by her kin to the family which has lost a male member so that the dead man can be replaced in this way.[103] That the intention of marriage alliances is to bind the two families with common descendants is shown clearly in Herodotus' story of Pisistratus' marriage to the daughter of his political enemy Megacles.[104] Pisistratus is said to have made the match in order to end fighting between rival factions and to secure his enemy's support. However, his failure to consummate the marriage properly, because he did not wish to produce offspring with Megacles' daughter, led to renewed enmity (Herodotus 1.60-1).[105] For the most part our ancient examples of marriage alliance, like this one, refer to ending of political feuds, but it was conceptually possible to give a relative in marriage to settle matters after a murder. Herodotus maintains that Alexander of Macedon married his sister to a Persian in order to bring an end to a dispute caused initially when some Persian guests were deemed to have insulted the women of Alexander's house. Unable to bear this offence, Alexander, together with other men of the house, killed their Persian guests (5.18-20). We are told that when the arrival of Persian troops seeking revenge for the death of their compatriots seemed imminent, Alexander arranged a marriage alliance for his sister with the leader of the troops, thereby bringing an end to hostilities (5.21). The benefits for each side are clear. The men do not have to risk their lives in battle, while the Persian leader secures for himself a wife who can bear children for him, as well as the valuable alliance with her brother that such a marriage signifies. Although some aspects of this tale are rather unlikely, certain key features are revealing.[106] The fact that Alexander is thought able to bring an end to the dispute in this way, even though he is dealing with far distant enemies, demonstrates a strong belief in the willingness of parties to settle disputes peacefully. The tale also demonstrates the significance of women both as vulnerable possessions who must be strongly protected and as useful resources who can be used for men's political advantage. These ideas will be discussed in detail in the next chapter. Similarly in myth when Agamemnon kills Tantalus, first husband of Clytemnestra, and their child, her brothers pursue him, but they are all said to be reconciled by Tyndareus, the siblings' father, when a marriage is arranged between Clytemnestra and Agamemnon (Euripides *IA* 1146-56; cf. Apollodorus *Epit.* 3.16).[107]

The suggestion that springs from the evidence of all these texts is that exile is the most likely response following a homicide and that blood revenge is unusual. However, there are considerable difficulties in understanding how the situation represented in the sources relates to reality. The prominence of political leaders and mythical characters in the examples skews the picture considerably and it is hard to deduce the behaviour of normal men who are largely ignored in the historical record. Parker has argued, based on the evidence of the early texts, that the blood feud did not exist in Greece, but instead killers either paid blood money or went into exile.[108] Seaford, on the other hand, is not convinced that the Homeric evidence suggests a strong tendency towards exile in reality. He imagines that feuding was rife in early Greece, but that it has been deliberately excluded from Homer to present an image of a unified aristocracy.[109] Certainly there is next to nothing in the textual evidence to suggest any protracted blood feud of the type where successive generations of opposing families take part in a cycle of killing and avenging.[110] Even in the various accounts of the early history of Attica, the emphasis of the texts is on the numerous exiles endured by the various political leaders who were out of favour (e.g. Herodotus 1.60-1; *Ath. Pol.* 14.3-4) and it is very unclear to what extent deaths and reciprocal killings were a key part in these political *staseis*. Seaford infers that reciprocal killings were a key part of early Athenian history, in particular as a result of the Cylonian conspiracy (*Ath. Pol.* fr. 8 Rose; Herodotus 5.71; Plutarch *Sol.* 12; Thucydides 1.126).[111] Although the accounts of this crisis differ, it does seem that an extensive and lengthy dispute arose in the city following the slaughter of the Cylonian conspirators. However, it is not clear from the accounts that this dispute involved reciprocal killings or could be categorised as a blood feud. Moreover, it is notable that the accounts emphasise that the family of those deemed responsible for killing the conspirators was driven into exile by the Athenians following a trial. This suggests that even in difficult situations such as this, attempts were made to prevent violence through recourse to trials and exile. Nevertheless, it is true to say that without the belief in the possibility of revenge, then the system of exile as Homeric characters explain it would immediately break down. This places the emphasis squarely on the importance of the credible threat of revenge as a mechanism for ensuring that communities do not sink too deeply into violence.[112]

While Seaford is right to emphasise the importance of revenge, this does not mean that blood feuding was necessarily a significant part of early Greek history. Evidence of conflicts in the early history of Athens and other Greek states, such as it is, suggests that people fought principally over land and political gain, not over homicides. In the opening paragraphs of his history Thucydides maintains that in certain parts of Greece violence was rife, in particular in fertile areas where people desired to acquire land (1.2.3-4). His belief is that early violence was principally driven by material concerns.[113] Moreover, he explains that people naturally gravitated towards Attica where there were fewer fights over the land. He maintains that this swelled the population to such a degree that it was necessary to send out colonies (1.2.5-6). The suggestion here is that while some were keen to fight to gain material advantages, many others desired to move away from violence and achieve greater stability.

I have previously suggested that most people are unwilling or unable to maintain long-lasting, bloody battles with their neighbours because of the costs they will have to pay themselves. If, as the texts and the theory suggest, people consider matters carefully before deciding whether they have anything to gain out of becoming embroiled in costly fights with their neighbours, then we might expect that revenge for homicide was the exception rather than the rule. Interestingly, in one Homeric example there is a suggestion that a man who has lost a brother or son simply mourns and goes on with his life. Apollo states that Achilles is treating Hector badly and that Hera, Athena and Poseidon are doing nothing about it. He says: 'Many a man, I presume, is likely to have lost an even dearer one than he has, a brother borne by the same mother, or maybe a son. He weeps and laments for him and that is the end of it, since the fates have endowed men with an enduring heart' (*Il.* 24.46-9). Achilles, on the other hand, is overwhelmed by anger and lashes out with excessive violence following the death of Patroclus. Apollo's statement perhaps implies that the silent majority of ordinary men would have made no response at all to murder other than grieving.[114] The suggestion here is that rather than hiding a history of feuding, the Homeric texts are really hiding a history in which revenge for homicide is taken rarely if at all.[115] In addition, it has been suggested that the true cycle of violence (in which life for a life is perpetuated potentially infinitely) belongs more properly in anecdote than in reality.[116] Although revenge for a killing might be cited as motivation, other incentives (such as material or political gain) are frequently in the background, meaning that some murders may go completely ignored if other compelling motives are not present.[117] Recently many anthropologists have argued strongly that the use of peaceful settlement has been much underestimated. This is particularly so in the case of disputes which occur within a community where the need for quick, peaceful settlement is greater.[118] Often, a man who is willing to compromise will find sympathy with third parties.[119] Gagarin has shown that in ancient Greece there is a strong tendency towards peaceful settlement even where there were no official law courts.[120] This tendency towards good relations in a community is explained by Daly and Wilson:

> Violent hostility is rarer than friendly relations even among non-relatives; people thrive by the maintenance of networks of social reciprocity and by establishing reputations for fairness and generosity that will make them attractive exchange partners.[121]

Seaford himself has placed considerable emphasis on the attempts of the classical *poleis* to control violence in order to ensure the interests of the whole community.[122] By extension, we can postulate that earlier communities (even though smaller) were also keenly concerned with maintaining reasonable levels of violence to ensure their survival. Certainly in the *Odyssey* the community in Ithaca is shown discussing homicides (24.421ff.) and the protection of personal property in an assembly (2.1ff.). Although Aegyptius suggests that an assembly might naturally be called for public issues such as the imminent approach of an army, Telemachus and the suitors' relatives both convene the assembly to discuss private grievances within their own families. Their aim is to rally the support of the community at large and so be able to accomplish their ends. By appealing to the men of Ithaca, Telemachus hopes that he can bring an end to the suitors' consumption of his property, either by gaining help to force them out or by the sway of public opinion. The significance of public opinion in controlling excesses is also noted by Antinous when he spots that Telemachus has avoided the suitors' ambush. His fear is that Telemachus will call the assembly and declare the truth about the suitors' plot to kill him. He then states that the people might harm them or send them into exile over this attempted homicide (16.381-2). The suggestion here that the people of Ithaca would act to drive out the suitors because they had threatened to kill a leading Ithacan implies a communal level of interest in avoiding violence in the *Odyssey*.

At the end of the *Odyssey* the suitors' relatives are thwarted in their desire for revenge by the intervention of the goddess Athena. This intervention is symbolic of the common desire that disputes should reach an amicable settlement, since a perpetual campaign of violence disrupts community life too severely.[123] If a particular individual or family is thought very disruptive and unnecessarily violent, they could be forced into exile or even executed. In other versions of the story, Odysseus goes into exile following the murders of the suitors.[124] Certainly this is the response which Eupeithes anticipates when he explains that the relatives need to attack quickly to prevent Odysseus' escape (24.430-7). Odysseus also mentions the possibility of exile (20.43; 23.117-22), but rejects it in favour of fighting, relying on the support of the gods.

In order for the families to stop fighting it is necessary for the gods to wipe their minds so that they forget about their losses (24.484). Loraux connects this settlement at the end of the *Odyssey*, with the amnesty against prosecution in Athens after the rule of the Thirty. She focuses on the importance of oblivion which will cause the participants to forget their woes.[125] Andocides (1.81) explains that the democrats from Piraeus could have elected to take revenge (τιμωρεῖσθαι) against the Thirty, but they decided instead to save the city. He states explicitly that this was because they placed the unity and success of the city before the need for private vengeance (τὰς ἰδίας τιμωρίας). Later he says that the Greeks thought it prudent that the Athenians did not take revenge (τιμωρία), but attempted to preserve the unity of the citizens (1.140). The author of the *Athenaion Politeia* adds that one man who did stir up grudges (μνησικακεῖν) was executed without trial in a bid to save the democracy (39.6-40.2). The amnesty covered all but prosecutions for murder committed with one's own hand (39.5-6).[126] The prohibition on prosecution left some citizens desiring revenge for the death of their relatives, but unable to achieve it. Leon's sons were unable to prosecute Meletus because of the amnesty, although it was known that he was responsible for arresting their father before he was put to death without trial (Andocides 1.94; cf. Plato *Ap.* 32c-d).[127] In this case the desire for revenge by relatives is thwarted by the need for a stable community in Athens. As in the decision of the Athenians 'not to recall woes', in the *Odyssey* too it is necessary for those who have been wounded not to recall their losses in order to bring about the peaceful conclusion of the poem.

The drive towards a peaceful conclusion brought about by the goddess Athena is not unique to this episode. Indeed, Athena appears to be closely associated both with helping heroes procure revenge and with preventing revenge in circumstances where the danger of drastic escalation would have a severe effect on the community. In the *Iliad*, it is Athena who helps the Pylians in their fight against the Epeans according to Nestor (11.714-21), but it is also she who stops the men from pursuing the fight any further, he says (11.758).[128] Elsewhere Athena intervenes to prevent her brother Ares from taking action, when he desires revenge (τίσασθαι φόνον) for his son killed in battle (15.115-18). This episode is excellent evidence both of the strong desire of kin to avenge their relatives (Ares declares that he will defy Zeus to achieve his end) and of the importance of rational decision-making and the drive towards peace in certain instances of homicide. Athena fears that if Ares disobeys Zeus, he will cause upheaval in the divine community (15.121-4). Hence she argues that he should forget his anger over the death of his son (15.138). As in the case of the suitors' relatives, forgetfulness is essential if revenge is to be dropped and peaceful conditions are to reign. This case is a particularly interesting one, since it illustrates that even the gods do not always have the power or the will to take revenge. Even they are portrayed as being driven by a consideration of the risks and benefits of their action. Ares forgoes revenge, although his heart desires it, because he is persuaded that he would be too harshly punished for his disobedience and that his revenge is not as important as he first thought. Again, this example suggests that taking no action at all following the death of a loved one is a possibility even when his relatives are strong. There is also further support here for the role of Athena as protector of community harmony and averter of civil strife.

It is no surprise then that Hera selects Athena to intervene when civil strife first threatens the Greeks in Book 1 of the *Iliad*. When Achilles is contemplating murdering Agamemnon, it is she who prevents him from drawing his sword and persuades him that he will receive compensation in the end (1.193-218). Although Achilles is angry with Agamemnon, he respects the goddesses and obeys at once when they urge him not to kill Agamemnon stating that a man is a fool to ignore the gods (1.216-18). Although it might be appropriate for Achilles to fight with Agamemnon who is a man of approximately the same status, he recognises that there is nothing to be gained from fighting against the gods.[129] In Attic tragedy too Athena plays a similar role. Most notably she calms the Erinyes and prevents their terrible revenge against Athens at the end of the *Oresteia*. She also intervenes to prevent Hercules' 'revenge' against Amphion by knocking him out with a rock (Euripides *HF* 1001-6). However she does not stop him killing his wife and children.[130]

Battlefield revenge

Throughout these texts there is a strong tendency away from lethal retaliation following a killing. However in wartime settings, cycles of lethal revenge are portrayed. Although Burnett has maintained that reciprocal killings on the battlefield cannot truly be classed as revenge, because there is no delay between the killings and no deception involved in the revenge act,[131] it remains the case that these killings are the ones most likely to be portrayed as followed by lethal retaliation.[132] Even if the logic of the situation demands that the killing of an enemy on the battlefield is a necessary part of warfare and, therefore, cannot be seen as a private act of revenge, nevertheless texts often portray these responses as vengeful attacks springing from anger and grief at the loss of a comrade. This is particularly so in the *Iliad*, where the poet frequently shows warriors participating in high-speed vendetta involving numerous reciprocal killings on the battlefield (e.g. 13.363-673, 14.440-505).[133] In other texts too acts of hostility between enemies are depicted as acts of revenge, even on the scale of inter-state warfare.[134] Nevertheless it is perhaps right to draw a distinction between battlefield killings and peacetime killings in that depictions of battle scenes frequently involve relatively extended 'feuds' with numerous reciprocal killings, extremely violent revenges and a tendency towards mutilation of corpses,[135] whereas it has already been seen that descriptions of responses to killings in peacetime situations tend to involve exile or other non-violent solutions instead. Tellingly, while Ascalaphus' companions are free to attempt revenge for him on the battlefield, his father Ares is restrained from achieving revenge for his son, although he desires it, because of the implications this will have for peaceable relations among the Olympians (13.520ff., 15.113-18).[136]

The vocabulary of payment and exchange is prominent in Homeric descriptions of battlefield retaliation, in particular in the boasts of warriors who have successfully killed an opponent following the death of a comrade. A key example appears at the beginning of a protracted 'feud' between the Greeks and Trojans in *Iliad* 13. The sequence begins when Idomeneus kills Othryoneus. When Asius attempts to rescue the body, he too is killed by Idomeneus. In response Deiphobus attempts to strike Idomeneus, but misses him and kills Hypsenor instead. That he considers this killing repayment for the death of Asius is made explicit in his speech over the body of Hypsenor, whose death he values as equivalent to that of Asius: 'So Asius does not lie unavenged (ἄτιτος)!'[137] Even on his way to the mighty gate-keeper Hades, I feel he will travel with a light heart now I've given him an escort' (13.414-16). Rather than showing Deiphobus simply killing an opponent in random fighting, as we might perhaps expect in a battlefield situation, the poet highlights the fact that this attack is borne of vengeful motives in several ways. By first aiming at Idomeneus, Deiphobus is shown trying to kill the very man who killed Asius. Although he misses his target, his use of vocabulary highlights that he is claiming his victim as a suitable exchange for his dead comrade. Then by stressing that his actions were motivated by a desire to please the dead man, Deiphobus associates the killing with a private revenge act rather than the killing of an enemy in battle. Most significantly the very use of a speech at this point in the narrative highlights that this act is conceived of as revenge rather than being a random or unrelated killing.[138] The sequence continues with Idomeneus' killing of Alcathous. In similar vein, he addresses Deiphobus directly, claiming this killing as payment for Hypsenor's death and modifying the calculation of the value of his comrade's life offered by Deiphobus. Instead of being worth one Trojan life, as Deiphobus maintained, Idomeneus claims that Hypsenor was the equivalent of the three Trojans he has killed (13.445-9).[139]

In Book 14, Ajax is portrayed making a valuation of the man he has just killed based upon his ancestry. After Polydamas kills Proethoenor, his boasts sting Ajax into attacking him. Although he misses his target he succeeds in killing Archelochus. He calls to Polydamas and invites him to consider the value of the two men's lives and whether this is a fair exchange of a life for a life: 'Think it over, Polydamas, and tell me frankly

26

– doesn't this man's death make up for Proethoenor's? To judge by his looks, he was certainly no coward or low-born – more like a brother or son of horse-taming Antenor. The family likeness is striking' (14.470-4). Ajax's comment indicates that a victim from a high-born family is valued as more significant and worthy of honour than a man from a less notable family. However, although Ajax appears satisfied with this exchange of lives, Acamas the brother of Archelochus is not and continues the 'feud' by killing Promachus as he tries to drag away his brother's body. Acamas boasts: 'You Greeks, loud-mouths, so free with your threats – trouble and misery are not reserved for us alone. We've had our losses: yours are coming. Look at your man Promachus, put to sleep by my spear in prompt repayment for my brother's death (ἵνα μή τι κασιγνήτοιό γε ποινὴ / δηρὸν ἄτιτος ἔη)' (14.479-83). This boast stings Peneleus in turn, and he attacks, killing Ilioneus who he claims is an equivalent of Promachus. Here the preoccupation with balance and equivalence in battlefield retaliation is manifested in poetic form. Peneleus equates the mourning of each set of relatives in his speech over Ilioneus' body: 'Trojans, do me a favour and instruct Ilioneus' father and mother to start lamenting him at home. After all, the wife of Promachus, son of Alegenor, will never have the happiness of seeing *her* husband return when we Greeks sail from Troy' (14.500-5).[140] Elsewhere the narrative plays with the notion of reciprocal killings by showing comparable modes of death. When Patroclus is distressed at the death of Epeigeus (killed by a stone thrown by Hector), he throws a stone himself and kills Sthenelaus (16.570-92).

These examples show that Homeric warriors were thought to desire revenge for their dead comrades and to take it by attacking any suitable target, not necessarily the original killer.[141] The notion that non-kin might desire revenge in this context is evident, in particular where the avenger is in a position of responsibility over the dead man. There is a certain difficulty in understanding to what extent this desire for revenge is driven by grief at the loss of those who have been slain and to what extent the avengers react to a perceived dishonour done to themselves.[142] Because their ability to protect and defend their subordinates has been thrown into doubt, the desire for revenge could arise more out of a need to show that they cannot be bullied and that they are not helpless.[143] As will be seen in the next chapter, feelings of this sort are frequently associated with the desire to protect the women of the family. Other motivations, such as desire for material gain, are also part of the mix.

The relationship of soldiers to one another has been much studied by Shay, who emphasises the bond which builds up between men who have seen combat together.[144] He stresses that the Vietnam veterans known to him saw their comrades as closer than family members as they needed each other to survive in battle.[145] The Homeric examples clearly demonstrate that unrelated comrades are involved in retaliatory killings on the battlefield in Homer. In particular, as Lendon has noted, physical proxim-

27

ity on the battlefield can be enough to lead a man to take revenge for a dead comrade.[146] However, in Homeric warfare combatants are not strangers to one another, but a group of men recruited from the same district, and relatives often fight side by side (e.g. *Il.* 2.360-8).[147] Ajax and Teucer, the sons of Telamon, are portrayed fighting side by side, while Hector frequently fights near his brothers or other relatives. He is encouraged to turn and make a stand against Achilles when he believes he is being supported by his brother, Deiphobus (22.229-47). Elsewhere the text indicates that relatives are positioned near to one another on the battlefield. When injured, Deiphobus is rescued by his brother Polites (13.533-9); Asius' son Adamas attacks Antilochus (who killed his father's charioteer, 13.394-401) after the death of his father (13.560-3); when the body of Harpalion is taken to Troy by the Paphlagonians, his father is among them (13.653-9).

Warriors are sometimes portrayed calling on a dead man's relatives to achieve revenge in battle. For example, Melanippus is rebuked by Hector following the death of his cousin Dolops (15.553-8). Hector's speech encourages Melanippus to action, although his attempted revenge fails and he is killed by Antilochus. Similarly Deiphobus calls on Aeneas to avenge his brother-in-law Alcathous (13.463-6). As discussed above, relatives are portrayed as keen to exact revenge for their kin, but can be thwarted through weakness or lack of opportunity or through calculations of expediency, as well as through a desire to maintain peaceful relations. On the battlefield, however, there is no pressure to settle with an enemy who has killed a relative and men are limited only by their own physical abilities in their attempts to achieve revenge.

The predominance of relatives involved in examples of battlefield revenge in the *Iliad* is notable. In battle, men are often said to attempt vengeance for their brothers. Hector makes for Achilles after he kills his brother Polydorus (20.419-23). Agamemnon is attacked by a man after causing his brother's death (11.248-50), as are Odysseus (11.426-45) and Antilochus (16.317-29). Antilochus is himself defended by his brother Thrasymedes. These vengeful attacks are said to be motivated out of anger and grief at the loss of a relative. Euphorbus refers to the joy which his grieving relatives will derive from receiving the head and armour of Menelaus, the man who killed his brother (17.34-50),[148] while Andromache fears that a Greek angered by the loss of a brother or son at Hector's hands will take revenge on Astyanax (24.735-8). The gods too are shown reacting in a similar fashion. For example, because of his anger at the death of his grandson Amphimachus, Poseidon is said to stir up trouble for the Trojans (13.206-9). In these instances conventional ideas about kindred in vendetta are played out, but in an unconventional setting. This notion is made explicit at the end of the speech of Acamas where he says: 'That's what a man prays for – a relative to survive him and avenge his fall' (14.482-4). This comment closely parallels Nestor's statement in the *Odyssey* regarding the revenge of Orestes for his father (3.196-8). The combination of all these factors (the involvement of kin, the description of the emotions which drive the heroes, the preoccupation with balance and equivalence, the language which the men employ and the use of speech in the narrative) further demonstrates that the poet intends to portray these acts as vengeance, not random killings of an enemy during warfare (contra Burnett).[149]

Guests (*xenoi*) feature strongly too and this is an aspect which is frequently underestimated. The guest-friendship relationship is described in terms which connects it closely to blood kinship.[150] For example, Alcinous says that a *xenos* is like a brother (*Od.* 8.546-7). Guests avoid fighting one another as kin usually do, as in the famous case of Glaucus and Diomedes (*Il.* 6.119ff.).[151] Kitts has argued well that the connection between the role of the Erinyes in punishing kin-killers and in punishing oath-breakers can explain why ritual relatives are defended and avenged in the same way as blood kin.[152] Men are also portrayed reacting angrily to the death of a guest and apparently attempting to achieve revenge for him in battle. Paris is said to fire his bow as an angry reaction to the death of Harpalion who was his guest (ξεῖνος). He succeeds in killing Euchenor with his arrow (13.660-72). Hector is also motivated to attack the Greeks out of grief for the death of his friend Podes with whom he used to share meals (17.575-92). Those who live under the same roof are also highly valued as being like kin. Ajax says that he and Teucer honoured Lycophron, who lived with his family, as much as their parents (15.439). With this thought in mind he exhorts his brother to fetch his bow and attack the Trojans following Lycophron's death in battle. Similarly, Aeneas is urged by Deiphobus to help his brother-in-law Alcathous, who looked after Aeneas as a child and lived at his house (13.463-6). These examples reveal a great degree of similarity between the portrayal of relationships of *xenoi* and of blood kin. The explanations attached to these killings demonstrate the warriors' feelings for their *xenoi* and for those with whom they had shared a dwelling as a child.

One of the most famous and most significant instances of vengeance in Homer is Achilles' attack on Hector following the death of his companion, Patroclus. Although Homer does not mention a family bond between the two men, he does say that they were brought up together in the palace of Peleus after the childhood exile of Patroclus for an accidental killing (23.84-8). It is therefore to be expected that similar feelings and emotions will be generated within their relationship as in those instances cited above of guests and men who live under the same roof.[153] That Achilles considered Patroclus as being like kin is implied in two similes.[154] Achilles is said to mourn for Patroclus as a lion mourns the loss of his cubs (18.316-23), and as a father mourns for his son (23.222-5).[155] Achilles also maintains that losing Patroclus is worse than losing his father or son, suggesting that he is as close to him as to his closest male agnates (19.321-7; cf. 24.44-52). Halperin argues sensibly that the poet uses these images of familiar relationships to explain the nature of the relationship between Achilles and Patroclus.[156] Another image which helps us to understand their relationship appears in Achilles' speech to the dying Hector. He tells him that his anger at what Hector has done to him is so great that he wishes he could eat him raw (22.345-7). A similar desire is expressed by Hecuba following the death of her son at the hands of Achilles. She wishes that she could eat Achilles' liver raw to make him pay for the death of her son (24.200-16).[157] This parallel image suggests that the anger of Achilles over the death of Patroclus and his desire for revenge against Hector is akin to that of a mother for her son.

Elsewhere it is suggested that the pair were actually related by blood. Eustathius claims that Hesiod made Peleus, father of Achilles, and Menoetius, father of Patroclus, brothers (*Hom.* 112.44ff.; Hesiod *Catalogue of Women* fr. 212a M-W). It seems possible that the expectation of revenge by blood kin was so great that it drove this interpretation of the heroes' genealogies. It is also possible that a kin relationship between the two men would have been understood through the choice of refuge for the child-exile Patroclus. Evidence elsewhere suggests that this choice would have been influenced by kinship. Orestes goes to live with his cousin when in exile. Pylades is the son of Atreus' daughter (Euripides *IT* 918-19) and Hermione is said to have been sent to live with her aunt and cousins in the absence of her parents (*Or.* 63-6). In Athens, Charmides was brought up from an early age in the home of his cousin Andocides (Andocides 1.48). Even if Homer's audience did not think that Achilles and Patroclus were blood kin, the longstanding quasi-kinship relationship between these two men as it is depicted in the *Iliad* is sufficient to explain their exceptional closeness in the poem. As in the cases of Ajax, Teucer and Aeneas, who are portrayed reacting angrily to the deaths of those with whom they grew up, Achilles' anger and desire for revenge against Hector is driven in part by his long-standing relationship with Patroclus, his 'foster-brother'.[158]

However, Achilles goes even further than this. He does not envisage Patroclus simply as kin, but as a version of himself (cf. *Il.* 18.82). He had imagined that after his death Patroclus would go home in his place and look after his son Neoptolemus (19.330-3).[159] This substitution of Patroclus for Achilles is also spelt out by the poet as Patroclus takes the field dressed in Achilles' armour. In this sense, as Nagy has argued, Patroclus is Achilles' 'alter ego' (cf. 18.82).[160] Achilles and Patroclus are so closely identified that when Achilles hears of the death of Patroclus he acts as if he had died.[161] He heaps earth on his head in the standard grieving ritual in which the mourner likens himself to the dead man and Antilochus grabs Achilles' hands to prevent him committing suicide (18.23-34).[162] This opens up the possibility that Achilles' revenge should be envisioned less as a means to secure the honour of his companion through the death of his killer, and more out of anger at himself, as well as a means to protect his own honour.[163] He has failed to protect his closest companion (ἐμεῖο δὲ

30

δῆσεν ἀρῆς ἀλκτῆρα γενέσθαι, 18.100), a man who has been likened to relatives he would be expected to protect (his ageing father and young son), and this has implications for the way others will view him.[164] In a speech addressed to his mother he berates himself for proving useless to his friends at their time of need, and labels himself responsible for the death of Patroclus (18.82-3).[165] He is aware of the risk he is taking in confronting Hector, but decides that it is better to die attempting revenge for Patroclus (Πατρόκλοιο δ᾽ ἕλωρα Μενοιτιάδεω ἀποτίσῃ) than to live on without him (18.90-4). His decision to take to the field is a particularly conscious one, in that Achilles is already aware of the implications of his actions.[166] He tells his mother that he is now aiming for glory, although certain death will follow (18.98-126). In choosing revenge over life, Achilles in a way exacts revenge on himself for causing Patroclus' death, but he simultaneously secures eternal renown for himself by his deeds.[167] This highlights the two key aspects of Achilles' revenge: his feelings about his own culpability in Patroclus' death and his desire to retrieve the honour Hector has taken when he killed Patroclus (symbolised by his seizure of Achilles' armour).[168]

A secondary motive for Achilles' battlefield rampage and slaughter of Hector is his desire to avenge and protect the Greek army as a whole. This motive is closely connected to the primary motives in that Patroclus is depicted as a member of the army who dies because of Achilles' neglect.[169] Achilles' relationship to the army is also depicted as parental in its nature (9.323-5). This motive is cited first by Achilles when he addresses Hector before their duel (νῦν δ᾽ ἀθρόα πάντ᾽ ἀποτίσεις, / κήδε᾽ ἐμῶν ἑτάρων, οὓς ἔκτανες ἔγχεϊ θύων, 22.271-2) and it is only after he deals Hector a lethal blow that he specifies the death of Patroclus in particular (22.331-6). The use of speeches here again highlights how the poet represents the warriors as taking revenge for specific past offences rather than killing men simply because they are enemy combatants. The vocabulary of payment used in Achilles' speech to Hector makes it clear that he conceives of Hector's death as a payment for the deaths of the Greek men he and the other Trojans have previously killed. Elsewhere Achilles highlights that he also conceives of the death of Hector as a payment for the death of Patroclus (ἀποτίσῃ, 18.93) and as payment to the Greeks for the insult (ἐπὴν τισαίμεθα λώβην) of Patroclus' death (19.208). Achilles also makes it clear to Hector that he is retaliating because Hector's actions have affected him personally (οἷά μ᾽ ἔοργας, 22.345-7). He conceives of the deaths of the Greeks and Patroclus as injuries to himself for which Hector has to pay him with his life.

However, Achilles does not consider Hector's death adequate payment for the death of Patroclus and the other Greeks. He values Patroclus much more highly than a single Trojan life (17.538-9). In addition to killing Hector, he sacrifices twelve young Trojans on Patroclus' grave as a price for his death (21.26-33; 23.19-23).[170] In his killing spree he also mentions

31

the deaths of the other Greeks and maintains that the Trojans in general will pay for them with their deaths (21.133-5). Achilles says: 'One by one you shall all die an evil death, till you have paid for the killing of Patroclus and the death of the Greeks you slaughtered down by their swift ships when I was away' (ἀλλὰ καὶ ὣς ὀλέεσθε κακὸν μόρον, εἰς ὅ κε πάντες / τίσετε Πατρόκλοιο φόνον καὶ λοιγὸν Ἀχαιῶν, / οὓς ἐπὶ νηυσὶ θοῇσιν ἐπέφνετε νόσφιν ἐμεῖο). Here again the vocabulary of payment is prominent as Achilles elucidates his motivation for killing Lycaon rather than accepting a ransom. Whereas in the past material compensation had been acceptable to him (even in this wartime scenario), Achilles' anger is portrayed as being so great that he will accept only payment in blood. Similarly he refuses to enter into any kind of negotiation with Hector and at first will not even consider ransoming his body because of his anger (22.340-7). Although Achilles initially seems to act as a man in a peacetime situation and accept compensation rather than kill captives, his anger at Patroclus' death causes him to reject any kind of settlement and to focus instead on extreme violence: Achilles initially desires to eat Hector raw, but settles for the attempted desecration and mutilation of his corpse, before finally capitulating, releasing his anger and returning his body for a ransom.

Achilles' attack on Hector and the other Trojans during his *aristeia* is portrayed by the poet as born of grief and anger at the death of a dear comrade (cf. 15.64-8). The vocabulary of payment used by Achilles highlights that he conceives of his slaughter of Hector and the Trojans as revenge for Patroclus and the other Greeks. At the same time his speeches which explain his motivations demonstrate that his actions are a reaction to the previous actions of the Trojans and were caused by them. Zeus too refers to the payment Hector will have to make for killing Patroclus (ποινή, 17.207). Even though Achilles might reasonably be depicted as slaying the Trojans because they are his enemies in a war, the poet does not choose to depict his actions in this way. Instead Achilles is shown acting out of a combination of anger at the loss of a loved one, guilt for failing to protect his 'dependants' and a feeling of dishonour that he might appear to be a weaker and less able warrior than Hector who has killed those under his care, 'without a thought' for him (22.332). If you appear to be no threat to potential enemies, like Achilles when he refrains from fighting, you risk attacks on your family by those who perceive you to be weak, as here when the Trojans attack and kill many of the weakened Greek army, characterised as the dependant kin of Achilles through the use of simile.[171]

Later Greeks were very interested in the revenge of Achilles and frequently discussed it as an act worthy of emulation by contemporary men. Socrates in Plato's *Apology*, Phaedrus in Plato's *Symposium*, Aeschines in *Against Timarchus* and Aristotle in the *Rhetoric* all refer to the passage in which Achilles prefers to take revenge and die than to return home safely without taking revenge (*Il.* 18.95-100). Aeschines declares that Achilles was driven to take revenge for Patroclus out of nobility of spirit (οὕτω δὲ μεγαλοψύχως ἠπείγετο τὸν φονέα τὸν ἐκείνου τιμωρήσασθαι) (1.145). He depicts the revenge as the virtuous act of a noble man and as worthy of emulation. Aristotle too argues that the decision is an honourable one, although not expedient for Achilles (*Rhet.* 1358b-59a). Socrates draws the conclusion that a man fighting in battle must run the required risks and die if need be rather than think of his own safety (Plato *Ap.* 28b-e; cf. *Hipp. Maj.* 292e-293a). His decision to expunge the lines in which Achilles apparently repents of his decision to die honourably in Hades (cf. *Od.* 11.488-91) is consistent with this thought (*Rep.* 386c). In the *Symposium* Phaedrus argues that Achilles took revenge out of love and that this was worthy of honour from the gods (179e-180b; cf. Plutarch *Pel.* 18). Later however, Diotima maintains that Achilles acted as he did in order to achieve eternal renown (208d). Xenophon in his *Symposium* focuses on the same passages, but determines that Achilles acted not out of love, but as a proper comrade should, in order to achieve glory (8.31-2). Here, as in my own reading of the Homeric passages, the ancient commentators focus on two aspects of Achilles' revenge for Patroclus: his love for his companion (sometimes interpreted as erotic love by the Athenians, rather than as kin-like or comradely love) and his desire to achieve honour and glory for himself.

Although scholarly debate has tended to focus on the nature of the relationship between Achilles and Patroclus, which is described differently in these classical sources, there is a consistent thread of admiration for the noble decision of Achilles to lose his life in order to achieve revenge.[172] Although some believe his motivation to have been love and others glory, nevertheless all agree that his action is worthy of praise. However, in one source the emotions of Achilles leading to his revenge are not so highly praised. In Plato's *Republic* Socrates denounces the excessive mourning and grief of Achilles. Gill has argued well that this reading of the *Iliad* is a subversion of conventional thoughts on Achilles' revenge.[173] It would appear from all this evidence that the classical Athenians tended to see Achilles' revenge on the battlefield as an ideal and that they were influenced by Homeric presentations of noble behaviour and revenge, especially when they took to the battlefield. Such influence can be noted in the presentation of classical war heroes such as Brasidas whose depiction in Thucydides appears to have been modelled on the Homeric Achilles (4.11-5.11).[174]

However, the picture is further complicated by the inconsistency between Homeric and hoplite styles of warfare. Socrates argues that Achilles can stand as a good model of valour and courage to an Athenian soldier because he chose to die rather than avoid battle, but aspects of his behaviour create difficulties for democratic Athenians, in particular his decision to sacrifice the collective army in favour of his own personal honour.[175] According to Michelakis this problematic side of Achilles' character was presented in Aeschylus' *Myrmidons*.[176] Instead of a clash between Achilles and Agamemnon, the play begins with the clash between Achilles and the army. Achilles is accused of treason by the Myrmidons (προδοσία) (fr. 132c20 R; cf. 132a8.5 R) and he refers to a decision to stone him (fr. 132c1-2 R) – apparently a collective reaction to his treason.[177] Here the tragic evidence appears to pit the individual against the collective, suggesting that what might be right for a lone hero, is not right for the army as a whole.

Classical war heroes such as the Spartan general Pausanias are depicted as espousing opposing ideals. In Herodotus' representation Pausanias particularly shines for apparently putting the honour of the Spartans as a whole above that of himself and his family. Unlike the heroes of Homer, he is represented as rejecting personal honour and excessive private revenge. In the aftermath of the battle of Plataea, Lampon of Aegina suggests that he ought to cut off the head of Mardonius and stick it on a pole, thus treating him in the same way that Xerxes treated Leonidas. This, he says, would gain him renown as well as personal vengeance for his paternal uncle, Leonidas (τετιμωρήσεαι ἐς πάτρων τὸν σὸν Λεωνίδην, Herodotus 9.78). Achilles' assertion that he will take the armour and head of Hector to put on Patroclus' grave as revenge for his death (*Il.* 18.333-5) shares a similar spirit as Lampon's suggestion. Herodotus makes it quite clear in his account that both the original outrage of Xerxes and the suggestion of Lampon are inappropriate. He characterises Xerxes' initial mutilation as excessive and barbaric by using the word παρενόμησε (7.238), and says that Lampon's counsel to Pausanias is most unrighteous (ἀνοσιώτατον, 9.78). Pausanias, on the other hand, is portrayed in a good light at this point in the narrative. He is shown rejecting Lampon's idea, saying that not only is it wrong to maltreat a corpse, but also that Leonidas has had sufficient vengeance (μεγάλως τετιμωρῆσθαι, 9.79), a view in which Herodotus concurs (9.64).[178] His rejection of the ideals of personal honour are also represented in his desire to gather the spoil for a special tribute to Delphi rather than allowing the men to collect it for themselves as a boost to their own honour (9.80).[179]

However, here we find a potential indication of where ideology differed from practice, for Herodotus states that the men actually stole as much as they could of the booty and sold it for profit. This implies that although Herodotus represents classical Greeks behaving very much according to a collective ideology, they were still most interested in personal gain and their own honour. Indeed Pausanias himself is later said to have been overcome by luxury and to have betrayed the Spartans for the prospect of a marriage alliance with the King of Persia's daughter; a suggestion that he too aimed at personal gain and aggrandisement more than the collective good (Thucydides 1.128.7-134.3). The model of the Homeric hero can be seen to have two aspects: he is noble and brave, yet at the same time self-seeking and a threat to the collective. That later texts used aspects of these characteristics to present contemporary war leaders is clear. It also

34

appears that classical Greeks were influenced by the Homeric presentations of heroic behaviour and were perhaps moved to emulate them even when this opposed civic values. That the problems associated with leadership in Homer were also thought to appear in the fifth century suggests that human nature was thought to overcome high ideals and to be a factor in determining behaviour for historical leaders too.

Shay sees the Homeric Achilles as an exemplary leader of men who exhibits concern for all the troops and who has successfully led twelve missions for the Greeks,[180] but who feels so betrayed by Agamemnon that he becomes uncontrollably angry to the extent that he threatens the very men he had previously protected.[181] By contrast Shay argues that Odysseus is depicted as a poor leader of men citing evidence for this claim from both *Iliad* and *Odyssey*.[182] When Odysseus leads his men away from Troy he still portrays himself in the role of a leader of troops, although he also tends very much to blame the downfall of the men on their own actions rather than on his leadership abilities.[183] However, certainly in the instance of the Cyclops in Book 9, Odysseus is directly to blame for the loss of six of his companions (and ultimately it appears for the loss of all the others through his taunting of Polyphemus). When Odyessus tells his story to the Phaeacians, this aspect becomes somewhat lost in the details of his triumphant escape plan. It is he who makes the decision to await the Cyclops in his cave against the advice of his companions who wish to abscond with as much plunder as they can carry. Odysseus claims that he was motivated to remain by a mixture of curiosity about the Cyclops and desire for treasure (9.224-9). Shay explains his apparently rash decision as typical of behaviour manifested by war veterans, who are attracted to dangerous situations even after they have returned home from war.[184] Certainly Odysseus does not seem, even by his own account, to have been thinking in great depth about the safety and well-being of his twelve companions during this episode. Instead his behaviour at this point seems self-seeking and self-centred. It is therefore open to debate whether Odysseus is motivated by the desire to avenge the lives of his slaughtered companions (as he sometimes maintains) or whether he acts more out of self-interest.

After his companions are killed and eaten by Polyphemus, Odysseus tells the Phaeacians that his first thought was of drawing his sword to kill the Cyclops (9.299-302). This reaction is closely akin to the initial idea of Achilles when he feels he has been publicly insulted by Agamemnon and the two passages share the phrase ὀξὺ ἐρυσσάμενος παρὰ μηροῦ’ (*Il.* 1.190, *Od.* 9.300). In each case the hero considers matters in his own head before acting – certainly Odysseus makes no mention of consulting his companions about the terrible situation they are all in or seeking their opinions. Again this detail points more towards the self-centred hero, than to a man who is principally concerned with the welfare of his comrades. In the *Iliad*, Achilles refrains from his attack because Athena asks him to reconsider.

Odysseus on the other hand claims that he himself realised that by killing the Cyclops he would doom himself and his remaining companions to death trapped as they were in the cave. Athena does play a role though as the goddess to whom Odysseus claims to have prayed to help him achieve his revenge (τισαίμην) on Polyphemus (*Od.* 9.316-17).

Because of the necessity of the escape plan, Burnett quite reasonably sees the acts of the Homeric Odysseus as defensive not vengeful.[185] Odysseus is very much driven by a desire to survive and the blinding plan achieves this where his original murder plan would not have. However, this account does not fully explain the behaviour of Odysseus, nor all of his proclaimed thoughts about the attack. Instead Odysseus' practically-minded patience in this episode is a telling element of how it is necessary to think carefully about the situation to establish the costs and benefits of any particular action. By devising a plan to deceive the Cyclops and to blind him while he is drunk, Odysseus manages to save himself and those of his companions who have not yet been devoured. His careful considera-tion before reacting to the Cyclops' attacks on his men is paralleled in several instances elsewhere in the epic. After his return to Ithaca he weighs up whether to kill Melanthius for his insulting behaviour (17.235-8). When he is fighting Irus in the palace he decides against a mortal blow so the suitors do not see his power (18.90-4). He also weighs up whether to kill his disloyal maidservants (20.10-13), but decides on patience.[186] In each case, his instinct is for self-preservation, even if this entails dishon-our. Rather than risking the loss of his life and his homecoming, Odysseus calculates that with patience he will be able to achieve revenge in the end.

But that is not to say that Odysseus was planning revenge for the sake of his dead colleagues. In his speech to the Cyclops after he and his companions have escaped, Odysseus vaunts his own prowess as part of his furious outburst. His tone suggests that he saw himself as the central figure whom Polyphemus was belittling by attacking his friends (9.475-6). Cast in this light his attack on the Cyclops was a way of redeeming his own sense of pride. In the same speech he credits the gods (and especially Zeus) with paying Polyphemus back (τῷ σε Ζεὺς τίσατο καὶ θεοὶ ἄλλοι) for his ill-treatment of guests (9.479),[187] although Zeus' rejection of the sacrificed ram problematises this claim (9.550-6). It is only later when Odysseus tells Penelope of his adventures that Odysseus' blinding of the Cyclops is said to be as revenge for his companions (ἀπέτισατο ποινὴν, 23.312). In both this speech and his tale to the Phaeacians it appears that Odysseus is using the idea of revenge for his companions to give a moral motive for his attack. But underlying this is the uncomfortable reality that Odysseus himself had jeopardised the lives of the men by rashly insisting on waiting to see the Cyclops. It is this episode, too, which apparently seals the fate of Odysseus and his men as stated in Polyphemus' prophecy (9.528-31) because of the curse Polyphemus utters against Odysseus and the conse-quent anger of Poseidon concerning the attack on his son.

These episodes from the Homeric epics suggest that although revenge often appears to be a key motive or is the stated motive for an attack, other reasons are involved as well. Both Odysseus and Achilles claim to be acting in order to take revenge for their companions, but it is clear that they also act for themselves to prove that they are not weak and that they are worthy of honour and leadership.[188] The extent to which these more selfish motives override the desire to take revenge for the sake of the dead is hard to evaluate. But it is worthy of note that without a combination of pressing motives, the texts suggest that revenge can be neglected in favour of settlement.[189] In fact, the examples suggest that revenge for a homicide outside warfare was not as common as we have been led to expect and that men might be reluctant to pursue revenge especially if it was not politically expedient to do so. Even in a wartime context, political expediency might be preferred to revenge as is stressed by Thucydides in his account of the Mytilene debate (3.36-49). In this debate Cleon argues for angry revenge against the Mytileneans saying that every man should be put to death for their treachery against Athens. His opponent Diodotus, on the other hand, wins the debate by arguing that taking revenge would not be expedient for the Athenian state in the war.[190]

'Women do most delight in revenge'[191]

By contrast, female characters are frequently shown calling for revenge and are associated with desiring revenge for its own sake. Female relatives are more likely to be depicted disregarding ideas of political expediency and peaceful settlements in favour of blood.[192] Authors suggest that their desire for revenge can make them ruthless towards their kin – they encourage them to take on the risks of revenge rather than avoiding trouble, even though this could mean losing them too. I have argued elsewhere that the association of women with the encouragement of blood revenge, especially in laments, leads to their depiction in literature as bloody avengers.[193] It is also possible that their lack of active political participation meant that they were not readily associated with preferring political motivations by male authors (although some evidence suggests that Greek women were interested in their male relations' political careers).[194] Although there is no evidence of women ever approaching the violence level of men in any society and no evidence of any culture in which men are less violent than women,[195] Greek literary texts often depict women as more bloodthirsty than their male counterparts.[196] Wilson highlights the case of Hecuba in the *Iliad* and compares her attitude to that of the goddess Hera. Wilson maintains that both of these female characters are depicted rejecting male attempts at settlement in favour of bloody reprisals.[197] Hera protests against the proposed settlement between the Achaeans and Trojans brokered in Book 3 and offers to sacrifice her own favourite cities in exchange for the annihilation of her enemies in

Troy (4.25-54). Hecuba does not want her husband to negotiate a ransom of Hector's body with Achilles, but longs for revenge against him (24.194-216).[198] As Wilson has noted in both instances, the women are said to want to eat their enemies raw in retaliation and to be willing to sacrifice their own loved ones to achieve this revenge (4.31-6, 24.212-14).[199] She concludes:

> It is reasonable to infer that the *Iliad* aligns accepting material settlements
> ... with the male and culture and denying material settlements and / or
> limits on *poinê* with the female and nature.[200]

In other texts too female insistence on blood revenge is emphasised[201] and women are even depicted taking revenge into their own hands. For example, Herodotus claims that Nitocris of Egypt achieved revenge for her brother's death by a trick. He says that while her brother was king, he was killed by a large group of conspirators who then forced Nitocris to take the throne, perhaps imagining that she would be more compliant to their wishes than her brother. However, she managed to avenge (τιμωρέουσαν) her brother's death by luring the nobles responsible into a trap and killing them all. She then threw herself into a pit of ashes to avoid retribution (ἀτιμώρητος γένηται) (2.100). Herodotus characterises Nitocris as duplicitous and single-minded in her attempts at revenge. The female protagonist of this tale cares more about blood revenge than her own political advantage. She is not thought to have been satisfied with the power she had gained following her brother's death, but to have desired revenge to such an extent that she was willing to sacrifice her own life.[202]

Pheretima is also depicted by Herodotus as being ruthless in her quest for revenge. Herodotus claims that when her son Arcesilaus was killed by conspirators in Barca, she went to the Persians to seek revenge (τιμωρῆσαι) for her son's death (4.165). Aryandes sent the Persian army to Barca allegedly as avengers (τιμωροί) for Pheretima (4.200). However, Herodotus conjectures (4.167) that the Persians did not act out of a desire to achieve revenge or justice (their expressed motive), but instead for political motivations (they wished to seize Libya).[203] Without this added incentive it is unclear whether Pheretima would have obtained help from them. Certainly she is earlier said to fail to obtain an army from Euelthon in Cyprus when she wishes to help her son to return from exile (4.162). Throughout Pheretima is characterised as highly supportive of her son, as well as violent and vengeful. When handed those deemed most responsible for Arcesilaus' death, Pheretima elects to have them impaled and hung around the city walls alongside the severed breasts of their wives (4.202). This revenge is particularly significant as it is the one which Herodotus singles out as being the most inappropriate due to its excessive nature. Pheretima is also said to have been punished by the gods because of the excessive nature of her revenge (ὡς ἄρα ἀνθρώποισι αἱ λίην ἰσχυραὶ τιμωρίαι

38

πρὸς θεῶν ἐπίφθονοι γίνονται) by being eaten alive by worms – a hideous end to match the hideous nature of her revenge (4.205).[204] Here, as in Homer, female characters are depicted manifesting such a strong desire to achieve blood revenge that it makes them act in excessive ways.[205]

In these examples powerful women are thought to seek revenge for their family members using whatever methods they can to achieve their ends. Nitocris relies on deception to kill her brother's enemies, while Pheretima relies on persuasion and the help of a foreign army. As previously noted, women were usually thought incapable of taking violent action against men without help and so they needed to rely on their ability to persuade others to aid them. Alternatively, women were thought capable of prevailing if they employed deception or set a trap.[206] Although there are problems with the historicity of these tales, they attest to the tendency to associate women with brutal revenge acts against their enemies.

In tragic plot-lines too, women are particularly associated with brutal acts of revenge.[207] However, while the women depicted in non-tragic texts are shown avenging their kin against enemies of the family, in tragedy women are typically depicted desiring and exacting blood revenge against *philoi*.[208] In this respect the tragedians appear to exaggerate and twist normal behaviour in order to create their plot-lines.[209] Not only do the plots focus on women taking revenge – a 'World Upside Down' type of plot as Burnett suggests in that women were not usually thought of as avengers,[210] – but the female avengers in tragedy also tend to attack friends, including blood kin, relations through marriage and guest-friends. Examples include Electra who attacks her mother to avenge the murder of her father,[211] Althaea who kills her son in revenge for the death of her brothers,[212] Alcmena who wishes to take revenge for her son and grandchildren on her cousin, and Hecuba who is depicted demanding and exacting revenge for her sons against *philoi*.

In tragedy as in Homer, Hecuba is closely associated with the desire for revenge and is characterised as a fierce defender of her sons' interests. In Euripides' fragmentary *Alexandros*, Hecuba is shown as an arch-defender of the rights of her sons, as well as being a vengeful mother.[213] According to the fragmentary hypothesis (P.Oxy. 3650) Alexandros was exposed by his parents following Hecuba's ominous dream, but was rescued by a herdsman. Twenty years later he was arraigned before Priam by fellow herdsmen because of his arrogant attitude.[214] Alexandros defended himself so well that he was permitted to enter the games established to commemorate his own death. When Alexandros triumphed in several events,[215] his brother Deiphobus took this as a great dishonour because he thought he had been beaten by a slave (cf. fr. 62a Kn).[216] In the hypothesis Deiphobus is said to have decided to ask his mother Hecuba to kill the troublesome slave who was actually her own unrecognised son.[217] Hecuba is said to have been on the point of killing him, when Cassandra recognised him.[218] The material in the hypothesis suggests that in this play Hecuba was depicted as so protective over the honour of her sons that she was willing to kill anyone who threatened their position.[219] Ironically, though, Hecuba's murderous attack in the play was actually aimed at her own unrecognised son.[220] Here, as often in tragedy, *philos* attacks *philos*, albeit unwittingly. Hecuba's desire to help and protect her sons leads to her near destruction of one of them. Even more ironically, the recognition of Alexandros and his acceptance into the Trojan royal family at the end of the play portends the doom of them all.[221]

In Euripides' extant *Hecuba*, the Trojan queen is characterised as equally keen to support her son and to achieve blood revenge for him, this time against a guest-friend. In some respects she is comparable to the Herodotean Pheretima whose constant concern is the welfare of her son Arcesilaus, and whose mother-love leads to very brutal acts of revenge. However, the tragic Hecuba attacks *philoi* rather than political enemies, as is apparent in *Hecuba* where she seeks help from enemies (the Greeks) to defeat a guest-friend (albeit a treacherous one) for the sake of her beloved son. In this respect the play toys with expectations and notions about friends and enemies, as is typical in tragedies (cf. 745-6).[222]

The play begins with the ghost of Polydorus, son of Priam, who has been murdered by the very man who was supposed to protect him and ensure the survival of the line of Priam after the fall of Troy. As noted earlier, the position of a guest in the house of his host was a vulnerable one, especially in this case where the guest is a young child incapable of defending himself.[223] The appearance of Polydorus' corpse at Troy leads Hecuba to seek revenge against his murderer. However, Hecuba too is in a particularly weak position. She has lost all her male relatives and is now a slave (159-64). She initially states that she would be unable to achieve her revenge without male help (οὐκ ἂν δυναίμην τοῦδε τιμωρεῖν ἄτερ τέκνοισι τοῖς ἐμοῖσι, 749-50). As we have seen, women would usually have to gain support from a male relative in order to achieve revenge and slaves were in a particularly weak position in that their masters would have to act for them (cf. 741).[224] The chances of the interests of a slave coinciding with those of a master or the interests of a woman coinciding with those of men outside her family are slim,[225] and this is the situation represented in the play. Hecuba approaches Agamemnon to try to persuade him as a 'relative' through Cassandra and as her master to take revenge against Polymestor (749ff.).[226] She also appeals to Agamemnon on grounds of universal traditions and customs claiming that Polymestor has violated *xenia*, has broken his oaths and has not given burial to the corpse of her son (786-97),[227] and she asks him to act as avenger on her behalf (σύ μοι γενοῦ τιμωρὸς ἀνδρὸς ἀνοσιωτάτου ξένου, 790-1). In a standard oath a Greek swore by his own life and that of his sons (e.g. [Demosthenes] 59.10; Pausanias 2.18.1), as the closely comparable story of Glaucus in Herodotus makes clear. In Herodotus' tale Glaucus consults the Delphic oracle about whether he should break his oath to a man who has left money with him for safekeeping (Herodotus 6.86). Although he tries to backtrack from his duplicity when he hears the oracle's reply that the man who breaks his oath sacrifices his descendants and future, he is not successful and his family dies out. Here as in the tale of Polymestor an oath is broken out of greed. The theme of the broken oath when first mentioned in *Hecuba* therefore portends the worst for Polymestor and his sons.[228]

Agamemnon is unwilling to act on Hecuba's behalf because he does not want to displease the army (861-3). He points out that Polymestor is a friend to the Greeks and Polydorus their enemy (858-9) and although he recognises that Polymestor's deed was terrible, he does not want to oppose the Greek army in order to uphold a principle.[229] For Agamemnon there is insufficient motivation to help Hecuba take revenge. Without a compelling motive of his own Agamemnon is not willing to act for Cassandra and Hecuba or even for universal laws and customs. Instead he is portrayed as considering the matter with care and electing to avoid any risks to himself. In the play Agamemnon is depicted choosing political expediency over claims for private revenge and theories of justice regarding *xenia*.[230] Euripides here plays on the association between the 'masculine' desire to look out for the common good and reject private revenge as opposed to the 'feminine' desire to pursue private interests and seek revenge. Earlier in the play Odysseus is also represented rejecting Hecuba's personal claims on him in favour of the public interest.[231] The arguments expressed by the pair closely reflect the arguments of the participants in Thucydides' trial of the men of Plataea, as has been shown by Hogan.[232] In the Thucydidean debate, the Thebans win over the Spartans through their appeals to political expediency, whereas the Plataeans' appeals to justice fail.[233]

In Euripides' *Heraclidae* too similar themes are presented. In this play, Hercules' old adversary and kinsman Eurystheus pursues the children of Hercules in the hope of eliminating them so that they will not return in maturity to compete with him for power (465-70, 1005-8). The children are taken to Marathon by their grandmother Alcmena where they supplicate the Athenians to help them and seek protection at the altar of Zeus. When Eurystheus is defeated in battle by Hyllus and the Athenians, and brought before Alcmena by Iolaus, Alcmena demands his death (1045-52).[234] However, it is not deemed right by the Athenians to slay a prisoner of war (961-80). Once again in this play *philos* is pitted against *philos* in controversial and difficult circumstances. Eurystheus is Alcmena's cousin (αὐτανέψιος, 986) and his herald tries to seize the children although they are suppliants (55-78). The play also emphasises very strongly the contrast between male legalism in which prisoners of war cannot be killed despite their former actions and female revenge out of personal interests.[235] Alcmena, like Hecuba and Pheretima, is represented as keenly supporting the interests of her son and grandchildren,[236] and she is willing to kill the man who threatens them herself (974).[237] By contrast the men of Marathon are troubled by Alcmena's insistence of revenge and are not happy to kill in revenge outside of warfare.

Like Alcmena, Hecuba too is forced to take revenge into her own hands when she can find no male avenger willing to help her.[238] Agamemnon does not prevent her from seeking revenge, but at the same time he does not believe that she will be capable of defeating a man (885). Hecuba manages to achieve revenge by relying on a combination of deception (δόλῳ, 884) and persuasion to lure her enemy, Polymestor, and his young children into her tent (968-75).[239] She also relies on the help of the other Trojan women whose collective power is a force to be reckoned with, comparable to mythical groups of women who killed men – the Danaids and the Lemnian women (886-7). The women acting together succeed in killing the children before blinding Polymestor (1034-6, 1049-55).[240] Meridor has argued that the murder of Polymestor's children was in the spirit of Attic law, because the Trojan women, rather than Hecuba herself, commit the murders.[241] However, as Gregory has pointed out, the play focuses on a problematic situation where legal institutions are absent and women take justice into their own hands.[242] Athenian women had little or no role to play in prosecuting and punishing in Attic trials and their role here should not be seen as normal. Instead the focus of the play is upon revenge in a highly problematic situation, involving a female protagonist seeking revenge, a dispute between *philoi*,[243] infanticide and blinding,[244] all typical tragic motifs, but not typical of classical Athenian life.[245]

At the same time Hecuba's revenge is carefully calculated to achieve equivalence for the terrible crime perpetrated upon her by Polymestor (cf. 1086-7). Just as Hecuba has been deprived of her last son by Polymestor, and is forced to live on knowing that her husband's family has died out, so too he is now deprived of his sons and future.[246] Hecuba's betrayal of her guest-friend Polymestor and murder of his sons while they are guests in her tent replicate Polymestor's betrayal of his guest-friend Priam and the murder of his son Polydorus.[247] Polymestor's greed, which led him to kill his guest, is now his downfall as Hecuba lures him by promises of more gold.[248] Although Polymestor maintains that what Hecuba did was worse than murder (1120-1), her revenge is very carefully balanced against his original attack. As discussed at the beginning of this chapter, an exact replication of the crime is not always felt to achieve an exact balance. By killing all Polymestor's sons Hecuba does more than take a life for a life. However at the same time she creates equivalence between her own position and Polymestor's position – both have now lost all their sons. Just as the man with one eye argued that a man who took his only remaining eye should lose both his eyes in return, here the man who took Priam's only remaining son loses all his sons in return.

An eye for an eye

The decision to blind Polymestor himself is also significant. Blinding in Greek thought is often symbolic of castration, a symbolism which makes perfect sense in this play.[249] In other tales blinding appears to be symbolic of castration and infertility.[250] Further evidence for this theory can be found in the parallels between this plot of *Hecuba* and the story of Hermotimus and Panionius told by Herodotus (8.104-6). In Herodotus' tale a man who was castrated by a slave trader later gets revenge on him by having him castrate his own sons, while the sons castrate their father. In both *Hecuba* and the Herodotean tale an apparent friend lures an enemy along with his sons into a trap by promising riches and prosperity.[251] Both stories feature revenge attacks on a father and his sons. And, I believe, in both instances the revenge aims at replicating the damage originally inflicted on the avenger by his victim. By castrating both father and sons, Hermotimus ensures that Panionius will share the same bleak future as him.[252] Likewise Hecuba aims to leave Polymestor the same bleak future that he has inflicted upon her family.

Herodotus maintains that the story of Hermotimus and Panionius contains the 'greatest revenge' (μεγίστη τίσις) known to him (8.105). Scholars have tended to interpret μεγίστη in this phrase as 'barbaric', 'most horrific' or even 'excessive'. However, Herodotus does not explicitly state that this revenge was inappropriate (as he does in the case of Pheretima, 4.205). While the Greeks would surely have been appalled at the castration in this story,[253] there is no evidence in the text that the revenge itself would have seemed inappropriate to them.[254] Indeed, in his 'avenger-style' speech where he explains his motivations for action, Hermotimus says that had he or his ancestors committed some form of wrongdoing against Panionius and his family, his treatment would have been explicable (8.106.3).[255] Further, he emphasises that he believes his action was divinely sanctioned as the gods placed Panionius in his hands so that he could execute revenge.[256] Moreover, the occurrence of μεγίστη with a 'revenge' word is normal in oratory where it does not have any of the negative connotations desired by the commentators for this story (Demosthenes 9.37; Isocrates 15.34; 20.6; Lysias 31.26). I believe μεγίστη should here be interpreted as 'fullest' and that Herodotus saw this revenge as a perfect kind of symmetry in which a man who perpetrated the worst kind of deed, suffered exactly the same fate himself. Further it is possible to postulate that the story is meant to be satisfying to the reader who applauds the neatness of the revenge act.[257]

Others have suggested that the revenge in Herodotus' tale is not balanced, but that attacking multiple victims instead of one should be seen as escalation.[258] However, this is to misunderstand the complex calculations that are needed to achieve balance in revenge.[259] If Hermotimus were to leave the sons of Panionius unharmed he would not cause Panionius to suffer the same fate as he has suffered. Hornblower further suggests (based on the use of the Greek word ἀποτέμνω) that the method of castration itself is not the same in each case, but that Hermotimus' attack involves a greater degree of amputation which would cause his victims to bleed to death – a 'dramatic escalation' as he terms it.[260] However, this reading, while consistent with Hornblower's theory that the tale at one level represents historical events between the Greeks and Persians in Asia Minor, implies that death would have been viewed as worse than castration.[261] It is not at all clear that this is the case. In fact, the castration of Panionius and his sons signifies the end of his family line, equivalent to his death.[262] Leaving him alive (as Hecuba leaves Polymestor alive, but blind) would mean he had to suffer throughout his life knowing that his line was doomed.[263] Here the metaphorical 'eye for an eye' is both equivalent to a 'life for a life' and yet more dire than a simple exchange of two lives. Miller finds (non-Greek) evidence in his examination of compensation payments that the reproductive capacity of either male or female is valued more highly than an individual's life.[264] The idea that the death of a man's line is deemed much more significant than the death of the man himself is familiar in Greek thought.

These stories are powerful testimony to the significance of offspring in the Greek world. In *Hecuba* Polydorus, the last son of Priam, is called the anchor of the house (80), the implement that prevents the ship / house going to its destruction. With his death the family is sunk. Significantly enough, a son is also the eye of the house, as Orestes is called by the chorus in Aeschylus' *Choephori* (ὀφθαλμόν οἴκων, 934). Similar imagery is employed by Atossa in the *Persians* in reference to her son Xerxes (ὄμμα ... δόμων, 169). Andromache also uses this metaphor in reference to her son in Euripides' *Andromache* (εἰς παῖς ὅδ᾽ ἦν μοι λοιπὸς ὀφθαλμὸς βίου, 406). Each of these instances refers to a son who is threatened with death and whose death would bring about the end of the family line. This fate comes to pass in Euripides' *Bacchae* where Cadmus laments the end of his bloodline along with the death of Pentheus. He too describes his grandson and heir in a similar way (1308).[265] The eye metaphor seen in these examples is further testament to the link between procreation and eye imagery. It is certainly possible to interpret the blinding of Polymestor in light of these examples. While the eyes are symbolic of offspring and the family line, his blind eyes in the play signify his lack of offspring and future hope. The light of the house has been extinguished for him. The central importance of offspring in Greek thought is evident enough from these examples. The part that violence and revenge played in securing reproductive resources for procreation and the continuation of the family line is the subject of the next chapter.

44

2

Adultery, Rape and Seduction

Acts of revenge stimulated by sexual jealousy are very familiar to us from stories in the media today. Examples of violent revenge, sometimes of the most excessive nature, are closely connected to instances of seduction, rape and adultery in ancient texts too and men are represented as being keenly interested in protecting their female relations from such attacks. Indeed, the Greek examples indicate that murderous revenge is associated more readily with these cases than with cases of homicide. Key mythical examples of this are Odysseus' revenge on the suitors for courting his wife and Menelaus' war against the Trojans because of Paris' theft of his wife. In this chapter it is suggested that these revenges abound in the mythical sources because of a male preoccupation with the importance of acquiring and protecting reproductive resources in order to ensure the continuation of the family line. Therefore Burnett is perhaps not wrong to see Odysseus' revenge against the suitors as the archetypal Greek revenge act, although her reasons for selecting this example are questionable. Instead of stressing the significance of the secrecy involved in the revenge act and the revelation of the avenger, the emphasis should rest much more heavily on the motif of 'rescue of a female relative' which Burnett has relegated to her 'favorite elaboration' section.[1] In my opinion the involvement of female relatives should not be seen only as an elaboration, but instead it is at the very heart of Odysseus' ruthless revenge and other key revenges. Both in mythical stories and in Attic law the most violent and deadly responses are associated with the protection of women and their reproductive resources.

The protection of women

The prominence of violent responses to protect women and their reproductive resources has been much discussed by evolutionary psychologists and anthropologists.[2] Daly and Wilson argue that male sexual proprietariness and rivalry motivate a substantial proportion of homicides everywhere.[3] They estimate that these killings could account for as many as half of all homicides.[4] This is because men tend to react strongly to any suggestion of sexual infidelity by their partners and are prone to violence and rage caused by this sexual jealousy.[5] Evidence for these theories can easily be detected in ancient sources. For example Isocrates says 'I know that all men value their own children and wives highly and are particularly angry at those who wrong them; that violence towards them is the cause of greatest evils, and that many private citizens and rulers are now destroyed by this' (3.36).[6] Demosthenes too maintains that 'we fight enemies to protect our women and children and we are permitted to kill even friends if they insult and defile them' (23.56). He also suggests that young men often exchange blows over women (54.13; cf. Lysias 4). The defence of women and children is also a significant factor in warfare as stressed in the *Iliad* (5.485-6; cf. 10.420-2) and the enslavement of conquered women and children features in both mythical stories and historical accounts.[7]

The ancients were much preoccupied with issues of female fidelity and the implications of this for male reproduction. Women's sexuality is an area where a woman wields particular power over a man and it is deemed threatening.[8] This power and the consequent anxiety it creates can be perceived in Herodotus' tale of Demaratus' mother. When others mock Demaratus and claim that he is the son of a stable boy, she responds: 'May the wives of those who say these things give birth to the sons of stable boys' (6.69.5). Her wish / curse here reflects the difficulty for men in preventing their wives from foisting upon them other men's children who might usurp the position of their own (perhaps unborn) children.[9] Consequently, there are some indications that Athenian brides were expected to express extreme modesty (cf. Xenophon *Oec.* 7.14).[10] The necessity for an unmarried girl to behave appropriately is highlighted in the *Odyssey* during Odysseus' encounter with Nausicaa. He decides against clasping her knees in order to avoid offence (6.141-7) and suggests to her that people would talk if she entered town with a male stranger (6.273-85). He further suggests that she herself would blame a girl who consorted with men before marriage (6.286-8). He also worries about the potential anger of Alcinous if he returns into the town openly with Nausicaa. He ascribes this worry to men's natural jealousy over their female relatives (7.305-7). Anthropologists have noted that adulterous woman and unchaste girls are unlikely to find suitable husbands in the future. If a woman cannot be given in marriage, and thereby create a good alliance for her family, she ceases to have worth, but instead becomes an economic burden for them.[11] Her father and brothers might then choose to kill her or cast her out.

In Athens, husbands refrained from killing their adulterous wives themselves, but they were compelled to divorce them ([Demosthenes] 59.87; cf. Lysias 14.28) and return them to their fathers.[12] The reason for this is that if a man killed his wife himself, he would risk angering her family.[13] Comparative evidence suggests that when the woman's father and brothers discovered the reason for her divorce, they could choose to kill her themselves as she had caused shame to the family and had lost them an important alliance.[14] However, anecdotal examples from recent times reflect the unwillingness of a father to kill an errant daughter.[15] It was apparently still possible under Solonian legislation for fathers to sell unchaste girls into slavery (Plutarch *Sol.* 23.2), thereby removing the economic burden on the *oikos* without resorting to killing. Although Mac-Dowell speculates that Athenians of the fifth and fourth centuries were unlikely to take such a step,[16] there is scant evidence regarding what treatment unchaste women received at their fathers' hands in Athens. The laws which state that an adulteress was not allowed to participate in state festivals and sacrifices (Aeschines 1.183; Demosthenes 59.86-7) seem to imply that many were not put to death or enslaved. However, there is little to suggest that anyone would prosecute a man who killed his own daughter in such circumstances.[17] Certainly Aeschines praises such strict behaviour towards shameless women when he refers to the tale of an Athenian citizen who found his daughter had been seduced before her marriage and walled her up in an empty house with a horse to kill her (1.182).[18] The scholiasts on this passage inform us that the man who did this was Hippomenes, a descendant of the mythical Athenian king, Codrus. Although Aeschines praises this killing, the example is of a mythical nature[19] and it is unclear whether Athenian men would actually have considered putting their errant daughters to death. Nevertheless, this rhetoric demonstrates that there was a keen interest in employing even the most extreme methods to ensure the chastity and fidelity of Athenian women and deter them from fornication or adultery. Similarly, in a fragment from one of Euripides' *Melanippe* plays, a speaker urges men to punish an unchaste woman (τείσασθε τήνδε) and not to hold back because of kinship. He says that failure to punish impure women causes corruption in others (Euripides fr. 497 Kn).[20]

The problem for ancient Greek men is that women are needed for bearing children to perpetuate the male line, but they cannot truly be trusted to remain faithful and obedient (cf. Euripides *Hipp.* 616-24; *Med.* 573-5; fr. 498 Kn).[21] Anxiety related to the problems of paternity is expressed in a number of ways. The horror of dying without any offspring is shown in numerous myths and anecdotes including the stories of castration discussed in the previous chapter and the myth of Jason and Medea discussed in detail further below.[22] Material considerations are also at issue relating to the proper inheritance of property and to the potential costs of raising children.[23] Because men invest heavily in rearing offspring, it is important for them to ensure that any children born to their wives are their own.[24] There are enormous gains to be made by an adulterer who succeeds in getting past the guard of a husband. If he eludes detection, another man will bear the costs of raising his child.

Sequestering mates is one possible tactic to avoid a competitor taking advantage of your resources to raise his child.[25] There are indications that this was a tactic employed by some Athenian men, although perhaps not very successfully (cf. Aristophanes *Thesm.* 788-99; Lysias 3.6).[26] In Lysias 1, there is mention of a lock which is placed on the outside of the door of the women's quarters (1.13; cf. Xenophon *Oec.* 9.5), although in the story which Euphiletus tells the court, it is (ironically) his wife who locks him inside. Euphiletus also tells the jury that he kept a good watch on his wife until she had borne him a son (Lysias 1.6).[27] By making this claim, Euphiletus is apparently protecting the interests of his son by suggesting that his wife did not have the opportunity to commit adultery before the child's birth. A child born to an adulterous woman cannot certainly be said to be the child of her husband, so it is important for Euphiletus to establish that the child is his legitimate son, if he has good reason to do so. Pomeroy has suggested that Euphiletus might have been motivated by his desire to retain his wife's dowry when he makes this claim.[28] She believes that even adulterous wives divorced under compulsion would take their dowry with them if the marriage were terminated without male issue. However, it is unclear that this would have been the case in this circumstance. The suggestion that fathers could be influenced by considerations of material goods when announcing the legitimacy of their children is certainly incompatible with the law which allowed lethal revenge against adulterers in order to prevent problems with paternity and inheritance in Athens. The fact that Euphiletus decides to kill Eratosthenes rather than accept his proffered monetary compensation might also indicate that he is not especially concerned about his material well-being. Elsewhere it is suggested that children could be stigmatised by their mother's adultery. In Euripides' *Hippolytus*, even though Phaedra has not committed any adulterous act with Hippolytus, she is worried that her children will be dishonoured by rumours about her. Her fear is that if she is thought of as an adulteress, then the paternity of her sons will be in doubt (419-23). Similar reasoning underlies Teucer's slur in Sophocles' *Ajax* that Agamemnon's mother was condemned to be drowned for being an adulteress (1295-7).[29] This insult implies that Agamemnon's paternity cannot be guaranteed because of the infidelity of his mother.[30]

An alternative tactic in protecting one's mate is demonstrating a credible threat of violence. Here, revenge or the threat of revenge has a deterrent effect.[31] A man who retaliates against an adulterer with extreme force ensures that no other men decide that it is easy to take advantage of him by cuckolding him. In this way a man protects his resources and his own honour.[32] Death is a common penalty for adultery, seduction, rape and abduction of women in both mythical and historical texts. This can be a private penalty exacted by the relatives of the girl, as well as being a state penalty which either permitted execution by relatives or prescribed death for this offence. The notion of death for men who commit offences against other men's womenfolk covers both time and space. Lysias maintains that death was a possible penalty for adultery throughout Greece (1.2) and cites the story of a brother of Agoratus put to death for abducting a girl in Corinth (13.65).[33] Tragic characters also hold these views. Orestes represents the murder of Aegisthus as the just penalty for an adulterer (Aeschylus *Cho.* 989-90).[34] In Euripides' *Hippolytus*, Theseus wonders whether his son died at the hands of a husband angered at his adultery with his wife (1164-5). Hippolytus himself is amazed that Theseus does not put him to death when he believes that he has been committing adultery with his wife (1041-4). Although Theseus does not kill his son himself, he does send him into exile and at the same time, curses him ensuring his imminent death. Theseus states that he would lose his reputation, if he were to spare Hippolytus after he had been so badly treated by him (976-80). By this he means that if he forgave his son, others would see him as weak and challenge his authority. Theseus believes that a strong response is vital for the protection of his household and status. As it happens though, the events of the play come about through the machinations of the goddess Aphrodite, and Theseus is condemning an innocent man to death, bringing misery on his own head in typical tragic fashion.

The necessity for an honourable man to avenge himself against someone who has attacked his wife is also demonstrated by a comment made in the Homeric tale of Bellerophon. When Bellerophon rejects the advances of Anteia she falsely tells her husband Proetus that Bellerophon wished to seduce her adding that he should either die or kill Bellerophon (*Il.* 6.157ff.). This thinking demonstrates that a man who is unable to kill sexual predators is symbolically dead. His inability to protect his reproductive resources could condemn him to a future with no progeny. This notion is paralleled with a twist in Herodotus' tale of Candaules' wife in which a foolish husband secretly hides a friend in his bedchamber so that he can observe his wife when she is naked. However the wife spots the interloper and insists that he make amends by killing her husband or dying himself. In this story the 'kill or die' comment is addressed to the potential seducer Gyges and not the husband (1.11). The fact that Candaules threatens his own wife's modesty in this tale and fails to protect her adequately is remarkable, as Gyges himself notes (1.10).[35] Candaules pays for his error with his life, losing as a consequence his wife and his throne. On one level this Herodotean tale appears to disguise a political wrangle between Candaules and Gyges.[36] On another level the story illustrates the dangers of failing to protect a wife properly by allowing another man to enter her bedchamber. This opens the possibility of betrayal by the wife and the loss of her reproductive resources to a rival.[37] Despite the fairy-tale quality of these stories, a kernel of truth is contained within them, expressing male concern about women's sexual power over them and their need to protect their wives strongly in order to ensure their own offspring's future survival. The universality of the themes of these stories, which are mirrored in many different cultures, indicates that these are widespread concerns for mankind and not only for the ancient Greeks.[38]

Similar themes are apparent in the tale of Clytemnestra who not only elects to commit adultery with Aegisthus, but is also implicated in the plot to kill her husband.[39] Here the loss of the man's reproductive future though the adultery of the wife is manifested in a mythic form by the wife killing her husband. In the *Odyssey*, the shade of Agamemnon repeatedly stresses that women are not to be trusted, even when they appear to be virtuous. For this reason, he encourages Odysseus not to be too open with his wife, nor to arrive home openly, advice which Odysseus later heeds (*Od*. 11.441-55). Indeed, it is made clear that some of the women in Odysseus' palace (if not Penelope herself) have become disloyal to him because they have been seduced by the suitors. The implication here is that the women are weak and are easily persuaded to betray their master. Clytemnestra herself is said to have been constant to her husband for a while. However, after Aegisthus disposes of her chaperone (a bard appointed to watch over her by Agamemnon), Clytemnestra easily succumbs to his advances (3.265-9). This story plays on the fear of men away at war for lengthy periods that other men are able to take advantage of their wives in their absence. The implication once again is that most women are too weak and immoral to guard their own modesty in the absence of strong male kin. Even in the case of a faithful wife, men still need to ensure that they are strongly protected. Despite her fidelity, Penelope is represented as being in a highly vulnerable position which requires manly protection. In the absence of her husband, with only a weak, young son to protect her, other men take advantage of the situation until Odysseus finally returns.

Responses to sexual offences against women

It is explicitly stated that the suitors fleeced Odysseus' household without fear because they thought Odysseus would not return (22.35-40; cf. 24.460). The suitors are said to be wasting the property of Odysseus and Telemachus without any thought of how they will repay it (1.372-8; cf. 22.35-41, 23.8-9). They appear to be eating constantly at Odysseus' house rather than at their own homes because there is no one strong enough to stop them doing so. Telemachus is too young and weak to handle the suitors on his own (2.58-62) and his attempts to get the people of Ithaca to intervene come to nothing.[40] The suggestion here is that the suitors are taking advantage of the lack of a strong male owner to use the house as they please. Notably the suitors think that Telemachus has gone to Pylos to get help for an attack against them, or that he will poison them (2.325-30), both women's methods of achieving revenge.[41] The suitors' attitude towards hospitality is illustrated in a most negative light through their treatment of Odysseus when he is dressed as a beggar.[42] Odysseus points out that they behave in an insulting manner (ὑβρίζοντες) and lack shame (οὐδ᾽ αἰδοῦς μοῖραν ἔχουσιν) (20.170-1). This behaviour is characterised as highly immoral and is thought to be the kind of behaviour that the gods avenge (τισαίατο λώβην) (20.169-71). The insults hurled at Odysseus are important as they drive him on to take revenge, by biting at his heart (20.284-6). He is similarly motivated by the insults to his wife and son (14.161-4).[43]

The nature of the insult to Penelope is highlighted in Antinous' comparison of Odysseus' request (which he imagines must be drunken) to attempt drawing the bow with Eurytion's drunken attempt to rape Hippodameia. This attempted rape resulted in revenge against him by his hosts and culminated in war between the Lapiths and Centaurs (21.299-304).[44] Antinous' objection is driven in part by the fear that Odysseus might humiliate him and the other suitors if he succeeds in stringing the bow where they have failed.[45] However, there is also the suggestion here that Odysseus would be attempting to make away with the bride inappropriately in that the contest of the bow aims to decide who will win the hand of Penelope. Ironically, though, it is in fact the suitors who are in the role of the drunken Eurytion as they try to woo a woman who is married to someone else in his own home. Further the idea of escalation here where the Centaurs march against the Lapiths because of an insult to one of them is mirrored in the response of the suitors' relatives after the death of their kin when it appears that the island will sink into a violent war.

The attacks on the women of the house rank particularly highly in Odysseus' estimation of the suitors' crimes and his decision to take lethal revenge.[46] They have been attempting to seduce his wife while he is still alive and they have seduced some of the maids in his house. These two crimes (along with the theft of his possessions) are cited by Odysseus in his speech to the suitors after he has killed Antinous (22.35-41).[47] This typical 'avenger-style speech' makes clear to all who are about to die that this is an act of revenge for specific named crimes rather than a random killing by an unknown man.[48] Similarly in his speech to Leodes before he kills him, Odysseus explains the exact nature of the man's crime. Although Leodes claims that he did not indulge in some of the greater excesses of the other suitors and was not disrespectful, Odysseus' anger is focused on the marriage this man was hoping for with Penelope. His speech highlights the significance of this motive in his decision to take deadly revenge and it throws further light on the reason. In hoping to marry Penelope, Odysseus claims that Leodes intended that she would bear his children. For this reason Odysseus says he will not escape death (22.321-5). This demonstrates clearly how the ideas of the evolutionary theorists are played out in Greek myths. Odysseus' reaction to this man is generated by his sexual proprietariness towards Penelope and his desire to protect her reproductive resources for himself. His extreme violence against the suitors is not atypical, but is representative of a desire to ensure the success of his bloodline in the future. This desire, which appears clearly in the Greek sources, is both embedded in Greek culture and significant in a more general way. Since Greek men had to rely upon their own abilities to defend their interests, the tendency towards violence in the protection of women and property is expected within Greek culture in a way in which it is not officially encouraged in the modern West. However, these tendencies towards violence are often associated with human males in circumstances such as these. This explains why incidents of domestic violence driven by sexual jealousy proliferate even when they are officially discouraged.[49]

Conversely the suitors believed that with little risk on their part, they could attempt to win valuable possessions and a noble wife. This becomes plain in their plots against Telemachus when it is suggested that the suitors would make substantial material gains if they got rid of him (16.383-6; cf. 2.332-6, 2.367-8). Removing the heir of the leading family of Ithaca would also have implications for those interested in promoting themselves in status and power on the island. It is said of Antinous that this was his main aim in courting Penelope (22.49-53) and Odysseus' strong response to the suitors and their relatives seems to be calculated as a method of firmly re-establishing himself as the leading figure on the island and of showing that others should not attack his household. Stress is also placed on the ending of the line of Arceisius in Ithaca, which would come about upon Telemachus' premature death (14.180-2, cf. 4.741). The death of Odysseus' only son and the marriage of his wife to another man combine to signify the symbolic destruction of Odysseus' reproductive powers. However the suitors' belief that Odysseus would never return is unfounded and their calculated risk does not work out.

Odysseus spends a deal of time planning and thinking about revenge, but does not rush straight in. At the beginning of Book 20 of the *Odyssey*, Odysseus lies in the hallway of his own home plotting troubles for the suitors who are afflicting his home, eating his livestock and wooing his wife. At this point he spots a group of women, who have taken the suitors as lovers, leaving his house. Odysseus is angered by the actions of these women and assesses carefully whether he should kill them outright or wait until the following day. As seen in the previous chapter, the careful consideration of the costs and benefits of actions is again prominent in Odysseus' decision-making process before he attacks. His anger does not drive him forward blindly, but he makes a choice based upon past experience. He refers to the episode with the Cyclops where he was also forced to consider his options carefully without rushing forward blindly in order to survive.[50] Just as in that case, it is implied, his life would be at risk if he were to act too hastily by killing the women when he had not made any proper plans to kill the suitors. Some further explanation for the nature of Odysseus' anger may lie in the simile which compares the 'growling' of his angry heart to the 'growling' of a protective bitch who wishes to defend her puppies against the possible attack of a stranger (20.14-16).[51] This simile depicts the nature of Odysseus' anger and reveals the emotional force behind his desire for revenge.[52] The image implies that Odysseus reacts strongly to the potential loss of his reproductive resources and that it is these and his progeny that he desires to protect. Eventually after the deaths of the suitors the twelve disloyal maids are put to death by Telemachus (22.437-73).

Odysseus lets none of the suitors escape death because all of them are guilty of sullying his honour and taking advantage of his family's perceived weakness during his absence. Although Eurymachus says that the suitors will pay compensation (22.55-9), Odysseus maintains that no remuneration is great enough to pay him back (ἀποτίσαι) except death (22.61-4). Instead, he must kill all the suitors to restore the balance of honour and demonstrate publicly that he is not weak. It is even worth risking one's life to achieve a restoration of honour after such insults (16.105-11; cf. 20.311-19). Odysseus' decision to kill all the suitors can be explained by his need to convince the people that no one should question his authority or make attacks on his household.[53] Odysseus realises that despite the danger (they are fighting against many of the important families of the district, 23.118-22; cf. 24.353-5), it is necessary for him to take risks in order to re-establish himself in power and regain the respect of the other leading families. Indeed, some of the citizens shudder at the prospect of fighting against Odysseus (24.450). For them his savagery and dominance in the fight against the suitors has the desired deterrent effect, although others (among them Eupeithes who is characterised as deluded) insist upon revenge (τίσεσθαι παιδὸς φόνον) (24.460-71). For the suitors' families too, the decision to attack is determined by their desire to avenge their kin (παίδων τε κασιγνήτων τε φονῆας τισόμεθ') (24.430-7), although their attempt is unsuccessful.

Odysseus' violent reaction to the threats to his family and to the undermining of his authority in his own house potentially influenced the behaviour of Athenian householders and their beliefs about their rights to protect their families and possessions. In a sensible article on this subject, Christ has suggested that the Athenians would have admired Odysseus as the model of manly excellence in his violent revenge on the suitors. He argues that an Athenian man's right to self-help in his own *oikos* harks back to the values portrayed in Homeric epic where the inviolability of the household was all-important.[54] The noble ideal of violent revenge against sexual predators as depicted in Homer combines with the ongoing need of Athenian men to protect their own households to explain why Attic law permitted the killing of a man caught in a compromising situation with another man's womenfolk (Demosthenes 23.53-5; Lysias 1.30; cf. Plato *Leg.* 874c).[55] The inclusion of concubines kept for the rearing of children alongside female relatives in the law of justifiable homicide suggests that the protection of reproductive resources was at the heart of this legislation.[56] This element of the law perhaps casts further light on Odysseus' rage at the behaviour of the maids in his palace.

Both in Lysias 1 and in the *Odyssey* the connection is made between dishonour done to husband and children by the acts of a seducer / seducers and the need for deadly retaliation (*Od.* 14.161-4; Lysias 1.4). According to Attic law, a man was also permitted to kill a thief in his house.[57] Odysseus clearly indicates that the suitors' attempts to seduce the women of his household and fleece him of his possessions are their two key crimes

(22.35-41), although their insulting behaviour is also relevant.[58] Significantly here Athenian laws allow a greater degree of violence in cases where women are threatened and the household is invaded, than in cases where a relative has been killed.[59] It seems likely that the decision to allow lethal retaliation in certain circumstances and not in others reflects earlier ideas and practice regarding appropriate levels of revenge. Certainly the decision to legislate against killing in the case of a homicide, but to allow it in other cases, is worthy of note. The implication of this decision is that these two types of revenge are conceptually different and require different responses. Moreover, the differences in response are not unique to Athens, but appear to be broadly similar throughout the available evidence. While the sources suggest a tendency towards non-violent resolution of killings outside of warfare in both mythical tales referring to the past and in classical Athens, violent revenge is regularly associated with threats to the household and is deemed to be a most just response to these threats (cf. Demosthenes 23.55; Lysias 1.29).

Exemplifying the appropriateness of lethal revenge in cases of seduction and rape is the aetiological myth of Ares who is said to have killed Halirrhothius for the rape of his daughter Alcippe. Halirrhothius' father Poseidon prosecutes Ares for murder, but Ares is acquitted of the crime at the Areopagus (Demosthenes 23.66; Euripides *El.* 1258-63).[60] While this story is told by Demosthenes and Euripides principally to demonstrate the sanctity of the Areopagus which even the gods are thought to respect and use in their disputes, it also demonstrates that lethal revenge against a man attacking a female relative is a firmly established principle. Even when the action shifts to the law court, murderous revenge in these circumstances is still considered to be appropriate and is questioned only by grieving relatives. Notably Poseidon is not thought to have attacked Ares himself in retaliation for the murder, but instead to have used the newly established court. Again the distinction between revenge for homicide and for sexual attacks is clearly demonstrated. On this point MacDowell asserts that the Athenians were 'primitive' for retaining the option of self-help against a man who stole one's property or one's wife, but 'progressive' in prosecuting killers rather than exacting blood revenge.[61] However, the evidence suggests that the tendency towards violence in one case and settlement in the other is traditional and there is no inconsistency here.

As suggested by the myth of Ares, although the laws allowed a man to kill in certain prescribed circumstances, the victim's relatives might still be expected to prosecute the killer in order to test the validity of his claims to have killed legally. In Athens, provision was made to try men who claimed to have committed homicide justifiably at the Delphinion (*Ath. Pol.* 57.3; Demosthenes 23.74; Pausanias 1.28.10).[62] Lysias 1 (*On the Murder of Eratosthenes*) appears to be such a case. Euphiletus is apparently being prosecuted by the relatives of Eratosthenes on the grounds that he did not kill Eratosthenes according to the law, but that he plotted the murder, perhaps for reasons other than adultery. In his speech, Euphiletus consequently spends much time attempting to establish that he did not plan to kill Eratosthenes out of prior enmity or to entrap him (1.4, 1.27, 1.43).[63] Instead he maintains that the killing was designed to eliminate a troublesome adulterer from the city (1.43-5). The stress he places on the deterrent element of his revenge (1.47) is consistent with the emphasis given to the deterrent function of revenge by scholars.[64] Just as Odysseus feels the need to react ruthlessly to reassert his position and protect his household, Euphiletus suggests that it was necessary for him to take lethal revenge not only to protect himself and his family, but also to defend other Athenian citizens from Eratosthenes' attacks. And just as Odysseus acts strongly to deter future attacks on himself, Euphiletus argues that by killing Eratosthenes, he is deterring would-be adulterers from committing the crime.

Like Odysseus, Euphiletus also gives a speech to explain his actions to the man he is about to kill, pointing out that Eratosthenes is not being attacked randomly, but that he is paying the price for his own misconduct (1.26). The significance of this speech is to highlight to the jurors that the killing is a legitimate retaliation against a man who has wronged Euphiletus' wife and children, as he states. In this respect his speech closely parallels Odysseus' address to the suitors where he points out their crimes against his wife and maids and tells them they will all die because of what they have done. However, there is an important difference between the two speeches. Euphiletus notes that he himself is not killing Eratosthenes, rather the law is killing him (οὐκ ἐγώ σε ἀποκτενῶ, ἀλλ' ὁ τῆς πόλεως νόμος). Herman has made much of this statement, arguing that it provides evidence that Euphiletus is trying to distance himself from notions of a revenge attack through his words.[65] Instead of being revenge, he argues, this should be seen instead as civic punishment.[66] However, as already seen, the connections made between this case and the tale of Odysseus closely associate Euphiletus' actions to the famous mythical revenge attack. Key characteristics typical of a revenge attack are present in Lysias' text including expressed feelings of dishonour, the rejection of a proffered settlement in favour of killing and, not least, the presence of an 'avenger-style' speech to explain Euphiletus' actions.[67] The fact that much stress is placed on the role of the law and of Athens in this speech does not mean that Euphiletus' actions should not be viewed as vengeful in spirit. Rather, he emphasises that his revenge killing is legitimate and should be accepted as such by the jurors.[68]

However, it seems that even if Euphiletus' story was accurate, he was treading on very thin ice in making his case, since he did not come upon Eratosthenes unexpectedly (although he tries to stress that he did, 1.37-42), but had been warned by his maid and had gathered witnesses from the neighbouring houses (1.23-4). The decision to gather witnesses is evidence of Euphiletus' need to prove to angered relatives (and to the jury) that he did not act inappropriately in killing Eratosthenes, yet at the same time this very element is suspicious since it implies a level of planning and calculation. The fact that Euphiletus elected to gather witnesses demonstrates that he knew that he would kill Eratosthenes and he was already thinking about the reaction of the dead man's relatives.[69] Odysseus too considers the reaction and potential pursuit of the suitors' relatives when he makes his plans of revenge against the suitors and sets in place suitable contingency plans to protect himself and his family. In order to convince the jury Euphiletus must carefully balance his need to prove that his actions were lawful with the expectation that killing of adulterers must be hot-blooded and not calculated.[70] Part of his strategy is to emphasise that killing was the only proper legal option, but scholars have noted that this is an exaggeration, since several other options were available to him, including prosecuting or publicly humiliating the adulterer.[71] He could also have accepted the compensation that Eratosthenes offered as others apparently chose to do.[72] Like Odysseus, Euphiletus rejects the proffered compensation with an indication that accepting it would be somewhat sordid and underhanded of him, while killing the adulterer is morally right and public spirited. Lysias' rhetoric suggests that honourable men and heroes like Odysseus take lethal revenge, while others who are less scrupulous accept money. Certainly it is implied in *Against Neaera* that Stephanus' alleged demands for money from Epaenetus for seducing Neaera's daughter are somewhat underhanded and ignoble ([Demosthenes] 59.65-6). Lysias apparently uses key elements from the *Odyssey* intentionally to demonstrate the similarity of Euphiletus' actions to the heroic and noble revenge of Odysseus. As such this speech implies that jurors would have been sympathetic to a man who killed an adulterer in such circumstances if his motivations were considered to be honourable like the heroes of epic.[73]

The decision to ignore an adulterous attack or to react to it may on occasions have been a difficult one, especially in cases where the law did not offer the kind of protection afforded to Euphiletus. For example in Herodotus' story of the inappropriate behaviour of Persian ambassadors towards women in the Macedonian court, Amyntas, king of the Macedonians, is prepared to accept the seduction of the women as a price for avoiding the risks of fighting against the Persians. However, his son Alexander refuses to accept the abuse of the women despite the risks. He calculates that it is better to kill the men than tolerate the seduction of the women of the household (Herodotus 5.18-20). He is said to react in this way, despite the inevitability of reprisal, as he feels that the insult is too great to bear.[74] It is notable that it is the young men who react violently in this tale, cohering with the evidence cited above that youths are more frequently involved in violent and lethal scuffles over women.[75]

Once again this story highlights a discrepancy in ways of dealing with disputes over the chastity of women and disputes over homicide. Alexander considers it is unacceptable to ignore the insult to his family's women or to settle this dispute peacefully. Instead he decides that death is necessary. However, the men on both sides are ready to settle the dispute over the homicide of the Persian ambassadors peacefully through the arrangement of a marriage alliance (5.21).[76] Herodotus suggests that the disputing parties prefer to come to an agreement without much thought for the loss of the ambassadors. In the agreement of the marriage alliance a female relative of Alexander is used as a sexual resource in his dealings with the Persians, but on this occasion because of the marriage agreement the sexual relationship between her and her Persian husband is a proper one, as well as being beneficial to both parties. Previously, on the other hand, the Persian ambassadors' relationship to the Macedonian women was not formalised and therefore their treatment of the women was viewed as so improper that a violent reaction was required. Although there are problems with the historicity of elements of this story, nevertheless the discrepancy between the participants' reactions to sexual offences against women and to homicide in this story is noteworthy.

Another possible response to a sexual attack on a woman is castration, which can be seen to be particularly appropriate in the circumstances. In the *Iliad* Phoenix maintains that his father cursed him with infertility because he had seduced his father's concubine (9.448-63).[77] The story pattern is replicated in Euripides' *Hippolytus* where Theseus believes that he and his son are competing over the sexual resources of the same woman.[78] He too curses his son, bringing about his death before he had experienced any sexual encounters (as is made clear through his rejection of Aphrodite in the play) and ending his chances of procreating and continuing the family line. This self-destruction of the family is typical of tragic plot-lines.[79] A similar response is also evidenced in one version of the castration of Gadatas, as told by Xenophon. It is said that the King of Assyria decides to take this drastic action because he thought Gadatas had made advances towards his concubine (*Cyr.* 5.2.28). Although this story is not reliable evidence for standard behaviour in such circumstances and it is suggested that the king acted unjustly and hybristically in his attack on an innocent man,[80] the response is symbolic of male reactions to seducers.[81] As seen in Chapter 1, castration is akin to killing and is often conceived of as being like death.[82] This response also neatly brings an end to the reproductive potential of a man who is thought to have been attempting to secure the reproductive resources of another man. As Xenophon's text makes clear there is also an aspect of dishonour and humiliation associated with being castrated.

The public humiliation of an adulterer or seducer is one of the possible responses to adultery attested in Attic sources, though it is unclear how often it was employed. Reference to 'radishing' occurs in Aristophanes (*Clouds* 1083, *Wealth* 168) and we can perhaps conclude that the humiliation of the adulterer in this way was something that the Athenians would have found amusing.[83] Certainly the male gods in Demodocus' song react with laughter to the humiliation of the adulterous Ares and Aphrodite when they are caught in an embarrassing trap by her husband Hephaestus (*Od.* 8.266-366). Brown suggests that the second burst of laughter by the gods (following Hermes' joke that he would be happy to be caught in such a trap with Aphrodite) shows that adultery among the gods is not such a serious offence.[84] Among the humans on earth on the other hand the implications for wooing another man's wife are far more serious, as the suitors will learn. However, there is a possibility of understanding all these revenge acts as pleasing and even amusing. Hephaestus' successful revenge is certainly satisfying in that the shame felt by the cuckolded husband is reversed and is felt by the adulterous couple. Where he felt he was being ridiculed by the behaviour of his wife and her lover, it is now their turn to suffer ridicule.[85] Odysseus' successful revenge can also be classified as satisfying for both internal and external audiences, in that the hero triumphs over the villains. Eurycleia is depicted as acting with great joy over Odysseus' revenge, although he rebukes her (22.408-13).

As Brown has shown, the theme of adultery in the tale of Demodocus is clearly related to the larger plot of the *Odyssey* in which the hero must overcome those wooing his wife.[86] The tale also shares some elements with Lysias 1. The role of the Sun who informs Hephaestus of the affair and acts as spy is comparable to the role of the two slaves in Lysias' speech. Hephaestus calls upon the other gods as witnesses just as Euphiletus summons his neighbours to witness his revenge on Eratosthenes. It is also implied in both cases that the wife in question is subsequently divorced and returned to her father. Hephaestus' demand that Aphrodite's father return the bride price seems to indicate this outcome. However, the episode differs in one important respect in that the immortals cannot perpetrate lethal revenge against one another. Hephaestus originally plans to imprison the adulterous pair forever – a form of revenge associated closely with divine punishment of other gods elsewhere.[87] However, Hephaestus eventually accepts compensation in the form of the adulterer's fine (μοιχάγρια) at the urging of Poseidon, who promises Hephaestus that Ares will make atonement (τίσειν ἄισμα) or that he himself will pay it (τίσω).[88] The peaceful resolution of this dispute and the decision to accept monetary compensation is paralleled in other tales of fighting among the gods.[89]

Wars over women

All these examples suggest that killing was seen as a just and heroic response to attacks on women, although accepting material compensation was also a possibility, if not a very honourable one. Another key way of responding was through a reciprocal attack on the women of your enemy. This method aims to replicate the offence in the revenge.[90] This response demonstrates clearly that the significance of the offence is its impact on men rather than on women.[91] The man whose wife, mother, daughter or sister is abducted feels dishonoured and desires to inflict the same feeling on the abductor. This reasoning is employed by Castor and Pollux, who are said to wage a war in order to rescue their sister Helen after she is abducted by Theseus and taken to Aphidnae.[92] In Theseus' absence the brothers conquer the city and retrieve Helen. At the same time, Apollodorus tells us, they elect to abduct Theseus' mother Aethra in revenge (3.10.7). This retaliation aims to make Theseus suffer in the same way as Castor and Pollux previously suffered. The loss of a female relative in this story is humiliating to the men involved and they are keen to retrieve their relative and to inflict a similar loss on their opponent.

This reasoning is also employed by Agamemnon when he decides that it is necessary for him to take the woman of another man after he is forced to return Chryseis to her father. He blames Achilles largely because of his role in persuading the army that Agamemnon should give up Chryseis and for that reason he elects to seize his prize Briseis. Achilles' anger following Agamemnon's appropriation of his woman is the pivotal factor around which the whole plot of the *Iliad* rotates and the significance of this fight over a woman should not be underestimated.[93] Achilles points out that Agamemnon has insulted him by taking his woman in the same way that Paris insulted Menelaus by taking Helen (9.337-43). Just as Menelaus is justifiably angry at Paris' affront, so too Achilles maintains that his anger towards Agamemnon over Briseis is justified. He feels that she is his by rights since he was the one who killed her husband and appropriated her (19.291-7; cf. Ovid *Heroides* 3). In some respects Briseis represents merely a prize and symbol of Achilles' military valour.[94] Pomeroy notes that 'an extra measure of prestige accrued to the warrior who possessed a slave who was once the wife or daughter of a man of high status'.[95] This is because she is visible proof of the victorious warrior's military ability and is a message to the world that he has overcome her husband or male relatives.[96] However, it is notable that women are highly valued by the Homeric warriors for their potential usefulness. Although Pomeroy has suggested that soldiers consorted with slave women merely for pleasure, the texts suggest that they intended to raise children with them. Patroclus apparently promised Briseis that Achilles would marry her on his return to Phthia (19.297-300). Just so, Agamemnon states that he likes his own concubine Chryseis as much as his wife Clytemnestra (1.112-15). In giving these values to the war captives, the men imply that they are considering them as potential child-bearers (cf. 1.31). When Agamemnon returns Briseis he swears that he has not had sex with her (19.258-65; cf. 19.175-6), demonstrating the significance of her importance as a future child-bearer for Achilles.[97] This is the fate of Andromache who is sent to the house of her husband's killer (like Briseis) and bears a son there for her new husband Neoptolemus (Euripides *Andromache*).[98] In Sophocles' *Ajax*, Tecmessa too is won by Ajax's spear and she bears a son for him. Ajax makes it clear that this boy will continue the family line in his place when he asks that his brother Teucer take the child home to their parents as a replacement for Ajax (567-70).[99] Teucer himself is portrayed as being the son of Telamon by Hesione, a woman he won while fighting with Hercules at Troy (Apollodorus 2.6.4). Although he may not be as highly regarded as Ajax, he still fights well alongside his brother and is depicted as a worthy warrior in the *Iliad*, in particular in the defence of the Greek camp, and is thought to bring glory to his father through his fighting (8.281-5). In Sophocles' *Ajax* it is also suggested that on the death of his brother, Teucer would inherit his household and position of power – a fact that might be seen as a motive for him to connive in killing Ajax (1012-16).[100]

The usefulness of women's reproductive abilities seen in these examples explains the decision to enslave the women of captured cities rather than kill them along with their men folk both in mythical and historical accounts.[101] Although the citizenship law of Pericles (451/0 BC) meant that raising children through captured slaves and concubines became problematic in classical Athens, since the law was intended to prevent these children from attaining citizen rights, evidence suggests that the practice still continued, perhaps because of the crisis during the Peloponnesian War.[102] In one anecdote, Alcibiades is said to have fathered a child with a Melian woman whose male kin he had been responsible for killing during the subjugation of Melos (Andocides 4.22-3).[103] Although this story is used to criticise the character of Alcibiades, who the orator claims is foolhardy to raise children in this way, it also shows how the resources of women captured and enslaved in war could be utilised by the conquerors.

The tendency towards wars of revenge over a woman in Greek versions of their early history is indicative of how they perceived the crimes of adultery and seduction. In the *Iliad* Menelaus brings with him a large Greek army to make Paris and the Trojans pay (τίσασθαι) for the abduction of Helen (2.590). As Menelaus takes aim at Paris during their duel, he prays to Zeus for revenge against Paris because he has wronged him and because as a guest he ill-treated his host (cf. Herodotus 2.115.4). This revenge is designed to have a deterrent effect on all guests who might think of wronging a host (*Il.* 3.351-4), so that remembering the death of Paris inflicted by the angry host he betrayed, these future guests will shudder and refrain from their crimes. In addition Menelaus' strength and ability to defend himself has been undermined by Paris' daring seizure of his wife, and so he needs to show that he is not weak and easy to attack.[104] By retaliating in force, Menelaus demonstrates to the world that he is not an easy target and at the same time re-enhances his own status at the expense of Paris.

While Menelaus is focusing on the death of Paris as a suitable payment for the wrongs done to him, other payments are also considered by the Greeks. Nestor suggests that every man must sleep with a Trojan wife in order to get vengeance (τίσασθαι) for the rape of Helen (2.354-6). This revenge replicates the attack made by Paris, but the scale has changed from one man to an entire city. The implication is that every Greek is in some way affected by the insult done to one Greek by one Trojan.[105] To this end, the Greek war effort aims not merely at the restoration of Helen and the death of her abductor, but at the annihilation of the city and the enslavement of the Trojan women. By killing the men and capturing the women the Greeks will bring an end to the bloodlines of the Trojans, thereby mirroring the fate which Paris might have inflicted on Menelaus when he stole his wife. This is a horrible fate for any ancient man as is made apparent by the oaths which men swore to demonstrate their trustworthiness. Before the duel of Paris and Menelaus, the soldiers swear solemn oaths that the side which breaks the oath will die, children and all, and their wives will go to other men (3.298-301). The breaking of this oath by a Trojan foreshadows the end of the war when these events will be realised.[106]

The competition for women in this story is heavily romanticised and historians have therefore been disinclined to believe in the historicity of this motive for war.[107] Interestingly, though, later Greeks were only too ready to believe that their ancestors would have been ready to launch an expedition for the sake of one woman. The Trojan War is cited as an example of how foreigners who steal women should be punished (Isocrates 4.181, 12.80, 12.83). Herodotus places the war in a chain of reciprocal abductions between Asia and Europe beginning with Io and Europe, followed by Medea and Helen (1.1ff.; cf. Euripides *Med.* 256).[108] Elsewhere in Herodotus women are abducted in revenge (τιμωρήσασθαι) when the Pelasgians seize Athenian women from Brauron and have children with them (6.138). His tale of the adventures of the Scythians and Amazons also emphasises that the male Scythians are keen to procreate with the captured female Amazons (4.110.1). These anecdotes reflect and are symbolic of the vital male struggle over women's reproductive resources.

Medea's sexual proprietariness

In his *Medea* Euripides explores the themes of marriage, sexual jealousy and procreation with an interesting twist: he places emphasis on the thoughts and reactions of a female protagonist. In the play Medea decides upon revenge after the man she deemed to be her husband elects to make a new, more advantageous marriage with a princess of Corinth. His actions are said to make her both angry at his betrayal of her and their sons (17-48, 98-110, 271, 286, 520-1, 589-90), and jealous of his new wife and future prospects (568-72). These emotions make Medea dangerous and drive her on in her desire to achieve revenge against her husband (πόσιν δίκην τῶνδ' ἀντιτείσασθαι κακῶν) for what he has done to her (259-63; cf. 163-5). As has been seen above, this combination of emotions is connected with male sexual proprietariness and evidence shows that female fidelity has been a key concern for men both in antiquity and more recent times.[109] Violence and rage caused by sexual infidelity is a strongly masculine characteristic, but in this play it is the rage of a woman aimed at her unfaithful husband that leads to the terrible acts of revenge depicted.[110] The focus on male sexual infidelity and the consequent anger and violence of a woman in this play adds an interesting twist to the conventional plot of unfaithful wife and irate husband. The element of male sexual infidelity and consequent female violence in the play creates an inversion of the gender roles. Commentators have frequently noted that Medea takes on masculine qualities in enacting her revenge.[111] In particular, the focus of scholars has been on Medea's preoccupation with her honour and the laughter of her enemies (381-3, 404, 797, 1049-50, 1354-5). Just as the Greeks are concerned with the way they are being mocked and dishonoured by the Trojans because of the abduction of Helen (Aeschylus *Ag.* 399-402, 412; Euripides *IA* 370-2, 1264-6), Medea too is portrayed voicing these same concerns. In addition Medea in some ways resembles the quintessential masculine hero Achilles before his revenge against Hector in that she contemplates suicide and refuses to eat (24, 145-7, 226-7; cf. *Il.* 18.23-34, 19.205-14).[112] Like Odysseus, Medea is shown taking time to calculate the potential costs and benefits of her actions. Rather than impetuously striking out, she coolly waits for possibilities to arise. However, she maintains that she would be willing to rush in with a sword and take her chances if necessary even if she were killed (392-4). Her violence generated by sexual rivalry and jealousy can be seen as further evidence of this trend towards gender inversion.

This play cleverly reverses and plays with some of what we have seen in the previous texts. Euripides emphasises the centrality of this reversal in his choral speech where nature itself is said to have been inverted (410ff.).[113] Just as Euphiletus attacks and kills his wife's lover rather than his wife, just so Medea lashes out at Jason's new love rather than attacking Jason. The nurse emphasises how Medea and her sons have been betrayed and dishonoured (17-20; cf. Lysias 1.4). In the world of Athens children born of an adulteress would be stigmatised and perhaps disinherited or disenfranchised.[114] As a wife who betrays her husband in adultery threatens the offspring of the marriage, so the future of Medea's children is threatened by the sexual infidelity of their father. Early in the play it is said that they will be disenfranchised and live in exile. In choosing a lover over her husband the Athenian woman would be rejecting her children and if she were caught and divorced, her relationship with her children would be at an end. Just so in the world of the play Jason's children are threatened with exile and seem to have been abandoned by their father

(86-8). By betraying his wife and children Jason makes himself an enemy of his own house.[115] Burnett has argued persuasively that Jason calls down his own doom on himself through his violation of the oaths he made to Medea at their marriage.[116] By calling for the destruction of himself, his house and children as a man did when taking an oath, Jason has called upon his own head the very destruction which is played out in the tragedy.[117]

At the heart of this play lies firm evidence of the tremendous significance of offspring.[118] The importance of having sons (490-1) is highlighted within the play in Medea's exchange with Aegeus who is depicted pursuing every possibility in his desire to sire offspring.[119] Jason's plan too is to increase his line and future progeny through polygyny (563-7). Initially Medea wants the children to die along with their father so the whole house will perish (113-14). However, she changes her mind in order to inflict the greatest amount of suffering on Jason (817) who must live on in humiliation and without future prospects, 'alive but erased' as Burnett notes – the very end with which he threatened Medea herself.[120] By killing his new bride along with Jason's sons Medea prevents Jason from having more sons (803-6) and accomplishes the complete annihilation of his line.[121] The assumption is that Jason's future marriage prospects would be irrevocably damaged by Medea's act. Medea's decision to kill the children but let Jason live on without future hopes is closely paralleled in Euripides' *Hecuba*, where Polymestor is forced to witness the murder of his children before he is symbolically castrated to prevent him siring any replacements.[122] At the same time Medea must destroy her own future happiness when she kills her children (1046-7; cf. 1025-37, 1247-50, 1361-2).[123] This act of self-destruction within the family is highly typical of tragic plot-lines.[124]

However, in some ways Medea's plot is quintessentially feminine in that she uses persuasion, cunning and poison to kill the princess.[125] Her association with violent revenge acts links her to the female avengers discussed in Chapter 1, although her decision to kill her children is in sharp contrast with the fierce devotion of those blood-avenging mothers to their sons.[126] However, Medea's targeting of the children is paralleled in other tragic revenge plots. The pattern is particularly common in those dramas which depict a man having sex with another woman or bringing a concubine into the house (e.g. Sophocles *Tereus*, Euripides *Ino*; cf. Euripides *Andromache*).[127] Just so in *Medea*, Jason's attempt to take a second wife leads to Medea's slaughter of his children. The effect on the audience is clear. Medea is a horrifying incarnation of the worst possible kind of wife. She is capable of the greatest acts of deception and witchcraft.[128] She is dangerous, powerful and 'manlike' in her outlook.[129] As has been seen, exceptionally strong retaliation by cuckolded men was often associated with attacks involving seduction and adultery in Athens. In the world of Euripides' play strong 'masculine' revenge for a sexual offences combines with the excessive 'feminine' vengeful desires to create one of the most notorious revenges in Greek literature.

The evidence seen in this chapter suggests that lethal revenge attacks are more readily associated in Greek imagination with reactions to adultery and seduction than to reactions against killers. In particular the Athenian laws, which permit a man to kill an adulterer or seducer caught in his home, but not to take blood revenge following the death of a loved one, are telling. It is my belief that the laws follow on from traditional practice and that epic poetry and myths concerning violent revenge against those who seduce women have no small part to play in this. The significance of offspring to a Greek man is vital in explaining why women's reproductive resources are protected in this way and why such violent attacks are associated with their protection. However, violent attacks are not only associated with the protection of women, but also with the protection of property, as seen in the myth of Odysseus and in Attic law. It has already been suggested that wealth is a factor in successful reproduction. The interconnectedness of these ideas will be further examined now in Chapter 3.

3

Raiding, Theft and Property Disputes

Revenge over the loss of material possessions lies at the heart of several mythical story patterns, in particular those connected with the theft of livestock and with the acquisition of weapons. This is because large animals such as horses, oxen, cows and sheep[1] and fighting implements such as armour and weapons are particularly valued for their practical importance. A ready supply of fine livestock and land means that there will be enough for a man to raise a large family, thereby strengthening his own position by creating allies for himself, as well as enhancing the chances of obtaining many descendants to follow in his bloodline. A plentiful supply of good weapons allows a man to protect himself and his family, as well as allowing him to fight to acquire further possessions. In addition to their practical applications, these items come to represent the status and honour of their owner.[2] A man with fine horses or an outstanding shield is noble and honourable, as is evidenced by the descriptions of fabulous items owned by the Homeric heroes (for example, Achilles' immortal horses and divinely created shield).[3] The ability to defend and protect possessions is, therefore, vital not just to allow a man to provide adequately for his family, but to ensure his honour is maintained. Equally robbers are driven not only by the desire to gain surplus goods (enhancing their own status and prospects), but also because through successful forays, they can quell potential rivals.[4] For these reasons, mythical scenarios tend to stress the importance of fighting to acquire and protect livestock and weapons. While revenge for theft is not always depicted as violent in the sources (for example counter-theft can be a satisfactory retaliation for a theft), death or even war are sometimes cited as responses to an initial loss of property.

The protection of property

As in the case of revenge for women, revenge over a piece of property can be seen to have a deterrent effect, persuading others that it would be foolhardy to try to remove any of your belongings. Those who steal gain the advantage conferred by ownership of the goods they have taken, but the possibility of encountering a violent avenger increases the risk for them. It is therefore essential for men to react as strongly as possible in order to gain a reputation for ferocity in defending themselves and their possessions. Texts emphasise the vulnerability of children without a father to protect them from exploitation at the hands of others. They are felt to be too weak to respond themselves and they often lack a strong defender.[5] This problem is made explicit in the *Odyssey* where Telemachus is portrayed as too young and weak to protect his absent father's property by himself (4.164-8). In the absence of Odysseus, the suitors feel free to intrude upon his home and squander its goods, as Penelope notes (17.537-8). Similarly, in the *Iliad* Andromache bewails the fate of Astyanax who, she thinks, will lose his lands to others and be driven from feasts because he has no father (*Il.* 22.489-98). Like Andromache, Tecmessa claims that Eurysaces will be defenceless and threatened with maltreatment by others without his father Ajax to protect him (Sophocles *Ajax* 511-12; cf. 986-9).[6] In all these examples the women of the house highlight their own weakness and comment upon the necessity of having a strong man present to protect his possessions as well as the interests of his family. Without such defence, the examples suggest, a man's sons are threatened with ruin, even to the point of starvation, when they have no father to protect their interests and to provide for them.

Comparable instances occur in lawsuits in Athens concerning guardianship of orphaned boys. Demosthenes emphasises his own youth and inexperience when facing his guardians in court (27.2). In one of his speeches against Aphobus he paints a picture of himself as a small weak child who was placed into the hands of unscrupulous men by his trusting father (28.15). His mother and sister are shown as particularly vulnerable, and all three are said to be threatened by penury (28.21; cf. 27.66, 28.19) and even by starvation (27.63) by the swindling guardians. In court Demosthenes appeals to the jury to help him regain his inheritance (27.3) and asks for redress for the wrongs that have been committed against him and his family (δίκην ζητῶ λαβεῖν, 28.18). He makes play with the fact that he is clashing with his own relatives in court (cf. 27.4-5), suggesting that their behaviour would be more suitable for enemies than kin (27.48, 65).[7] He says that their treatment of himself and his family appears to be that of men who have been ill-treated in the past (27.64),[8] hinting that revenge through embezzlement would be a possible response for a disgruntled enemy, but that in the absence of former enmity their behaviour towards their wards is outrageous. Similarly, in Lysias' speech *Against Diogeiton* two orphaned boys bring a case against their guardian, who is also their maternal grandfather and paternal uncle (32.12),[9] suggesting that he has misappropriated their inheritance and left them destitute (32.10). Here, too, as in the Homeric instances (upon which Lysias probably drew in creating this speech), it is the mother of the boys who stresses that they have lost their inheritance because they are too young and weak to react (32.12-18).[10] But like her Homeric counterparts, she is incapable of preventing the exploitation of the children on her own. Even though the law aims at offering protection to orphans to prevent guardians exploiting them, their mother cannot pursue the matter in court by herself.[11] Instead

Lysias portrays her as appealing to other male relatives to help her children.[12]

These cases suggest that, despite the existence of laws to protect them, orphaned children were still in a particularly weak position and in need of assistance from other family members to try to protect their rightful inheritances. Without the presence of strong male avengers, the rhetoric in these texts suggests that women and children were exposed to exploitation leading to penury and even starvation. The appearance of a man willing to take revenge (as in the case of Odysseus) can reverse the trend in the favour of those who have been exploited. These examples demonstrate the necessity of developing skills which can be used in defence of attacks on property, be it skill at fighting in the heroic epics to drive off invaders who threaten the household, or skill in rhetoric at Athens to achieve justice through the courts.

Cattle-raiding

Heroic myths suggest that the skills necessary to acquire and defend property can be developed through cattle-raiding. Cattle-raiding myths, which are common to a wide range of cultures,[13] are particularly connected with the heroic age in Greece.[14] The existence of raiding in certain parts of modern day Greece[15] suggests that there is no reason to doubt that the myths reflect a genuine practice. However, it is unclear to which historical periods raiding belongs. Some suggest that it was a key feature of Mycenaean Greece, others believe that it was characteristic mainly of dark age Greece and others argue that it could date to the archaic age.[16] Instead of seeking to place raiding in one particular historical era, though, it is perhaps better to emphasise that it is a practice that occurs among men who specialise in pastoralism rather than in agriculture.[17] Hence it is possible that at different times and in different places throughout antiquity raiding occurred where herding was the predominant mode of farming. Thucydides certainly believes in the historicity of raiding (both by land and sea) and that it was still current in certain places during the classical period.[18] Rather than pointing to the significance of pastoralism, though, he chooses to highlight the incidence of weapons (1.5.3-1.6.3).[19]

Cattle-raiding myths tend to focus on the important link between a man's abilities as a warrior/hunter and as a provider and protector.[20] These myths frequently reflect a man's transition from boyhood to manhood where he first proves his mettle and wins the shield and spear with which he can fight to defend his family.[21] Walcot has argued that the story of Nestor, as told to Patroclus in *Iliad* 11, conforms to this pattern.[22] In his tale of youthful heroism, Nestor reports first how he proved himself able to procure livestock from his father's enemy and then how he successfully protected it in battle. The strife between the Eleans and Pylians in Nestor's account begin with the theft of his father Neleus' prize-winning

67

racehorses by King Augeas at the games in Elis (11.698-700). Augeas is said not only to have taken the horses, but to have insulted the chariot driver and sent him packing. Racehorses are of high importance in the Homeric texts because (as will be seen further below) the speed of horses in battle made them particularly prized. By publicly insulting Neleus and stealing articles of particular status-value to him, Augeas apparently aims at diminishing Neleus' honour and standing. Augeas' insult functions as a challenge to Neleus. If he cannot respond, then he must admit that Augeas is his superior.[23] Nestor maintains that Augeas acted in this way because he perceived that the Pylians had been seriously weakened by their war with Hercules (in which eleven out of the twelve sons of Neleus were killed, 11.690-3) and that they are therefore incapable of responding to the theft and insult (11.694-5). Although there is no description of the dispute between Hercules and the sons of Neleus in Homer, Isocrates says that this dispute also started with cattle-rustling. Neleus and his sons are said to have stolen from Hercules the cattle which Hercules took from Geryon as his tenth labour. In retaliation for the theft Hercules is said to have killed all of the sons of Neleus except Nestor who had taken no part in the raid (Isocrates 6.19). Hercules' aggressive attitude towards the defence of the cattle is paralleled in other versions of the tale where he is said to have killed all those who attempted to take them from him (Apollodorus 2.5.10).[24]

The risks involved both in herding cattle and in trying to rustle them are high in these myths. Those who desire to steal are willing to kill to achieve their aim. Hercules kills the owner of the cattle as well as the cattle-herd and his dog (Apollodorus 2.5.10; Hesiod *Theog.* 287-94, 979-83).[25] Conversely the thieves risk death at the hands of a retaliatory raiding party, as happens to Neleus' sons.[26] By stealing the cattle Neleus' sons aim to acquire greater wealth and status for themselves and for their father as is suggested by Pausanias' account of cattle-rustling in the past (4.36.3). However, because of their failure to stand up to a lethal retaliatory attack, they leave their father and the other Pylians open to attacks from others who perceive them to be too weak to respond. Fortunately for Neleus, though, his youngest son Nestor remains alive and has just reached an age where he is able to retaliate for the theft of his horses and the losses of the other Pylians (*Il.* 11.674-6, 688-9). In a night-time raid on the Eleans, Nestor reports that he managed to drive away enormous numbers of sheep, cattle, goats, pigs and horses (11.677-81).[27] In order to achieve this he killed Itymoneus, who was defending his cows, and terrified the other local people so that they did not stand up to him (11.672-6). At home the Pylians divide up the spoils so that everyone who has lost something to the Eleans is repaid (11.685-705).[28]

The Pylians have recouped their losses, but now it is the Eleans' turn to respond to the attack in an attempt to recover their lost property and to make the Pylians pay for what they have done. Rather than launching another counter-raid, though, they decide upon an attack on Pylos by the full strength of Elis (11.707-9). Although Neleus forbids Nestor to fight, he secretly takes to the field without his horses and chariot and successfully procures these items from the enemy by fighting on foot (11.737-44). With the help of Athena, the Pylians prevail and the Eleans are forced to leave empty-handed (11.714-17). In seizing the chariot and horses, Nestor neatly rounds off the whole affair which began (in Nestor's account at least) with the theft of Neleus' chariot and horses.[29] Through his successes on the battlefield Nestor is also able to prove as a fighter so that his father can no longer claim he is not old enough to fight for Pylos (11.717-21).[30] In the events narrated by Nestor, his accomplishments as a raider are swiftly followed by his success as a warrior and his acceptance as the leading fighter of Pylos. As such his raiding exploits are his initiation into the world of adult fighting and his experiences on the battlefield, where he must win military equipment for himself, confirm that he has now reached maturity. Not only does the story make the link between ability at raiding and ability on the battlefield, but it also emphasises the importance of effective retaliatory action when threatened by enemies. Failure to retaliate to the insult of Augeas could have led to a series of such insults and attacks from all comers. The participants in the tale all assess the situation carefully and take risks accordingly. Augeas calculates that he can procure the horses of Neleus at no cost to himself and his people, but he does not reckon on the abilities of the as yet untested youth Nestor. Conversely Nestor is not prepared to accept Augeas' theft, but calculates it is worth the risk of retaliating in order to recoup their losses.

This story also demonstrates the way in which violence is thought to escalate. Initially a non-violent insult causes a violent response teamed with a raid to recoup losses. However, this brings in other members of the hostile group when their horses, sheep and cattle are rustled which in turn leads to warfare.[31] Similarly in the *Odyssey* Eupeithes is said to have taken refuge with Odysseus when Ithacans desired his blood for raiding the Thesprotians with whom they were at peace (16.424-30). The implication of this tale is that raiding by one man can lead to counter-raids or a war of retribution against the community at large. The possibility of launching a war in retaliation for the loss of animals is also alluded to by Achilles when he says that he feels no strong motivation to fight against the Trojans since they have not raided his livestock or burnt his crops (*Il.* 1.152-6). Likewise Sarpedon emphasises that he is fighting the Greeks simply in order to be helpful to the Trojans, since the Greeks are not looting his possessions (5.480-4). In both these statements, retaliation for raiding is assumed to be a strong motivation for fighting a war. As with the initial decision to insult or to retaliate, the trajectory of the feud is something which must be calculated by participants at the beginning. Each man knows the risk of escalation and of his own death, but these risks must be balanced against possible future advantages – gaining goods and honour, and, hence, power and a high social position. At each stage, the participants aim to achieve the maximum possible strength and honour at the expense of others. Once achieved, these advantages must be maintained by presenting a strong public persona to suggest that swift retaliation will follow in the event of attack. If a counter-raid does not swiftly follow a raid, a man potentially faces the loss of all his livestock and ruin for his family. These examples hint at the existence of a kind of vendetta motivated by disputes over property (rather than disputes over homicides) and drawing in ever increasing numbers of people.[32] This association of violent retaliation and escalation to the point of warfare with property disputes mirrors that found in the cases of disputes over women, as discussed in the previous chapter.

Another mythical cattle-raid in which a youth demonstrates that he is worthy of acceptance by his male peers is described in the *Homeric Hymn to Hermes*.[33] Iles Johnston has argued that this tale, like the tale of Nestor, has close connections to initiation rites as well as to athletic competitions.[34] According to this interpretation Hermes must earn his place in the pantheon and the honour which goes with it.[35] In the hymn, the infant Hermes determines upon a raid of the cattle of Apollo on the very day he is born. Like Nestor, Hermes launches his raid by night and in secrecy. Much attention is given to the tricks he contrives to hide the theft of the cattle (75-81; cf. 210-11). Trickery and thieving are intimately connected to the character of Hermes, as to other famous raiders, including Odysseus' grandfather Autolycus and Odysseus himself.[36] Secrecy is a difficult issue for raiders, as they need to achieve the raid without alerting anyone, but at the same time there is an opposing desire to reveal the raid and display their ability at raiding.[37]

After stealing the cattle and hiding them, Hermes returns home where his mother Maia rebukes him and tells him that Apollo will bind him in retaliation for the theft (155-8). Imprisonment is a typical choice of response for a god (e.g. *Il.* 5.385-91, 8.296ff.), since death is not a possible threat for an immortal. However, imprisonment is also a response associated with mortal thieves both in myth and in Attic law.[38] Enraged by the loss of his cattle, Apollo threatens to throw Hermes into Tartarus (254-9), another typical divine threat with implications of imprisonment.[39] Harrell has argued that to the audiences of the hymn the mention of Tartarus would have been resonant of Theogonic myths in which Zeus threw his rivals into Tartarus.[40] By defeating and imprisoning his rivals to power, Zeus confirmed his authority and right to rule. Similarly, Apollo's threat of Tartarus signifies the competition and rivalry of the two sons of Zeus over property, power and honour.[41] Other ancient evidence suggests that brothers were thought the most likely of kin to fight over these things.[42] In his essay *On Brotherly Love*, Plutarch cites inheritance as the most likely cause for disputes between brothers (*Mor.* 478a-92d).[43] In the Homeric hymn, Apollo also specifies that Hermes will rule over other boys in

Tartarus, suggesting that he will never reach manhood.[44] The significance of this jibe is that Hermes will have failed in his quest to prove his maturity and hence to achieve acceptance among the other gods. This theme is further elaborated towards the end of the hymn when Apollo does finally attempt to bind his brother. In his speech to Hermes before he applies the cords, Apollo addresses his brother as an infant, although he acknowledges his strength. However, when Apollo discovers to his amazement that Hermes is too strong to be held (409-14) he must reconsider his initial assessment. Hermes' ability to escape the cords with which he is bound finally confirms his divine power and skills. Instead of being treated as a mere baby, he deserves recognition as a god worthy of equal honour.

Interestingly, despite his anger and his threats, Apollo does not exact revenge from his younger brother, but he is first persuaded to take the matter to Zeus so that it can be settled peacefully (312-28) and is then placated with the offer of gifts (436-62).[45] Similarly, although Hermes threatens to make his brother pay (τίσω) for his violent incursion on his home and for bringing him to court (385-6),[46] he is happily reconciled with him after the decision of Zeus. Instead of becoming enemies and perpetuating the cycle of raid and counter-raid or launching lethal attacks upon one another as occurs in the heroic myths, or even retaliating against each other with further legal actions as in Athens, Apollo and Hermes are reconciled and become friends. Various possible reasons have been put forward to explain this. It has been suggested that the response in the hymn is closer to historical reality than events portrayed in heroic myths.[47] Certainly historical instances of reconciliation after raiding have been recorded in modern Crete where it is possible for a youth to gain acceptance through raiding the flocks of his elders.[48] The story of Theseus and Peirithous (Plutarch *Thes.* 30.1-2), in which the young Peirithous steals the cattle of Theseus from Marathon in order to prove himself and is accepted as a friend by Theseus for his daring and courageousness, also conforms to this pattern.[49] However, given that revenge and even homicide are possible responses to raiding in Crete, these pieces of evidence are inadequate to prove that friendship was the norm after raiding in antiquity. Instead there appear to be different modes of raiding, one in which potentially violent retaliation follows a theft and the other in which a settlement is brokered. It seems likely that different circumstances decide individual participants on whether to fight back with strength or settle the matter and be reconciled. In the case of Hermes and Apollo, the fact that they are gods surely influences how they are represented. Although the actions of the gods in myth are usually based on actions typical of men, the immunity of the gods to lethal revenge means that killing the thief is not an option. In this respect the hymn constitutes a problematic source for deciding what the usual response to cattle-raiding was in reality. Moreover, the blood kinship between Hermes and Apollo is highly significant, as raiding between close agnatic kin is not the norm and this factor must be seen as significant in their decision to settle their dispute peacefully. Speakers in the courts at Athens emphasise that it is improper for relatives to fight in public, although this does not always stop them (Demosthenes 48.1; Lysias 32.1). Instead family arbitrations, as happens in the hymn, are preferred (see Lysias 32.2).[50] This interpretation makes the portrayal of the fraternal relationship central to the hymn.[51] The dispute first arises out of brotherly vying for privileges and is settled peacefully when each sibling feels he has gained what he is due. By his raid the infant Hermes challenges Apollo for a share in his cult and at the end of the poem he has achieved this aim with the exchange of gifts.[52]

In these examples the initiatory significance of the raids has been emphasised, but the instances also refer to the more practical significance of stealing livestock. Hermes is said to have set out on his quest for the cattle because he desired meat (64). Here the hymn indicates the importance of attaining cattle for sustenance as well as for personal honour. However, despite his hunger Hermes does not eat the meat (131-3).[53] Instead he sacrifices two oxen and creates twelve portions, thus including himself among the other Olympians in honours (116-30). Because he is a god, smelling the scent of the sacrifice is more appropriate for him.[54] For men, though, the desire for sustenance is a key motivating factor in raiding, especially when they are far from home. Armies voyaging at sea or laying siege to a city are in need of supplies and these can be attained by raiding.[55] Thucydides emphasises this motive for raiding, along with acquisitiveness and the quest for glory, in his account of piracy and banditry in early Greece (1.5.1).[56] However, this tactic can be a highly risky one as the owners of the livestock are liable to respond violently to the theft of their animals.

A key example of this in the *Odyssey* is the theft of the cattle of the Sun by Odysseus' companions which leads to their destruction (1.7-10). When they are becalmed on the island of Thrinacia, the companions decide to seize the cattle and eat them against the instructions they have received from Odysseus (who has previously been warned against touching the cattle by Tiresias, 11.104-17 and Circe, 12.127-41). They are motivated to act in this way out of fear of starvation (12.340-2). In Odysseus' account of events, Eurylochus plays a key role in encouraging the other men to eat the cattle.[57] He believes that they will be able to appease Hyperion by building a temple to him and filling it with offerings on their return to Ithaca (12.345-7). Alternatively he thinks it would be better to drown than to starve to death if the god decides to avenge the loss of his cattle (12.349-50). Eurylochus acknowledges that the god will be angered by their actions and will require repayment, either in blood or through honour and possessions. In deciding to sacrifice the cattle the men take a calculated risk. They decide that the threat of death is so imminent that they had better take the chance that the god will accept their proffered material compensation. At the same time they hope to postpone their deaths till a later point and perhaps to achieve a quicker and less painful death.

However, like Odysseus when he kills the suitors, Hyperion is not interested in material compensation. He is outraged when he learns of the death of his cattle (12.376) and he goes straight to Zeus and the other gods to demand revenge (τῖσαι) on Odysseus' companions (12.378). He charges that the companions were insolent to kill his cattle (12.379) and threatens the gods that he will no longer perform his function, if he is not paid for the insult to his honour and for the loss of his property (εἰ δὲ μοι οὐ τίσουσι βοῶν ἐπιεικέ᾽ ἀμοιβήν, 12.382). By threatening to go and shine in Hades instead of on Earth, Hyperion equates his lot as the victim of a theft to that of a dead man who requires help from others to avenge his loss. In order to appease him and ensure his continued presence on Earth, Zeus promises to strike Odysseus' ship with his bolt bringing about the death of the companions (12.385-8), but sparing Odysseus who was asleep at the time of the theft (12.338, 366, 371-3).[58] In this example, the thieves make the mistake of stealing from a god who is undoubtedly in a good position to take revenge on them, although interestingly Hyperion does not avenge the loss of the cattle himself, but applies to a higher power for help.[59] In this respect, the companions' gamble is very high, but this is explained by the misery of their situation and their belief that they will die anyway if they do not act quickly.

While material goods are important to ensure basic survival, wealth (and the power which attends it) also allows a man greater access to women and their reproductive resources. The more wealth a man has, the greater scope he has for acquiring a good wife and, through her, a strong alliance with her kin. Theognis' complaint that people prefer money to noble birth in choosing a spouse (183-96) is indicative of this mentality.[60] Likewise, in the *Odyssey* Penelope's brothers and father are said to be pressing her to marry Eurymachus because he is offering the most gifts (15.16-18). A man with plentiful resources makes an attractive husband for a woman planning to raise a family.[61] A wealthy man also makes a good ally for his prospective father-in-law. The need for plentiful possessions in order to attain a sought-after wife is evidenced in the tradition of the bride price where a man gives a substantial quantity of goods, often including valuable animals, to secure his bride (e.g. *Il.* 11.244-5, 22.472). The price paid for brides can be measured in cattle and girls occasionally bear cow-related names which apparently indicate the worth of the girl in cattle to her father and husband.[62] The interconnectedness of cows and women is made explicit in the myths associated with Castor and Pollux. In one version the pair seize the daughters of Leucippus from their bridegrooms Idas and Lynceus who pursue them for revenge and kill Castor (Theocritus *Id.* 22.137ff.; Hyginus *Fab.* 80; Ovid *Fasti* 5.709). In another version Castor is killed by Idas and Lynceus in a fight over cattle (Apollodorus 3.11.2; Pindar *Nem.* 10.60). The alternate use of death in revenge for the theft of two girls and death in revenge for the theft of cattle demonstrates the interrelatedness of these two notions. The apparent equivalence in responses to these offences is also noteworthy. Theft of animals and women alike is answered with lethal revenge. Although the stories are mythical, they nevertheless attest to the value placed on these commodities and to a mentality which praises risk-taking to attain and defend such precious property.[63]

In myths, fathers like to test the abilities of prospective suitors for their daughters' hands before agreeing to the marriage. For example, Pelops must show his skill at chariot-racing (and ruthlessness) in order to win his bride from her father (Apollodorus *Epit.* 2.4-8; Pindar *Ol.* 1.67-90; cf. Pausanias 5.10.6-7, 5.17.7).[64] Othryoneus is also tested by his intended father-in-law Priam who is willing to accept him as a son-in-law without any bride price in return for his service in the Trojan army (*Il.* 13.363ff.). However, he does not achieve his goal of marriage. Instead, his death in battle marks his failure as a warrior and defender of Priam's daughter. Through consideration of this story, it is possible to interpret Achilles' abrupt refusal of Agamemnon's proposal of a marriage alliance. In his offer of gifts to Achilles, Agamemnon stipulates that Achilles may choose any of his three daughters as a wife without the need to pay bride price (9.286-9). However he is not offering his daughter without strings attached.[65] Rather Achilles (like Othryoneus) would need to pay for the match in military service. This implicitly questions both Achilles' ability to pay the bride price for Agamemnon's daughter and his ability as a warrior through a test of his military prowess. Another example combines the payment of the bride price with a trial of a man's ability to procure sustenance for his family while simultaneously proving his resourcefulness and skill at fighting. Neleus demands the cattle of Phylacus (or Iphicles) as bride price for his daughter Pero (Apollodorus 1.9.12; *Od.* 11.287-97; Pausanias 4.36.3).[66] Instead of paying for the girl out of his own wealth, her prospective husband must secure the cattle of another man. By doing so he can prove his ability to support his new wife. In this respect, stories referring to testing before marriage are closely comparable to the myths where youths are tested to prove their manhood. There are some indications that such tests were also preferred by rich fathers in reality. Herodotus tells at length of how Cleisthenes of Sicyon selected a husband for his daughter, judging the many suitors on their athletic ability and manliness, as well as on their general demeanour (6.126-30).[67] Although van Wees maintains that the testing of suitors is a folk-tale motif rather than a custom, the connection is, nevertheless, made in these stories between a man's suitability as a bridegroom and his ability to provide for and defend a wife and family (cf. also *Od.* 14.211-13).[68] As such, although tests of this nature may not have been customary, the tales highlight the importance of these skills and leave open the possibility that prospective grooms might well have been judged on criteria such as these, even if they were not tested on them.

74

3. Raiding, Theft and Property Disputes

According to Pherecydes the cattle demanded by Neleus had originally belonged to his mother Tyro (3F33 Jacoby) and therefore this tale demonstrates again the expectation of counter-raids following on from original thefts. Notably, though, this myth does not refer to lethal revenge as a response to cattle-rustling. Instead, Melampus is imprisoned when he is caught trying to make off with the herds. Again, as discussed above, it is unclear to what extent this would have constituted a typical response in such circumstances. However, the mention of imprisonment indicates that killing was not an automatic response and that more than one acceptable method of retaliating against thieves existed.

Property disputes in classical Athens

In Athens, too, several procedures existed for dealing with thieves. Demosthenes emphasises that different procedures could be chosen according to an individual's own preference and belief in his ability to react (22.26-7). Strong men, he says, are capable of arresting the thief themselves, while weak men can bring a written indictment or bring the case to a public arbitrator where the risk is low.[69] Here, as in myth, individual participants decide upon a response according to the level of risk they are willing to take. Interestingly, the main penalties for theft cited by Demosthenes (24.113-15) are death, fines and imprisonment, paralleling the responses found in the myths. The public nature of the imprisonment and the humiliation of the bound thief is emphasised here, reflecting the reasoning behind this choice of punishment.[70] Death was cited as a possible penalty in a variety of scenarios, including for those caught stealing at night (Demosthenes 24.113), for thieves who took valuable goods (Demosthenes 24.114; Lycurgus 1.65) and for temple robbers (Isocrates 20.6; Lycurgus 1.65-66).[71] That ordinary people desired lethal revenge against those who stole from shrines is made explicit in Herodotus' tale of Artayctes who stole the treasure from Protesilaus' shrine and treated it sacrilegiously. Although he offers compensation in return for sparing his life, the people want revenge for Protesilaus and urge the Athenians to put him to death (οἱ γὰρ Ἐλαιούσιοι τῷ Πρωτεσίλεῳ τιμωρέοντες ἐδέοντό μιν καταχρησθῆναι). The Athenian general is in sympathy with them and Artayctes is executed along with his son (Herodotus 9.120; cf. 7.33).[72] It is implied in the narrative that the infliction of death in such circumstances is understood as a way for the gods to punish errant humans through human actions. Clearly too the local people hope to honour Protesilaus, whose shrine had been desecrated, through their revenge on Artayctes.[73] The evidence suggests that there was no glory to be found in looting sacred places and temple robbers ran extreme risks to acquire their booty.[74]

Classical texts imply that contemporary cattle-raiders were not held in high esteem either. In Isocrates' version of the story of Hercules and the sons of Neleus (6.19), Nestor is called prudent for not taking part in the raid, whereas in the Homeric account Nestor appears simply to have been too young to participate. Similarly, Thucydides' comments on plundering in early times show that he felt there was a discrepancy between views held in earlier times and in contemporary Athens (1.5.1).[75] He supports his arguments by referring to the way in which people ask openly 'Are you pirates?' in old poetry (1.5.2). This question is placed into the mouth of Nestor in the *Odyssey*, who asks Telemachus and his men if they are traders or pirates who risk their own lives to bring evil to others (3.71-4). The Cyclops asks Odysseus and his men exactly the same set of questions (9.253-5). Nevertheless, there was still a large degree of admiration in Athens for the heroes of myth and for their exploits, which in all probability had an impact on Athenian attitudes and behaviour towards their property and the property of others.[76] Although Odysseus is clearly an excellent example of a roving pirate and raider of the kind condemned by Thucydides, his cunning and trickery in achieving revenge were still much admired by contemporary Athenians. Moreover, as seen in Chapter 2, Odysseus' violent revenge against those who threatened his property and family provided inspiration for Athenian citizens.[77] Athenian householders, like Odysseus, could be expected to react violently to any attempts to make off with their property. Demosthenes suggests it would be terrible if Athenians were not allowed their traditional right to protect their possessions in this way (23.61).[78]

The principle is carried into Attic law which allowed men to retaliate violently to 'unjust and forcible' attacks on their property (*IG* 1³.104, 36-8).[79] A thief who entered another man's house was understood to be violating the household and the masculinity of its *kurios*, just like an adulterer, and lethal retaliation in such circumstances was permissible by law (Lysias 1.36; cf. Aeschines 1.91; Demosthenes 23.60).[80] Athenians hated to be humiliated by another man in their own homes, especially in front of female relatives (Demosthenes 22.53; cf. 21.78-9; Lysias 3.6-7). In modern times too men (but not women) tend to resist robbers who have broken into their houses in part because they cannot tolerate being humiliated in this way in their own homes by another man.[81] Public sympathy is often with those who attack a burglar in their house, even when their violence exceeds the bounds of the laws. Christ believes that Athenian jurors were also highly sympathetic towards manly protection of home, women and property.[82]

The tendency for intrusions into another man's house to result in violent scuffles and even death is noted in a number of orations. Particular problems arise where litigants have been awarded compensation or the right to seize goods from an opponent. In these cases there is a clash between the right of one man to seize property and the expectation that Athenians will protect their homes against incursions by other men. As Christ notes, the problem of collecting fines owed to you is that you could be treated like a thief.[83] A man who is too meek in his attempts to collect what he is owed risks failure. Speaking angrily might not be enough to secure what you want and more dynamic action might be necessary (Demosthenes 35.31). However, a man who is too violent in his attempt could be prosecuted in turn and face violent repercussions.[84]

Demosthenes 47 (*Against Euergus and Mnesibulus*) illustrates these problems clearly. The dispute described in this case was originally over the collection of naval equipment needed by the Athenian state. The speaker in this case, who was responsible for securing the equipment, first employed legal means to attempt to procure the items. When Theophemus still refused to co-operate, the speaker claims that he went to his house in order to seize the necessary goods (47.38) in accordance with the Council's vote that the goods should be procured by whatever means possible. When the speaker attempted to remove the goods from Theophemus' house, however, he apparently met with resistance and the two men resorted to physical violence. Theophemus then charged the speaker with assault and was supported in his case by his brother and brother-in-law, Euergus and Mnesibulus (47.64). Theophemus, with the help of his witnesses, was apparently able to convince the jurors that he was struck first and he was awarded damages against the speaker (47.7-8).[85] It is possible that the jurors felt sympathetic towards a man who was protecting his home and possessions against the incursion of another man. The speaker, on the other hand, is at pains to demonstrate that he was struck first, and he emphasises that it was only natural for him to respond physically to the violent attack of his opponent.[86] He also alleges that the two witnesses did not tell the truth in the assault suit against him (47.51, 64).

The situation is now reversed and Theophemus, along with his brother and brother-in-law, go to the speaker's estate in order to seize the damages awarded in the assault case. We are told that Theophemus and his friends first seized fifty sheep and a shepherd, a slave boy and a bronze pitcher (47.52). This action can be compared to the heroic cattle rustlers who seize property in retaliation against their opponents. However, in this Athenian version the men openly take the animals after a legal judgement in their favour. Next the men enter the house and take furniture and other possessions (47.53-6). In the absence of a man to protect the property, the female residents of the house apparently attempted to defend the possessions to the best of their ability, although not very successfully. Their inability to fight back is made very clear by the speaker who emphasises the uneven nature of this dispute compared to his own manly clash with Theophemus earlier on. The speaker's wife is said to have objected to the men verbally, pointing out that some of the goods were part of her dowry and that the men had already seized more than they were awarded by the court judgement. She also promised the men they would receive the full debt in cash (47.57). However, the speaker claims that the men ignored her. Meanwhile the speaker's old nurse attempted to hide a cup in her bosom to prevent the men seizing it. In the ensuing scuffle over this cup, the woman was so badly injured that she later died (47.58-9). The speaker alleges that he considered prosecuting for homicide following the nurse's death, but he was advised against this course of action.[87] It seems likely that his desire to prosecute arose not only out of a desire to avenge the dead nurse (as he states), but also because it provided him with an excellent means to exact revenge against his opponents for their treatment of him.[88] Instead of prosecuting for homicide, he decides on a suit for false witnesses against two of his opponents.

This case provides clear evidence that violent disputes could easily erupt when a man entered the home of another man in order to seize property, even following a legal judgement allowing him to do this. Both physical attacks and legal attacks feature in this prolonged disagreement, and the men are also willing to involve others in their attacks in order to achieve their own ends (the nurse who is killed and the witnesses who are prosecuted). The desire to achieve revenge after a man has entered your home and taken your property is very noticeable in this case, as the participants fail to reach a settlement at any point, but continue attacking one another through a variety of means. Similarly, in *Against Nicostratus* Apollodorus makes it clear that he desires revenge for the removal of property from his house following a court judgement against him. He stresses that he felt he ought to avenge himself (τιμωρεῖσθαι ᾤμην δεῖν) against his neighbour ([Demosthenes] 53.15, cf. 53.1) because the original court judgement was incorrect and so he plans to prosecute Nicostratus' brother Arethusius for false citation as revenge. Here too, as in Demosthenes 47, the revenge plan involves an attack on a relative of the original opponent, as this is seen as the best way to achieve a desirable outcome. Arethusius in turn reacts to the proposed prosecution by going to Apollodorus' estate by night and attacking the trees and vines more destructively than an enemy in wartime, as Apollodorus suggests (53.15).[89] Apollodorus eventually wins a conviction against Arethusius (53.17), although his opponents allegedly try several ruses to prevent him taking the case to court including sending a citizen boy to pluck roses from his flowerbed so that he might be indicted for assault if he hits him (53.16) and trying to throw him into a stone quarry (53.17). In this case it seems that a series of physical and legal attacks were made by the participants in a long-term dispute over money.[90] The level of violence between the men is again noticeable as they threaten one another with death (either through murder or through being condemned to death by prosecution) at various points. That men felt strongly about their property and money is not surprising, but that men are so willing to become involved in violent fights over property in Athens alerts us to the fact that these resources were just as highly valued by the Athenians as by the heroes of myth and that the Athenians too were prepared to become involved in violent revenge over their property. It is also likely that they were inspired by the mythical heroes when they made their decisions about how to react in a

78

property dispute. As in the case of Nestor and some of the other raiders discussed above, the disputes in these cases do not end easily, but continue through a range of attacks and counter-attacks.

The significance of weaponry and armour

The cattle-raiding myths reveal some of the most basic requirements for being a man, including the need to fight for and protect food sources, and the need to demonstrate these skills to pass into adulthood as a proven warrior or into a good marriage as a worthy bridegroom. Also important in these myths is the acquisition of armour and weapons, especially those taken from a defeated foe, to demonstrate the superiority of a man as a fighter. Without access to a good supply of weapons and tools, a man loses advantages both in raiding and in war. Hence it is not surprising that military equipment, just like cattle, can be represented at the heart of passionately fought battles and can be the cause of lethal revenge attacks.[91] As is clear from both Homeric epic and classical texts, weapons and armour have both practical and symbolic importance – they are useful and necessary for fighting, and they can confer honour upon fighters who wield and capture them.

The warriors at Troy frequently attempt to strip their fallen foes of their weapons, rushing in after they have killed them and trying to remove certain articles (e.g. *Il.* 11.99-100, 110-11, 246-7) or taking the body behind their own lines to strip it (e.g. 13.197-202). The typicality of this action is shown through the depiction of Ares, the Homeric god who embodies the brutality of war and the behaviour of warriors, stripping the body of Periphas whom he has killed (5.842). Conversely, the dead man's friends attempt to shield him from this plundering (e.g. 4.532-5; 5.297-8; 17.1-8) and to carry his body back behind friendly lines (e.g. 5.668-9; 11.257-8; 13.195-6). The fierce protectiveness of a man's comrades while fighting to shield his body means that even the great heroes sometimes have to back down and retreat without managing to strip him of his armour (e.g. 5.621-26; 13.509-11). Similarly the aggressiveness of Hector's attack on Menelaus, who is protecting the body of Patroclus, makes Menelaus back down (17.82-105).[92] The warriors are shown taking extreme risks in order to acquire this booty as they are frequently left vulnerable to attack by retaliators angry at the death of their comrade as they bend to take his armour from him. For example, Diomedes is injured by Paris' arrow while taking Agastrophus' armour and must retire from the field (11.373-8). Hector too opens himself up to an attack by Ajax when he attempts to strip Amphimachus, but his helmet saves him (13.188-94). Elephenor is not so lucky. He is fatally stabbed, while trying to drag off and strip the body of Echepolus (4.463-9).[93] In light of this risk, Nestor's instruction that the Greeks should not strip bodies, but engage wholeheartedly in attacking and take spoils only after the fighting is over, would seem to make good sense (6.68-71).[94] The loss of a valuable fighter like Diomedes from the battle has serious implications for the efforts of the Greeks. However, Nestor's plea does not seem to have a great deal of impact. The text depicts Greek warriors attempting to seize armour even when they are most pressed by the enemy during Hector's attack on the Greek wall (e.g. 11.333-5; 12.195). Even though the Trojans are on the point of breaking through the defences and reaching the Greek ships, Teucer is so intent on stripping Imbrius of his arms that he rushes in and exposes himself to an attack by Hector (13.182-3).[95]

The risks the men are willing to run in order to try to seize arms demonstrate the high importance placed on the acquisition of weapons and armour in the Homeric mode of fighting. The value of the weapons and armour is primarily as practical tools which can be used against the enemy. After breaking his own spear in battle Meriones asks Idomeneus if he can borrow a spear from his tent. Idomeneus willingly offers him one of those he has captured from the Trojans. He also mentions that he has a large collection of other items including shields, breastplates and helmets all taken from the enemy in battle (13.255-65). In this instance the collection of booty from defeated foes ensures the prompt return of a Greek fighter to the battle. By removing the items, the fighters are also depriving the enemy of useful equipment. When Hector dons the armour of Achilles which he has stripped from the body of Patroclus he is demonstrating his military prowess as well as depriving Achilles of this vital equipment. Without his armour, it is necessary for Achilles to wait until he can procure more before he re-enters the battle (17.710-11; 18.127-37). These pieces of military equipment have additional value as status items which confer honour upon their owners demonstrating that they are great warriors and enhancing their standing both among their peers and in the eyes of the enemy (cf. 5.275, 17.131).[96] This is made explicit by Euphorbus who tells Menelaus that he stands to gain glory among the Trojans if he seizes the spoils from the body of Patroclus. He therefore threatens Menelaus with death if he does not step back from the body and allow him to strip it (17.12-17). In Euphorbus' imagination taking the arms of Menelaus would also be a significant part of his revenge for his brother and would bring consolation to his relatives (17.34-40). The warriors often have their eye on weapons which belong to particularly high-ranking members among their opponents. For example, Diomedes desires Aeneas' armour because of its renown (5.434-5), while Hector has his eye on capturing Nestor's shield because of its fame and value.[97] He also aspires to take Diomedes' armour at the same time. He believes that if he captures these, the Greeks will flee in their ships and no longer wish to fight (8.191-7). In this case, wielding the shield or wearing the armour of a great hero publicly demonstrates the superiority of the soldier who possesses it, as he has managed to defeat its owner in battle. If Hector can defeat two such great heroes, he believes he will convince the other Greeks that they stand no hope of overpowering him. Herein lies the significance of Zeus' comments on Hector's decision to wear the armour of Achilles, which he has taken from the body of Patroclus, although he has not defeated Achilles himself (17.198-208).[98] Armour taken from a defeated foe symbolises the strength of the wearer over the owner whom he has defeated. However in this case, as Zeus comments, Hector is foolish to believe that he is stronger than Achilles or worthy of wearing his armour.

A display of enemy weapons can also be used to prove the magnitude of a victory for all to see. Hector announces that if he wins his duel against Ajax he will hang the arms of his enemy in the shrine of Apollo where they will stand as a memorial to future generations of his great deed (7.81-90). Trophies made of enemy spoils erected on the battlefield and dedications to the gods displayed at their temples were common in later times.[99] Dedications could consist of a collection of weaponry and armour (e.g. the spoils from Marathon dedicated to Apollo, GH1² no. 19) or of an artwork paid for from the sale of captured men or spoils (e.g. a chariot made from the ransom of captive Chalcideans and Boeotians, Hdt. 5.77.4) or both (e.g. the Phocians dedicate captured Thessalian shields and statues made from the proceeds of their spoils at Abae and Delphi, Herodotus 8.27.4-5). After naval battles ships might also be dedicated to the gods (Herodotus 8.121.1; Thucydides 2.84.4, 92.5). Trophies were usually a set of wooden poles holding enemy armour and weapons placed at the site of a victory in battle.[100] Just as the Homeric heroes targeted the equipment of the greatest heroes, so too classical soldiers liked to make trophies from the weapons of a defeated leader. When the Spartan general Brasidas dropped his shield into the sea during the assault on Pylos, the Athenians picked it up and used it for the trophy which they set up after this attack (Thucydides 4.12.1). Such trophies are signifiers of victory, which graphically illustrate the scale of the enemy defeat and humiliation.

Horses and chariots are also a key target for the Homeric warriors. Nestor's acquisition of horse and chariot through killing Augeas' son-in-law Moulius allows him to enhance his own chances of success in battle and through their use he says he was able to kill many enemies (*Il.* 11.737-44). Horses are especially desirable if they are speedy, as they can whisk a man out of perilous situations (e.g. 16.866-7). They are also a mark of wealth and standing. On their night-time spying mission / raid Diomedes and Odysseus decide to take Rhesus' horses because they are told of their splendour: they are beautiful, swift and strong (10.436-7; cf. 544-52, *Rhesus* 616-21). Dolon also claims that Rhesus' chariot and armour are made of precious metals and would be appropriate for the gods (10.438-41), but the pair does not have time to seize these items (10.503-11). For similar reasons, Dolon desires the horses of Achilles as his prize for spying on the Greeks (10.321-7; cf. 391-9, *Rhesus* 182-3). Hector also desires them, but is dissuaded from trying to take them by Apollo (17.75-8; cf. *Rhesus* 184-90). These horses are particularly outstanding (cf. 10.401) since they are immortal, beautiful and exceptionally swift. Likewise, Diomedes desires the horses of Aeneas because they are bred from the horses of Tros, which are of divine lineage and superior to his own. He tells his charioteer to take hold of these horses and drive them back to the ships if he captures them (5.260-73). This Sthenelus dutifully does after Diomedes has killed Pandarus and wounded Aeneas (5.319-27). Diomedes exchanges the horses for his own pair because they are faster to enter and leave the battle (8.105-8). Their excellence also bestows glory on Diomedes (5.273) both because of the high quality of the animals, and because his ownership of them demonstrates his skill at defeating renowned warriors in battle. A fine warrior has fine horses and they are recognisable to the other fighters (cf. 5.181-3). By driving Aeneas' horses into battle Diomedes brings with him visible evidence of his victory against one of the leading Trojans. Diomedes also collects the horses of Echemon and Chromius, sons of Priam, and sends them back to his ships (5.159-65).

Ajax and the perverted cattle-raid

This discussion of the Homeric heroes' attitudes towards weapons and armour serves as a preface to explain why Ajax becomes so angry when he is not awarded the arms of Achilles. The value of the arms of Achilles lies partly in their manufacture – they are unique and beautiful, crafted by the god Hephaestus – and partly in their status value as the weapons of a great hero. As seen in the examples from the *Iliad* cited above, these are exactly the type of arms that men are most prepared to risk their life for on the battlefield. The possession of these items would enhance the reputation of their bearer by showing his prowess as a fighter. Arms taken from a dead enemy signify the superior military strength of the bearer and so in this case Ajax feels entitled to the arms since he is the best living warrior among the Greeks. Here too there is a connection between the practical significance of the arms and their application. The finest arms should be in the hands of the finest warrior. In addition losing the competition to Odysseus, an inferior warrior, is humiliating for Ajax who feels insulted by the decision.[101] His response to the insult is not detailed in Homer, although Odysseus alludes to his suicide when he says that Ajax died because of the contest and the Greeks were disadvantaged by his loss. In Hades Odysseus pleads with the shade of Ajax asking him to forget his anger over the contest, but Ajax maintains his anger and refuses even to acknowledge his rival (*Od.* 11.541-67).

Implacable anger and stubbornness are also key characteristics of the hero of Sophocles' *Ajax*. In this play, Ajax's reaction is to plan a revenge attack, not only against Odysseus, but also against the other Greek leaders whom he blames for deciding the contest in Odysseus' favour (441-6). His revenge is driven by great anger (χόλῳ βαρυνθείς, 41) and he feels dishonoured and insulted by the decision in the contest, partly because the award of the arms leaves him without tangible proof of his honour in the form of a prize and partly because he has been rated as inferior to another fighter (98, 463-5).[102] The significance of his revenge would be to demonstrate his superiority as a fighter visibly and he could reclaim the prize he believes is rightfully his. By killing the Atreidae, he would ensure that they were never able to dishonour him again in the future (98-100). He also hoped to prevent them from treating others in this way (447-9). His attack on Odysseus aims, in particular, to humiliate and harm his enemy, since he was the man who defeated him in the contest and, hence, it is necessary for him to belittle his opponent in order to re-establish his own supremacy. Rather than killing him outright he planned to hold him captive and whip him (101-13) in order to make him pay appropriately (κεῖνος δὲ τίσει τήνδε κοὐκ ἄλλην δίκην, 113). This is a particularly significant choice of revenge, for whipping is the punishment of a slave. The whipping of a free man is, therefore, a particularly humiliating and belittling act which serves to place the avenger in a position of superiority (cf. Demosthenes 21.180).[103] Many of the key characteristics of a revenge attack are associated with Ajax's demented attack on the animals in Sophocles' play. Like the Homeric heroes who seek revenge, Ajax expresses strong emotions and is motivated by a sense of dishonour to attack his enemies. His aims are personal and he does not consider what is best for the army as a whole. He hopes to humiliate his opponent as he has been humiliated and thus to restore the balance of honour. Tecmessa also alludes to his speeches of triumph over the supposed Atreidae and Odysseus in which he mocked them and explained how he had achieved revenge (301-4).[104] However, although Ajax believes he has successfully achieved revenge, he has been thwarted by Athena who caused him to kill cattle instead of the Greek leaders.

When Ajax learns that his attack was not on his enemies, but on harmless animals, he laments that his disgrace is even greater than before. For, although he is a powerful warrior capable of destroying noble and worthy enemies, he has turned his strength against weak and harmless beasts (364-7).[105] Ajax is also strongly motivated by his sense of honour when he decides on suicide, since, he believes, he will not be able to face his father again without proving that he is an honourable man (462-4). He rejects other methods of proving his mettle, including dying in a glorious battle against the Trojans, as this would only enhance the cause of his Greek enemies, the Atreidae (466-9).[106] Instead, he determines upon a course which will show his father that he is not a coward (470-2). Ajax still desires to kill Odysseus and the Atreidae before he dies (384-5, 387-91) and significantly, before killing himself he curses the Atreidae, praying to the Erinyes that they will die at their own hand (killed by their own offspring) as he has died at his own hand (835-43).[107] Nevertheless, as Burnett has pointed out, the suicide-curse is usually associated with the weak, especially women, and it is indicative of Ajax's inability to achieve revenge through the strength of his hand.[108]

In this play there is another interesting inversion of the norms of heroic behaviour through the motif of the distorted cattle-raid. Whereas the typical mythical hero raids the cattle of the enemy to prove his manhood and to feed his army, in this tragedy Ajax falls on the cattle of the Greeks and is greatly dishonoured for his act. While Teucer is on a genuine raid against the Trojans (342-3), his half-brother Ajax is mistakenly occupied with an attack on the Greeks' own livestock (25-8). As in the myths of typical cattle-raids described above Ajax attacks by night (47, 285) and kills the shepherds looking after the animals (27).[109] He also drives some cattle away, although at the time he believes them to be human captives (61-5, 296-300). However, his slaughter of the cattle without an accompanying feast is indicative of his madness and of the distortion of his acts.[110] In typical tragic fashion his revenge is turned against supposed *philoi* instead of against enemies.[111] This attack for highly personal reasons makes no attempt to consider the greater good or the well-being of the Greek army as a whole, but focuses exclusively on Ajax's personal honour and his feelings of humiliation. Rather than considering what is politically expedient or seeking a settlement, his attack concentrates only on achieving revenge for his own satisfaction. In trying to kill fellow Greeks, he is treacherously hoping to destroy his own comrades.[112] His destructive cattle-raid is an excellent metaphor for this internecine conflict. By killing the animals, which symbolise food and survival to the army, Ajax is shown to be destroying the army from within.

As in the instances involving women, both mythical and historical examples indicate that disputes over property could become violent and that revenge attacks involving property could be lethal. Once again as in the case of sexual offences against women, counter attacks and retaliatory violence appear to be more readily associated with disputes over property than with homicides. That wealth and property were thought important for a man in raising and protecting his family is clear. The examples also indicate the great significance attached to notions of honour which possession of certain pieces of property can symbolise. Men's reaction to insults to their honour is the subject of the next chapter.

Insults, Status and Power

As established in the etymologies given in the introduction, honour (τιμή) is a key concept for an analysis of revenge.[1] Honour can be manifested and earned in several ways, including through leadership qualities, eloquence in public speaking, athletic skills and hunting abilities, but it is particularly associated with military prowess. If someone manifests these qualities he is thought capable of defending himself and his family. These abilities are also vital in conferring social status and power on a man. Great sensitivity to insults to honour in a variety of guises appears throughout the ancient sources. Insults can be verbal or physical and may be aimed both at the man himself (e.g. an accusation of cowardice or of weakness) and at his family (in particular insults regarding the chastity of his womenfolk).[2] The capacity to take revenge when insulted, attacked or deprived of power is important. Although avoiding confrontation and refusing to rise to the bait can be a way of dissipating a fight,[3] a man who always fails to react to insults (in particular intentional insults) can open himself up to attacks from others who perceive him to be weak.[4] Similarly a man who fails in his attacks also risks attracting unwelcome attention. As Miller has stressed, it is not necessary to react violently to every insult, real or imagined, as long as the threat of violence is always apparent.[5] Hence men are frequently shown calculating whether or not they should retaliate to an insult and making rational decisions about the most appropriate course of action for them in a given situation.[6] Friendship or kinship between men can prevent conflict following an insult.[7]

Responses to insults and the protection of honour

The connection between honour and revenge has been much studied with regard to Mediterranean societies, where men's decisions are frequently said to be affected by the perceived importance of maintaining or enhancing their honour.[8] Anthropologists working in the region have described how men put a great deal of emphasis on their personal honour which can be gained and lost through appropriate or inappropriate responses to insults and attacks. A man who loses honour through a public insult or slight can restore it by reacting appropriately. A man who fails to react to an insult, on the other hand, can appear weak and without honour.[9] Fighting between men (especially young men) over matters of honour and seemingly trivial insults is rife even today and not only in so-called

'Mediterranean society'.[10] Indeed, Daly and Wilson cite statistics to demonstrate that in the USA murder is often precipitated by a drunken insult or argument.[11] In Wolfgang's 1958 study, the highest cited motives for murder were insults, cursing and jostling. Daly and Wilson suggest that this fighting over insults can be viewed in terms of a competition for social standing where it is possible to gain honour and status by manifesting behaviour deemed to be 'honourable' when challenged in public.[12] The measuring of honour and social ranking through a man's public reputation means that insults and offences which occur in public are usually deemed far more serious than those which occur in private.[13] If a man is insulted publicly, he might feel the need to react strongly to demonstrate his capability to defend himself, his family and property.[14] He has been belittled in front of others and needs to find a way to prove his worth and hence regain the honour lost through the insult. Revenge in these circumstances aims at readjusting in favour of the avenger the levels of honour which the original attack or insult has left unbalanced.[15] Ignoring the offence could leave the victim open to attack by all-comers for weakness. Conversely, swift retaliatory action can restore a man's lost honour and allow him to maintain or even enhance his social standing. Therefore, revenge following an insult is frequently immediate and violent, such as a punch, and seemingly minor insults to honour can even lead to the taking of a life. Victims of insults often make what may seem to be excessively vehement responses to trivial insults. By reacting strongly they demonstrate manifestly that they are worthy of public deference from their inferiors and that opponents should think twice before confronting them.[16] So it can be that even a small insult spurs terrible revenge if it occurs in front of others, whereas a private incident can be more easily forgotten. It is also important that an avenger identify himself publicly in order to reclaim fully honour he has lost in a public forum. A secret response may satisfy the individual avenger, but does nothing to restore his public image.[17]

Daly and Wilson explain this need for swift, public revenge as a way of maintaining 'a credible threat of violence' to ward off competitors. Where men perceive that their interests are threatened by rivals, it is necessary to display sufficient force to deter them. They explain: 'Effective deterrence is a matter of convincing our rivals that any attempt to advance their interests at our expense will lead to such severe penalties that the competitive gambit will end up a net loss which should never have been undertaken.'[18] It is important to present a 'credible threat of violence' because a man can deliberately set out to insult another man with the intention of dishonouring him.[19] This is a calculated risk and is dependent on whether someone is seen to be too weak to respond. Difficulties arise in particular in cases where men are near equals, or have comparable claims to honour.[20]

Daly and Wilson have argued that the key reason that men risk their lives over apparently trivial matters is that the loss of honour and status is a threat to their reproductive success.[21] By their argument heightened social standing allows men to acquire more 'wives' and therefore, potentially, more children. Conversely severe loss of social status could result in a man being condemned to bachelorhood, because those who have higher status are monopolising all the women. This reproductive competition occurs between men rather than women because there is a limit on the number of children each woman can produce.[22] Such an interpretation throws light on the dispute between Agamemnon and Achilles in the *Iliad*, which is much discussed as a key example of how the principles of honour and deference work in the Homeric epics.[23]

When Achilles is publicly dishonoured by Agamemnon, his immediate thought is whether he should attack him physically (*Il.* 1.188-92). This action would repair what Achilles sees as lost esteem when Agamemnon seizes his prize. Achilles won Briseis through his fighting ability and Agamemnon's decision to seize her implicitly attacks his skills as a fighter and ability to protect and defend his possessions and womenfolk. By defeating Agamemnon in a duel or killing him, Achilles would demonstrate to the army that these qualities should not be challenged. This would be a risky strategy though, as Achilles might not have the support of the large host of men around him if he were to kill Agamemnon. Nevertheless, he seems intent on the killing (1.205) until Athena dissuades him with the promise of considerable material reparation in the future (1.213-14). Since Achilles feels that his contribution to the successes of the armed expedition are being underestimated and that the prizes he receives for fighting are small compared to his efforts, the promise of material gains should not be underestimated. Material goods and power are of great consequence in the estimation of a man's status. Moreover, as suggested by Daly and Wilson, this Homeric example clearly shows how a man who has both power and material possessions can better hope to acquire a ready supply of women. Achilles gains his through fighting, while Agamemnon gains his through his status and position of power over the army.[24] Notably, although Achilles bows to Athena in her request, he attempts to ensure that no one will mistake his decision for weakness by threatening to kill anyone else who seeks to take his possessions from his hut (1.300-3). He also maintains his anger against Agamemnon and plots an alternative form of revenge against him with the help of his mother and Zeus. Agamemnon, on the other hand, seeks to assert his superiority over a man who appears to be lacking in deference towards him. He says that even Zeus honours him along with the other nobles, but Achilles alone is disloyal (1.174-8). By taking Briseis, Agamemnon is making a show of his power and status in front of the whole army. His action is designed to challenge Achilles and to show everyone that he is more powerful and important. He also intends to deter others from setting themselves up against him (1.184-7).[25] The significance of honour in this episode is emphasised in the text by the use of a host of τίω- and τιμάω-related words.[26] The implacable anger of the pair, which allows neither man to retract, is also of great importance here.[27]

Although Achilles does not take lethal revenge against Agamemnon at once, his decision to refrain from the fighting wounds Agamemnon's credibility as a leader. Without Achilles, the Greek troops founder and the Trojans advance on their ships, killing many men. Achilles' aim is to make Agamemnon regret his treatment of him (1.241-4) as well as to suffer humiliation in the same way that he has done (9.378-87). For this reason, Achilles refuses to accept Agamemnon's offer of gifts in Book 9, since he feels that no amount of gifts can compensate him until Agamemnon has paid in full, i.e. by being humiliated as he has been.[28] He claims that Agamemnon dishonoured him although he is honoured by immortals (9.110). Accepting the gifts would place Achilles on a lower footing than Agamemnon as a man who can be insulted and then paid.[29] Refusing the gifts allows Achilles to revel further in Agamemnon's humiliating losses as leader. There is also a deterrent quality to Achilles' revenge against Agamemnon, as he wishes the rest of the Greeks to bear witness to what has happened to him and to prevent Agamemnon from acting in a similar way in the future (9.369-72). By undermining Agamemnon's ability as leader, Achilles might also hope to prevent Agamemnon from acquiring other prizes from the army and, therefore, his supply of women. If he is universally considered to be a poor leader, he could lose his status and position and with them his access to prizes.

A similar encounter occurs in the *Odyssey* when Eurylochus speaks out against Odysseus' plan to investigate Circe's house. He accuses Odysseus of folly and of leading his men to ruin. Odysseus takes this as an insult to his status and position as leader. Eurylochus has publicly challenged his leadership abilities and questioned his competence to maintain his position of leader of the Ithacan troops. Through his intervention here, Eurylochus implicitly suggests that he would make a better leader of the troops (a position he takes elsewhere in the absence of Odysseus) because he is more thoughtful of their welfare. Odysseus' immediate thought is of killing Eurylochus, although he is his relative of his (*Od.* 10.441). The mention of the relationship between the two men implies that their alliance through marriage creates a special bond between them which Odysseus considers when deciding whether to avenge himself for the insult. However, in his tale he suggests that it was not their relationship which saved Eurylochus, but the other men who pleaded for him. Unlike Achilles, Eurylochus is frightened and cowed by Odysseus' angry response and follows him dutifully, demonstrating his subservience (10.428-48). Interestingly, though, Odysseus' apparent lack of skill in leading his men does eventually culminate in the death of them all and Odysseus' reduction to penury in the storm at sea.[30] Here his lack of prizes and possessions on arriving in Phaeacia is mirrored in his lack of men to honour his position and status. The story also highlights Odysseus' exceptional access to women. While his men are turned into swine by Circe, he is able to overcome her because his heroic status ensures a good relationship with the gods. His domination over her is made clear in their sexual union in which she promises to be submissive. Eurylochus, who demonstrates his cowardliness and inferiority to Odysseus in heroism in this episode, has no comparable opportunities.

Such confrontations are not unique to Homer. Xenophon portrays Cyaxares and his nephew Cyrus engaging in a similar dispute over honour, military success and power in his *Cyropaedia* (5.5.26-34). This example compares particularly well to the dispute between Achilles and Agamemnon because of the age and power difference between the two participants and is perhaps based on the Homeric paradigm.[31] In the story Cyrus takes an army of his uncle's men and with them manages to annex further territory for the Medes. He expects his uncle to be pleased by his exploits because of the gain for the people as a whole. However, Cyaxares' reaction indicates that he feels that his nephew's military success reflects badly upon his own ability as leader (5.5.33). He feels that Cyrus' achievements dishonour him (ἀτιμάζεσθαι) and he maintains that he has gained nothing if he increases his realm, but loses his honour (5.5.34). Because he himself did not fight in order to make these gains, he feels he will be viewed as unworthy of leadership in the eyes of others. His perspective provides interesting insight into Agamemnon's attitude towards Achilles' successes. Although Achilles is performing tasks that are of overall benefit to the Greeks led by Agamemnon, because Agamemnon himself did not participate in these raids others might regard him as somehow inferior (a notion which Achilles himself highlights, *Il.* 1.225-32; and which is later voiced by Thersites speaking for the normal soldiers, 2.239-40).[32] When challenged by Achilles, it is therefore particularly necessary for him to demonstrate publicly that Achilles is subservient to him and he is still unrepentantly insisting on Achilles' deference when he sends the envoys to persuade him to return to battle (9.158-61). Just so, in the example from Xenophon, Cyaxares is keen that Cyrus demonstrate his subservience to him. Significantly Cyaxares compares the behaviour of Cyrus in making the Medes love him more than their leader to the behaviour of a seducer who makes a wife love him more than her husband (5.5.30; cf. Lysias 1.33). The power of this statement lies in the horror felt at adulterous attacks on wives.[33] The comparison of kingly power to husbandly power makes clear the association of a man's strength and autonomy in protecting his household with his honour, status and power.

In his speech Cyaxares echoes the sentiments of Sarpedon and Achilles who purposefully make the choice of fighting for honour, albeit with risks, in order to demonstrate that they are worthy of their social position (5.5.33-4; Sarpedon: *Il.* 12.310ff.; Achilles: 9.410-16; cf. Ajax: 15.560ff.).[34] Homeric heroes are keenly aware that retreat from battle will be viewed as dishonourable and that they ought to hold their ground to maintain their reputations as pre-eminent heroes and deserving leaders of the people. When Odysseus contemplates whether he ought to flee from battle when faced by overwhelming odds, he decides that only a coward would flee and that he as a hero must stay and fight (11.403-10). Menelaus too contemplates whether he should stay his ground against Hector or face the disapprobation of the Greeks by withdrawing from protecting the body of Patroclus (17.90-105).[35] In this case, though, Menelaus does decide to withdraw as he perceives that Hector is being aided by the gods and he calculates that it would be foolish of him to fight against the gods.[36] Just so, when Zeus hurls his thunderbolt before Diomedes and Nestor to make them withdraw from battle, Diomedes feels he must retreat before the wrath of the gods, although he is grieved at the prospect of being dishonoured and insulted by Hector and the Trojans (8.146-50). Withdrawing from battle, even when it is prudent as here, is associated with cowardice and dishonour in the minds of these heroes and therefore Diomedes is highly reluctant to leave the field. Hector does indeed insult his honour by accusing him of being no better than a woman (8.163); a typical insult, which draws on the standard antithesis between male courage and female weakness, in particular in military situations. Hector himself faces a similar dilemma when confronting Achilles. He knows that if he does not fight Achilles, he will be criticised by his own people and will lose face, but he is also aware that he is risking everything by entering into combat with him.[37] He briefly considers the possibility of negotiating with Achilles, but realises that if he were to attempt it, Achilles would slay him 'just like a woman' (22.98-131). Here the parallel is again drawn between cowardice in battle, as Hector hopes to avoid fighting, and being likened to a woman. Just so, Cyaxares says that he has been made to look like a woman (namely lacking in military ability and power) by Cyrus' actions (*Cyr.* 5.5.33).

Insults which compare a man to a woman are intended to belittle him and denigrate his physical power and military strength (cf. *Il.* 7.233-43). The power of the insult lies in the fact that women are typically non-combatants and are unarmed.[38] Although women are occasionally depicted fighting in a battle, their association with cowardice is so strong that it can shape the picture of the warrior woman unfavourably. A key example appears in Herodotus' version of Artemisia's role in the battle of Salamis. When all seems to be going disastrously, Xerxes believes that he spots Artemisia sinking an enemy vessel and cries out in praise of her, likening her to a man in his exclamation 'My men have become women, my women men!' – a phrase that clearly plays on the association of women with cowardliness and lack of military skill. Herodotus, on the other hand, points out that Artemisia is sinking a friendly ship in order to escape from a tight situation (8.88). Here Herodotus' portrayal of Artemisia matches the general expectation that women are not only weak and cowardly, but also exceptionally devious.[39] Similar associations appear in tragic versions of Agamemnon's murder by Clytemnestra. This story provides a new take on the notion of being 'worse than a woman'. While Agamemnon is successful in battle at Troy, he is 'worsted by a woman' at home through her treachery and guile and is judged by his children to have died dishonourably (Aeschylus *Cho.* 345-53, 479; cf. Euripides *El.* 7-9).[40] Significantly the children use the shameful nature of his death to taunt him in the grave in the hope that he will assist them (Aeschylus *Cho.* 490-5). The use of taunts and insults, especially by women, to rouse a man to revenge is frequently associated with ritual lamentation.[41]

Typically men react strongly to such insults so as to overturn them as quickly as possible and prove that they are worthy of honour through their military skills and strength. Herodotus says that when Mitrobates (governor of the province at Dascyleium) sneers at Oroetes (governor of Sardis) suggesting that he is not a man, because he could not take Samos, his response is to demonstrate that this insult is not true. He takes Samos and crucifies its tyrant Polycrates. He does not make the utterer of the insult pay (τίσασθαι) immediately (3.120), but kills him later, after the capture of Samos (3.126). In this way, he demonstrates to Mitrobates that his insult was unfounded, as well as restoring his honour.[42] Similarly when Masistes insults Artayntes by saying that he is worse than a woman, Artayntes' immediate response is to draw his sword, although the man he is attacking is the brother of Xerxes (9.107). This killing would not only prove that the insult had no grounds, but it would remove the insulter and thereby restore the victim's lost honour. However, Xenagoras of Halicarnassus anticipates his attack and prevents it, gaining by doing so the gratitude of Xerxes who made him leader of Cilicia as a reward. Artayntes' reaction is closely comparable to Achilles' initial response to Agamemnon's insult to his honour when he contemplates drawing his sword to kill the king, but is prevented from doing so by the intervention of Athena.[43] The perceived need to put oneself in a position of such high risk emphasises the perceived importance of responding decisively to insults of this nature.

Insults which attack a man's ability at hunting or in athletics are also portrayed as eliciting violent responses both in the Homeric epics and in later texts. The connection of athletic and hunting ability to military skill (as seen in Chapter 3) explains why this is a sensitive area. This connection is demonstrated clearly in the Homeric story of Tydeus who is said to have challenged the Thebans to an athletics contest and to have triumphed in every event. The Thebans are angered by their losses and immediately attempt to counteract the humiliation they feel by sending out a party to kill Tydeus (*Il.* 4.387-98).[44] By killing Tydeus, the Thebans hope to prove conclusively that his physical and military skills are not as strong as his successes on the field of athletics suggest. However, their failure to defeat Tydeus in battle demonstrates instead his superiority over them. The fact that he is able to defeat all the Thebans in both athletics and in combat indicates that his military and athletic ability are on a par. This story is paralleled in a twisted way in Xenophon's tale of the (unnamed) mad Assyrian king. Gobryas tells Cyrus that his son outdid the king at hunting by killing two beasts which the king had failed to hit. The king is humiliated by the better performance of an inferior and reacts ferociously. This time he does not miss, but successfully brings down his prey with a spear as if he were a wild beast (*Cyr.* 4.6.3-5).[45] By killing the young man, the king removes his rival and demonstrates his own power and murderous capabilities. Similarly, the exiled Scythians in Cyaxares' court are said to feel wronged by him when he insults them because they return empty-handed from the hunt (Herodotus 1.73). Again their reaction is extreme and mirrors a successful hunt in a twisted way. By killing a boy and serving him as a meal to Cyaxares, the Scythians treat him as a piece of prey from the hunt. Elsewhere responses to insults to athletic ability are counteracted by less violent methods. Odysseus, who reacts furiously when someone suggests he is poor athlete, seeks to disprove the insult by outdoing all the Phaeacians at discus throwing and by challenging them all to other contests (*Od.* 8.178-85). Odysseus' successful throw and fearless challenge inform all those who are present that he is not as weak as he might appear and that they should be wary of attacking him.

The gods too are portrayed as reacting strongly to such insults by mortals. When a man sets himself up as an equal to a god, the gods are thought, like their powerful human counterparts, to defend their position aggressively and take violent revenge on anyone who questions their superior status.[46] Thamyris is punished by the Muses for claiming his own skill at music is greater than theirs. In the *Iliad* the Muses are said to have deprived him of his skill, a tidy revenge which removes the grounds for his boasting and demonstrates the superiority of the goddesses (2.594-600).[47] Niobe's boast that she has more plentiful children than Leto results in the death of those children at the hands of Leto's pair Apollo and Artemis (24.602-9), again a neat revenge where the superiority of the divine children is manifested clearly in their ability to overcome all the mortal children despite their numbers. In Sophocles' *Ajax* Athena is angered by Ajax' boast that he does not need her help in battle (764-9). His rejection of the goddess insults her and she proves her power is greater than his by thwarting his plans for revenge against the Atreidae and by humiliating him in front of all the Greeks.[48] Similarly, numerous myths stress the folly of failing to defer appropriately to a god and offer them the proper sacrifices and honour. In the prologue of Euripides' *Hippolytus* Aphrodite explains that the gods too enjoy honour (7-8) and that those who dishonour her will pay (5-6). The play is an account of her successful revenge against Hippolytus because of his neglect of her in his worship (20-2).[49]

In these examples the gods are depicted following similar principles to humans in preserving and enhancing their status. They are shown immediately and decisively acting to defend their position from any threats by inferiors. In Euripides' *HF*, Hera drives Hercules mad saying that if he is not punished, then god is nothing (840-2).[50] In the *Bacchae* Dionysus avenges himself in like manner against insults that Zeus is not his true father and he is not a god. Although Cadmus maintains that Dionysus has acted justly (ἐνδίκως) in taking revenge against Pentheus, he believes that the revenge taken was excessive (ἀλλ' ἄγαν), especially since the god hit out at his own kin (1249-50).[51] Interestingly the gods' reactions tend to be much harsher than their human counterparts who are much more likely to show restraint following an insult rather than to lash out violently. This discrepancy can perhaps be explained by the ability of the gods to avoid all retribution from humans.[52] Hence there is no need for them to calculate the risks of action when they attack humans. Nevertheless the actions of the gods are based on human principles and are not thought to be uniquely divine. Significantly, Agauë complains that Dionysus' revenge against her family is too harsh saying that gods ought not to be like mortals in wrath (1348). Similarly, in Euripides' *Andromache* the messenger comments that Apollo is acting like a man remembering old quarrels (1161-5), when he brings about the death of Neoptolemus for his insult to him (49-55, 1002-6). Here, a direct comparison between the behaviour of gods and men is brought to the fore. Although the gods are said to behave like humans, it is important to stress that humans do not always behave in the same way. Unlike gods they need to consider the ramifications of their actions and decide whether to risk revenge. The gods' ability to take revenge on any mortal who displeases them with no fear of retaliation places them in a different league. Only when the fighting is among the gods is it necessary for them to compromise,[53] although it is possible for gods to take revenge (of the non-fatal variety) on one another. In the *Hippolytus* Artemis promises that she will get revenge (τιμωρήσομαι) on Aphrodite by smiting one of her favourites (1416-22). This revenge would exactly reciprocate the loss of honour which Artemis now suffers from the loss of her worshipper, Hippolytus.

All these tales demonstrate the significance placed on taking revenge following insults across a wide variety of literary genres. The examples suggest that there is a large degree of variation in the type of response according to who is involved and the circumstances of the insult; an important factor which suggests that not everyone was thought to react in an identical way to insults. Evidently there was a perceived need to act rationally and calculate the most appropriate response in a given situation while weighing the advantages and disadvantages of failing to react or overreacting. On occasions, though, characters are repre-sented as miscalculating and acting foolishly or excessively.[54] It should also be noted that the depiction of reactions to insults in later accounts certainly derives much from the presentation of honourable responses in Homer. Nevertheless, these accounts still present evidence of an interest in honour among the classical Greeks, especially in its association with military prowess.

Men competed for honour on the battlefield in the classical period and military prowess was as valuable to citizens of the classical *polis* as to Homeric warriors.[55] In the texts, praise is given in particular to men who hold their posts through manly courage – e.g. the Spartans at Thermopylae (Herodotus 7.220), the Chians at the battle of Lade (6.15), or the Samian ship which remains and fights despite the order to flee (6.14). While death in battle was deemed honourable, abstinence was seen as dishonourable (9.17.4).[56] The Spartans were reputed to be particularly sensitive to questions of personal honour (cf. Plato *Rep.* 545a2-3). Ancient writers stress that Spartan warriors thought it dishonourable to withdraw from battle even when heavily pressed or outnumbered. Instead, they profess willingness to die rather than retreat (Herodotus 7.104.5; 7.220; Xenophon *Hell.* 1.6.32; Tyrtaeus fr. 10 West; cf. Thucydides 5.9.9). Spartan women were also said to share a fierce interest in the honour of their sons, encouraging them to die in battle rather than return alive in dishonour (Plutarch *Mor.* 240-1).[57] Failure to fulfil these ideas is said to cause some Spartans to commit suicide out of shame at their dishonour. Of the Spartans who happened to miss the battle at Thermopylae, Herodotus tells us that one reacted to the persistent insults of his fellow citizens by fighting suicidally at the battle of Plataea, while another felt so ashamed to have missed the battle that took his own life (Herodotus 7.231-2).[58] Similarly Thucydides says that Timocrates committed suicide out of shame when his ship was sunk in the first sea battle of the Peloponnesian war (Thucydides 2.92.3).[59] This perception of Spartan attitudes towards military honour is highlighted in Thucydides' account of the shock felt when some Spartan hoplites chose to surrender to the Athenians after becoming trapped on Sphacteria (Thucydides 4.40). Significantly in this case dishonour on the field of battle led to civic dishonour when it was decided that the men involved should be deprived of their right to hold public office (*atimia*) (Thucydides 5.34.2). This demonstrates that the connection between success as a warrior and social status was equally pronounced for the classical Greeks as for Homeric heroes.

Insults, honour and status in the Athenian law-courts

In Athens, too, a deserter, coward or shirker could be disenfranchised, making him *atimos* (literally without honour) and hence without status or political power (Aeschines 1.28-32, 3.175-6; Andocides 1.73-4; Lysias 10.1, 14.6-9).[60] Accusing a man of dropping his shield in battle (meaning that he fled in a cowardly way from the field instead of holding his position in the line) is a common insult. This insult occurs frequently in comedy[61] and is also used to discredit political rivals in oratory. Aeschines repeatedly refers to an incident in which his rival Demosthenes supposedly fled the field at Chaironeia.[62] His use of this insult in public is an attempt to discredit his opponent and make him seem unworthy of public office.[63] However, this statement (along with certain others, including accusations of patricide) was also considered to be slanderous by law and could be prosecuted (by δίκη κακηγορίας), although, as Carey suggests, Athenians may well have been reluctant to pursue this kind of case in the courts.[64]

The evidence suggests that Athenians were able to use the courts to prosecute following an insult to themselves or their families, and speakers frequently refer to the insult that has been done to them and their hopes of achieving revenge through the laws.[65] Insult is interpreted broadly and can include acts of physical violence, taunts and attacks on the chastity of female relatives.[66] Rivals occasionally indulge in a series of counter-prosecutions related to insults (Lysias 10.1, Isocrates 17.21). Yet, although Athenians had the option of pursuing insults to their honour through the courts, and some of them took advantage of this possibility, this did not eradicate violent responses to insults or other slights in Athens.[67] Van Wees' suggestion that violence decreased in Greece because of a rise in population has some merit, as the rise of concentrated communities living together in *poleis* does seem to have brought about efforts to prevent violence within the community.[68] However, the idea that violence decreased significantly in classical Greece is a problematic one. First, as van Wees himself argues, the Homeric epics exaggerate the level of violence in society as they depict ideals for the most aggressive men and focus almost exclusively on the activities of the elite warriors.[69] Even among the great heroes there is a remarkable lack of violent responses to insults (other than on the battlefield) in Homer and a great deal of restraint.[70] Second it is by no means clear that classical Greece was a place lacking in violence. Instead, violence seems to have been used extensively, as a means of coercing court judgements or in drunken brawling at Athens, as well as to subjugate allies or defeat foes in international relations.[71]

In his speech *Against Meidias* Demosthenes cites two cases of honour-related violence as part of his discussion of whether violent retaliation following an insult is appropriate for Athenians. In one incident involving Euthynus and Sophilus (both athletes) a perceived insult leads to instant retaliation which kills the man (αὐτὸν ὑβρίζειν ᾤετο, ἀμυνάμενον οὕτως ὥστε καὶ ἀποκτεῖναι, 21.71).[72] In the second incident Eueon is said to have killed Boeotus because of a punch. Demosthenes explains that he reacted out of anger at the perceived dishonour (ἀτιμία) caused to him by the blow. He adds that the original blow constituted an act of *hybris* and therefore a violent reaction was not a surprising response (21.71-2).[73] Gestures, tones and looks are all said to enhance the insult in the eyes of the victim (21.72). It is also maintained that it is the feeling of dishonour brought about by a blow, rather than the blow itself which rouses anger (21.72; Isocrates 20.5-6). Anger is central to these episodes. It is aroused by what the angry man perceives to be insulting behaviour and it provokes violent responses from him (cf. Demosthenes 53.16).[74] Both these incidents are said to have occurred at parties in the presence of other guests and after the consumption of alcohol (21.73). The speaker of Lysias 3 emphasises that drunken brawls and fighting are commonplace in Athens especially in disputes over lovers (3.42-3; cf. Demosthenes 54.13-14).[75] In the examples cited from *Against Meidias* Demosthenes suggests that violent responses to insults were normal in Athens, although presumably it was much rarer that such brawls resulted in a death. Significantly, he notes that violent retaliatory reactions are worthy of sympathy (to the extent that many jurors apparently voted to acquit Eueon out of sympathy for his reaction), although he argues that men should retaliate through the laws, as he is attempting to do, rather than retaliating violently (21.74-6; cf. Isocrates 20.8). Based on the reaction of the jurors at Eueon's case it is possible to posit that violent retaliation for insults was tolerated in Athens provided that it was not deemed to be excessive (cf. 21.75).[76] Moreover it is possible that some of the jurors felt that Eueon's response constituted legally permissible self-defence because his opponent could be shown to have initiated the fight. Throwing the first punch is elsewhere synonymous with culpability in fights of this nature (Demosthenes 23.50; 47.7-8, 15, 38; Lysias 4.11, 15; cf. Antiphon 4.2.2-3; [Demosthenes] 59.15).[77] This means that a man can be held responsible for his own death, as argued by Antiphon in his third *Tetralogy* (4.4.3), if he was the one to throw the first punch.[78] Read in this way, Demosthenes' decision to prosecute rather than to respond violently to Meidias could be seen as atypical.[79] Indeed, the speaker of Lysias 3 refers to his disinclination to prosecute Simon for assault out of fear of being derided in public and of this having negative implications for his social standing (3.9, 40).[80]

Cohen has suggested that Demosthenes was in a difficult position because he needed to persuade the jurors that his failure to retaliate violently to Meidias' insult was not a sign of his own weakness or of the triviality of the incident. Instead he carefully paints restraint as a virtue. The orator makes much of his forbearance, saying that men ought not to take revenge into their own hands, but should bring the case to court in order to get revenge through the laws (21.76). In this way he attempts to be perceived not as a passive victim, but a man of honour who restrained himself.[81] Demosthenes is indeed in a difficult position. His failure to react in anger to Meidias might imply that the attack was insignificant (cf. Isocrates 20.5). However, by reacting violently in such a public arena Demosthenes would have run a considerable risk. In a fight matters easily escalate, endangering the fighters' lives, as seen in the examples cited above.[82] Moreover, the legal ramifications of seriously wounding or killing a man in a brawl could be considerable, including the death penalty, exile and loss of political status (cf. Lysias 3 and 4). The fact that the slap did not take place at a party, but in a civic, religious context is also relevant to Demosthenes' decision to restrain himself. By deciding against retaliating in kind, Demosthenes does not necessarily show that the Athenians respected restraint above violence, as Herman has argued.[83] Rather, Demosthenes, like Achilles in *Iliad* 1, makes an assessment based on the possible risks and gains of the particular situation.[84]

Demosthenes apparently perceives his chances of overcoming the wealthy and powerful Meidias as slim and he implicitly admits his physical and social inferiority when he fails to retaliate violently. With his subsequent legal response, he would have had the chance to win back this ground, by inflicting death or disenfranchisement on his opponent through the courts (21.182).[85] However, Demosthenes allegedly dropped his suit against Meidias. Aeschines slurs his rival by saying that he gave way to Meidias and gave up his honour for the sum of 30 minae (3.52).[86] Plutarch's fuller account maintains that Demosthenes was wise to yield because of the difficulty of defeating a strong man with great wealth, eloquence and many friends. He adds that Demosthenes was still young at the time of this case and that he would never have submitted if he had felt able to overcome Meidias (*Dem.* 12.2).[87] Christ speculates that Demosthenes decided on this course of action because he was afraid that Meidias would retaliate against him violently if he attempted to collect any fine awarded to him.[88] In this case Demosthenes is in a position of inferiority and his actions and words confirm this.

Similarly, Pittalacus allegedly dropped his lawsuits against the men who burst into his house and whipped him because he felt he could not defeat them and he wanted to avert a worse fate for himself (Aeschines 1.58-64). In this case, Pittalacus' inferior social standing is made explicit and his inability to defend himself against the attacks of socially and physically stronger men means that they can treat him harshly with impunity.[89] A similar situation is illustrated in the *Odyssey* when Odysseus is forced to sit quietly and submit to both the insults and physical assaults of the suitors in order to maintain his disguise as a beggar (17.453-87). We are also informed that he thought carefully about whether he should react violently when Melanthius accused him of being a poor athlete and soldier, but he decided that he could not react to Melanthius without revealing his identity (17.217-46). The example shows clearly that those of low rank without warrior abilities are expected to submit to humiliation without reacting, whereas a powerful man has the ability to defend himself and presents a threatening figure whom others would be reluctant to insult.

Equally Demosthenes portrays Meidias as a most powerful man who can successfully achieve what he wants by manipulating the system. He alleges that because of his wealth he can bribe or cajole magistrates into postponing his cases giving himself an advantage in court (21.112; cf. 21.140).[90] He is also powerful enough to achieve revenge against those who have thwarted him, such as Strato of Phalerum the arbitrator who ruled against him by default when he failed to appear on the day of his arbitration with Demosthenes (21.83-101). According to Demosthenes, Meidias first attempted to bribe and cajole the magistrates and arbitrator into recording a verdict in his favour. When they proved immune to his bribes and Strato refused to rule in his favour, Meidias began to threaten them. Finally he denounced Strato and caused him to be disenfranchised (καθάπαξ ἄτιμος γέγονεν).[91] The connection is made here between Strato's inferiority to Meidias in social standing, wealth and power, his inability to better his opponent either through legal or extra-legal methods and his dishonour (expressed through the term *atimos* signifying his disenfranchisement). Because of his disenfranchisement, he can no longer speak for himself in court and he is therefore weakened and unable to defend himself.

The inability to make your own case in court makes a man no better than a woman or child, since they require an adult male to speak for them in legal proceedings.[92] As seen above, being 'no better than a woman' is a common slur in military situations, where it is implied that a fighter is physically weak and unable to defend himself adequately.[93] At the same time the ideas of cowardice and avoiding a fight are also applied in legal contests, especially with reference to the need to defend weak family members ([Demosthenes] 59.12; cf. Lysias 10.3).[94] Just as warriors feel the need to avert and avenge attacks on themselves and their families, so too speakers in the Attic courts refer to the necessity for them to avenge through the courts wrongs done to themselves and their families. This parallelism between the need for ability at speaking and at fighting to confirm manly honour is telling. Lack of ability in these areas condemns a man to inferior social standing and he is forced to accept harsh treatment by his social superiors (as in the case of Pittalacus). In Plato's *Gorgias* (486a-c) Callicles says that a man who cannot speak to defend himself in court is vulnerable to attacks from all-comers. Men feel that they can slap him in the face and not have to pay.[95] Failure in lawsuits can also lead to disrespect by opponents (cf. Demosthenes 54.43). The speaker of Lysias 3 claims that Simon only decided to bring his case against him after the speaker had failed to win in a private suit (3.20; cf. 3.39). The implication of this statement is that the speaker is deemed to be ineloquent and incapable of speaking persuasively in court and winning his case. His public humiliation through the loss of the suit makes him appear weak and an easy target for Simon. Elsewhere, Lysias states explicitly that, while the strong can insult whom they please with impunity, the weak are unable either to defend themselves against attacks or to make such attacks themselves (24.18). Conversely Meidias' power and status are such that he is confident in his ability to do what he pleases, while others appear to be afraid to stand up to him or attempt revenge against him (Demosthenes 21.131).[96] Similarly Lysias implies that the strong are able to resist requital, when he asks whether an opponent thinks himself so powerful that he can avoid revenge at the hands of those he has wronged (ἢ τοσοῦτον δύνασαι ὥστε οὐδέποτε οἴει τοὺς ἀδικουμένους ὑπὸ σοῦ τιμωρίας τεύξεσθαι; 10.13).

Cohen has argued that Demosthenes 54 (*Against Conon*) can be read in a similar way to *Against Meidias*. In his speech Ariston needs to justify why he is bringing the case to court (54.18-19) and must face the charge from Conon that he is reacting inappropriately in a case of normal youthful rivalry (54.42).[97] He too makes much of his modesty compared with his opponents' aggression. Herman has suggested that this offers proof that the Athenians would not have approved of Conon's behaviour.[98] However, as Carey has pointed out, this rhetoric could be disguising the speaker's role in inciting the incident and there could be some truth to Conon's claims of youthful rivalry between Ctesias and Ariston. It is further possible that political motives underlie this case and that matters are not as straightforward as they first appear.[99]

In both Demosthenes 21 and 54 we get a glimpse of the way in which politicians could use court cases to further their social standing and to embarrass their rivals. Because a man who was convicted in court lost honour, the courts had the potential to play a significant role in allowing Athenian citizens to compete publicly for honour.[100] However, any political motivations underlying the lawsuits are not always made obvious by the participants. In the same way, as Christ has noted, litigants tend to play down potential financial motives and emphasise honour instead. He deduces: 'This tendency suggests that the Athenian audiences were more comfortable with the defense of manly honor than with the naked pursuit of financial and political ends.'[101] This argument closely matches the one made by Ferguson regarding publicly cited motives for fighting among the Yanomami as opposed to privately held motives which are not voiced.[102] On this view the pursuit of honour and revenge are held to be 'moral' motives which find sympathy among the people at large. Intended material gains or political manoeuvring, on the other hand, are not received so sympathetically and do not generate the same level of public support. However, it is important to emphasise that these motives are not unconnected. The public perception of a man's honour is essential for his political and social standing and, therefore, the pursuit of honour and revenge is not apolitical. As discussed in the previous chapter, wealth and material goods are also important in determining social status and allowing a man to maintain his position in society and protect his family. Hence the pursuit of financial or political goals, even under the guise of pursuing honour, tends towards attaining an elevated social position and the privileges which attend this.[103]

Insults and power disputes in the
Theban plays

All these themes are apparent in Sophocles' plays about Oedipus and his family, although they are presented in a way typical of tragic plot-lines.[104] Oedipus' story starts with a drunken slur at a banquet in Corinth. When someone accuses him of not being the son of his father he is angry, but does not react violently. Instead he questions his parents and the oracle at Delphi.[105] During his subsequent journey he meets a party of travellers in the road and a dispute erupts. It begins with blows between Oedipus and Laius' herald and culminates in an all-out attack. Oedipus claims that Laius tried to drive him from the road by striking him on the head with a goad,[106] but that he made him pay, though not equally (οὐ μὴν ἴσην γ' ἔτεισεν), by killing him and his companions (800-12). Here Oedipus expresses the unequal nature of his revenge – in return for a blow, he responded with murder. The likelihood of this kind of escalation in angry confrontations and brawls is attested in the stories from oratory above.[107] Elsewhere Oedipus reaffirms the naturalness of his response saying that it is not normal to ask a stranger if he is your father when he has insulted you. Rather it is normal to strike back at once (*OC* 991-4). This justification alerts us to the perceived difference in retaliating against your father and against a stranger. While a man who is angry might be expected to retaliate violently against another man whom he considers to be a social equal, especially one who struck the first blow (cf. 270-2; 991-6), there would be no justification at all for an attack against his father.[108] Typically again, this tragic plot-line is twisting what might be considered average behaviour and turning it into something perverse and shocking. Although it is true that Oedipus did not recognise his father, his angry response here is the beginning of his troubles. In *Oedipus Tyrannus*, Sophocles' portrays Oedipus as a man who believes in his own intelligence, but who does not think deeply enough before becoming excessively angry. This is made evident by his confrontations with Creon and Tiresias in the play. Rather than thinking through the implications of his actions, Oedipus reacts vehemently when he confronts the strangers on the road. Yet, this reaction is not the only possible option, although perhaps submitting himself to the insults of Laius and his men would have seemed intolerable for haughty Oedipus. Sophocles' depiction of Theseus in *Oedipus at Colonus* on the other hand is quite different. Although he is greatly angered by Creon's arrogant behaviour, he maintains that he will not himself wound Creon physically as he deserves. Rather he will attack him with the law (*OC* 904-18). Although an attack on Creon by Theseus would not be problematic in the way that Oedipus' attack on Laius was, still he prefers to resolve the dispute without recourse to violence.

As in the examples discussed earlier, there is in *Oedipus Tyrannus* an encounter between an older and a younger man each feeling that if he were to back down he would suffer dishonour. Similarly, too, the dispute between father and son here is paradigmatic of the dispute between the older and younger generation over property and power. In each case the fear of the older man is that the younger will manage to seize some or all of his share of power and property by dishonouring and insulting him. The younger men all desire to demonstrate that their abilities merit greater honour and, with that, a greater share in the status and power of their elder. The fact that in the myth Oedipus ascends to Laius' throne after killing him is testimony to this idea. It should not come as a surprise either that the consequence of Oedipus' success in this fight is that he wins for himself Laius' wife.[109] The tragic twist is, of course, that she is his own mother.

Laius' initial fears of being killed by his son are realised in a violent way, just as the succession of the gods is supposedly achieved through violence. As Strauss has argued, the predominant idea of the importance of filial piety is backed up by a secondary notion concerning generational competition in which the son will eventually succeed his father and continue in his place.[110] That this problem was felt to influence and affect autocrats more than other men is evidenced in a wealth of examples of disputes over thrones (many between brothers).[111] The problem faced by feuding relatives in these cases is that an appropriate avenger may not be available. Oedipus is both the most likely avenger and the attacker of his father and usually revenge would not be expected in these circumstances, as in the Homeric version of the tale (*Od.* 11.273).[112] In Sophocles' play, though, Oedipus is unwittingly his father's avenger when he curses himself as killer of Laius.[113] This curse destroys his status – he loses the honour he gained through saving the kingdom along with the throne and he goes from the land as a beggar without honour.[114] His sons Eteocles and Polynices remain to dispute who should rightfully take the throne.

In this dispute, the tragic paradox of friend who is foe comes to the fore. This idea is picked up by Antigone in her lament over Polynices (φίλος γὰρ ἐχθρὸς ἐγένετ᾽, ἀλλ᾽ ὅμως φίλος, Euripides *Phoe.* 1446). While revenge against an 'enemy' is unproblematic, the conflict between the brothers in these plays is represented as a moral problem, especially when they face one another in single combat and die at each other's hand (Aeschylus *Septem* 680-2; Euripides *Phoe.* 1364-9). The brothers themselves do not always recognise this problem, but prefer to see themselves as traditional enemies. Polynices asks his brother, just as Oedipus asks, who would strike and not expect to receive the same treatment in return? (*Phoe.* 594-5). He refuses to withdraw from battle because he feels ashamed to be mocked by his younger brother for cowardice (Sophocles *OC* 1422-3).[115] The traditional role of revenge against an enemy for wrongs done is twisted so that brother now takes revenge against brother and the family self-destructs as is typical in tragedy.[116] This retaliatory aspect of the struggle for power is emphasised by Aeschylus in the two sisters' lament

for their brothers at the end of the play (*Septem* 961, παισθεὶς ἔπαισας / σὺ
δ' ἔθανες κατακτανών). In leading an army against Thebes, Polynices
speaks frequently of his hopes for revenge against his brother for exiling
him (*Septem* 636-8, 1049; Sophocles *OC* 1326-30), although his chief
motive is clearly his desire to return to power from being a dishonoured
outcast (Euripides *Phoe.* 427-9; Sophocles *OC* 1295-307).[117]

That the desire for status and honour causes many disputes in ancient
examples across all genres is evident. The discrepancies between different
reactions in different circumstances can be explained as the portrayal of
decisions made by individuals in specific circumstances, although Oedipus' attack on his father in tragedy stands out from the other examples as
being highly abnormal. The strong tendency towards reconciliation is
evident throughout the sources, but it is also understood that young men
can get carried away when fighting and that the situation can easily
escalate out of control.

What Motivates Orestes?

Orestes' story is usually seen as a classic case of blood revenge in which a son avenges the murder of his father as soon as he has reached maturity. In particular Aeschylus' rendering of the tale in the *Oresteia* trilogy is often understood as an examination of the role of blood revenge and feuding in early Greek society and its replacement with 'justice' through the establishment of legal procedures at Athens.[1] However, as we saw in Chapter 1, the evidence does not reveal that blood feuding was a major force in Greek society, a conclusion that challenges this standard reading of the *Oresteia*. Instead men appear to have preferred to find more peaceable methods of resolving matters after the death of a relative. Moreover, although it is frequently noted that Orestes is driven by a variety of motives, nevertheless modern commentators usually assume that the desire for blood revenge is the dominant motive for his murder of Aegisthus and Clytemnestra. A careful reading of the sources reveals that this position is not as obvious as it first appears. The stated motives of Electra and Orestes are not always identical, for example. Indeed, Orestes himself frequently cites return from exile and reclaiming his inheritance (both wealth and power) as his aim. Certainly the feud over power between siblings and cousins of the house of Tantalus is key to this story through several generations. As seen in Chapters 3 and 4, relatives are thought most likely to attack one another during feuds over inheritance and power. In addition, issues of paternity and the continuity of the male bloodline are central in the different versions of this myth and, as such, Clytemnestra's infidelity is a major factor in the different sources. Orestes' violent response to Aegisthus and his mother is driven in large part by their adultery and the way in which their affair dishonours his father and himself. As we saw in Chapter 2, very violent responses and lethal revenge are readily associated with instances of seduction and adultery, and killing in these circumstances is both a mythical and historical norm.

The tragic Clytemnestra also has multiple motives for her murder of Agamemnon, some explicit, others more suppressed. Although she often claims her act constituted revenge for the sacrifice of her daughter Iphigenia by Agamemnon, which she believes gives her moral authority for the murder of her husband, she gains other advantages through his death (specifically money and power).[2] In Sophocles' and Euripides' plays, her stated motivations are questioned by her daughter and she is accused of using revenge for Iphigenia as a pretext to achieve other ends. This reading is also implicit in Aeschylus' trilogy where Clytemnestra has assumed power with Aegisthus in the absence of her husband.

The Oresteia story in Homer and tragedy

In Homer the story of Orestes provides a foil for the story of Odysseus, with Orestes as an example for Telemachus, the suitors compared to Aegisthus, and Penelope contrasted to Clytemnestra.[3] Athena in her disguise as Mentes notes that Orestes has gained honour by killing his father's murderer Aegisthus and urges Telemachus to do honourable deeds and make a name for himself as well (*Od.* 1.296-302). Nestor repeats this advice and utters the famous phrase that it is a good thing for a man to leave a son behind to avenge his death (3.193-200). This statement suggests that fathers (such as Nestor) take comfort from the notion of having sons to avenge their deaths, but this does not mean that the sons are motivated solely out of a desire for blood revenge. While both Athena and Nestor make clear the connection between Orestes' actions and the murder of Agamemnon by Aegisthus, other motives are also apparent. Notably the speakers feel that Orestes is a suitable example for Telemachus even though Telemachus does not need to avenge his father's death. Instead, as his own reply to Nestor makes clear, he hopes to gain honour like Orestes by attacking the men who are threatening to take his mother, his property and his power.

The significance of offences against women in driving men to kill is central to the plot of the *Odyssey*, as seen in Chapter 2. Just as Odysseus is motivated to kill the suitors primarily because of their attempts to seduce Penelope and the women of his household, so too Orestes' murder of Aegisthus is prompted in large part by his adulterous affair with Clytemnestra. This is made clear in Zeus' speech at the beginning of the *Odyssey* where he cites Aegisthus' adultery with Clytemnestra alongside the murder of Agamemnon as reasons that Orestes put his life at risk. Moreover he notes that Orestes wished to kill Aegisthus in order to return home and retake the throne of his father (1.29-43). Telemachus too is motivated by a desire to regain possession of his father's house and wealth when he begins to think about the possibility of dealing with the suitors. As seen in Chapter 2, the suitors' plan to eliminate Telemachus springs from Antinous' desire to seize power. He, like Aegisthus, plans to attain this power by marrying the wife of the ruler. However, both Aegisthus and Antinous take considerable risks in their bid to attain power. Aegisthus' decision to remain in Mycenae after killing Agamemnon, rather than going into exile, makes him vulnerable to Orestes' attack when he comes of age and wishes to retake the throne. However, through Clytemnestra's complicity he does succeed in ruling in Mycenae for seven years before Orestes returns (3.306-8). Antinous on the other hand fails in his efforts to achieve power and is slaughtered along with the other suitors before he manages to convince Penelope to marry him.

In Homer, Clytemnestra's motives for being complicit in the murder of her husband are relatively simple. She is portrayed as an unfaithful wife who has succumbed to the advances of another man. Her adultery is what men who have been absent from home for a considerable period fear, while Penelope's constant fidelity despite the circumstances is an ideal wifely response in the same situation. The fact that Agamemnon is murdered by Clytemnestra's lover on his return from war further adds to the anxiety felt by men unable to offer adequate protection for their wives. An adulterous wife, it is implied, does not only create anxiety about the paternity of her husband's children. She can also become involved in plots to kill him. The close connection between a wife's adultery and the destruction of his line (symbolised by the husband's death and the scattering of his legitimate children who are replaced by the children of the adulterer) is a major topic in tragic representations too (e.g. Euripides *El.* 914-17; *Or.* 195-200; Sophocles *El.* 587-90).

Much debate has focused on the extent of the role of Clytemnestra in the *Odyssey*, mainly because of the apparent differences between her part in the murder in Homer and in Aeschylus. When the story is used to encourage Telemachus to take revenge for his father (1.298-302; 3.193-8), the role of Clytemnestra is not mentioned and the emphasis is on Aegisthus. However, Agamemnon in Hades later emphasises the role of Clytemnestra in the murder when he converses with Odysseus. This is because he is attempting to warn Odysseus about the dangers of returning home openly (11.421-56), whereas the earlier passages encouraging Telemachus focus on the bravery of Orestes.[4] Neither is there any specific mention of the matricide in Homer (although the burial of Clytemnestra is mentioned at 3.309-10). Again, this is partly related to the context of the story where it is offered as a paradigm first to Telemachus, who is in the position of Orestes, but does not need to act against his mother, and then to Odysseus, who is in the position of Agamemnon. Moreover, the differences between the tragic and heroic Orestes hang on this issue. In Homer the focus is on Orestes' murder of Aegisthus the murderer, usurper and adulterer. In tragedy Clytemnestra becomes the central character and Orestes is forced to consider the problems associated with killing his mother.[5] By comparison the murder of Aegisthus in the plays is straightforward as it is in Homer.[6]

The dispute over the throne of Argos between the cousins Agamemnon and Aegisthus is at the heart of Aeschylus' *Oresteia* trilogy and the other tragedies which revolve around the myth of Orestes. This conflict is a continuation of a family feud for power initiated by the brothers, Thyestes and Atreus, in the previous generation (Aeschylus *Ag.* 1090-2; Euripides *El.* 699ff.; *IT* 192ff., 811-14; *Or.* 1-14, 807-18, 995-1012). Angry about his lack of power, Thyestes decides to attempt to seize power by persuading

Atreus' wife to help him get the throne. To achieve this end, he commits adultery with her and she willingly betrays her husband. The seduction of ruler's wives in order to acquire power has already been noted above in the stories of Aegisthus and Antinous.[7] In tragedy the particularly bitter nature of the brothers' dispute is reflected in its culmination: the cooking of his nephews' by Atreus who dupes his brother into eating his own sons to get revenge on him (*Ag.* 1095-7, 1214ff., 1583ff.; *Cho.* 1065ff.).[8] The eating of his own children in this story is symbolic of him eating and thus destroying his own future.[9] In one version of the myth, Aegisthus kills Atreus and returns power to Thyestes (Hyginus *Fab.* 88). In another version, Aegisthus is saved when his brothers are killed and returns from exile to kill Atreus' son, Agamemnon. He takes control of the land with Agamemnon's wife Clytemnestra (Aeschylus *Ag.* 1497-504; Euripides *El.* 8-10).

Aegisthus and Clytemnestra have different grudges against Agamemnon, but they unite against a common foe to achieve a joint revenge (Euripides *El.* 1046-8). By aligning himself with the wife of his enemy, Aegisthus gains better access to Agamemnon (Aeschylus *Ag.* 1636-7), while Clytemnestra can rely upon Aegisthus' help and protection in killing her husband (1434-6).[10] It is also possible to see Aegisthus' union with Clytemnestra as a way of legitimising his rule.[11] In tragedy Clytemnestra's motivations for killing her husband are complex. Her anger is raised by Agamemnon's sacrifice of their daughter Iphigenia, and in some versions by his murder of her first husband and baby. Significantly Apollodorus says (*Epit.* 3.16) that Tantalus, the first husband of Clytemnestra, was a son of Thyestes adding further layers of kin-killing to the tale. This version perhaps seeks to explain Clytemnestra's rationale in deciding to ally herself with Aegisthus, her first husband's brother. In tragedy Agamemnon's relationship with Cassandra is also at issue, not to mention her own love for Aegisthus and the power she has achieved during Agamemnon's absence at Troy.

Although Clytemnestra justifies her actions by citing Agamemnon's treatment of their daughter, this does not appear to have been her main reason for killing her husband, even according to her own account.[12] Instead she states that Agamemnon should have been exiled for the terrible sacrifice (Aeschylus *Agamemnon* 1414-20).[13] She maintains that he deserved to die at her hands because of his relationship with Cassandra and the other women at Troy (1438-46). Cassandra too represents herself as the cause of Agamemnon's death in Euripides' *Trojan Women*. She claims that through her marriage to Agamemnon she will be the avenger of her brothers and father (359-60, 404-5). She means that Clytemnestra will kill Agamemnon in anger because he has returned from Troy with another 'wife' (cf. Euripides *El.* 1030-4). Clytemnestra, like Medea (discussed in Chapter 2), undergoes gender inversion in Aeschylus' trilogy and is called manlike (Aeschylus *Ag.* 11).[14] These explanations are further suggestions that exile was thought more typical in cases of murder, while death was associated more readily with cases of adultery. Moreover, in the *Electra* plays of Euripides and Sophocles, Electra claims that avenging Iphigenia was merely a pretext and that Clytemnestra was actually driven by other motives (Euripides *El.* 1069ff.; Sophocles *El.* 584ff.). Electra maintains that her mother's love for Aegisthus and her desire for power were both significant in her decision to murder her husband (Euripides *El.* 1086-90; Sophocles *El.* 520-5; 560-2, 583-90). Otherwise, she would not have committed adultery with Aegisthus and she would have permitted her son to ascend to the throne and take his rightful inheritance rather than exiling him.[15] Aeschylus' play also refers to the wealth and power which Clytemnestra and Aegisthus acquire upon the death of Agamemnon. The chorus suggests that tyranny was their ultimate aim (*Ag.* 1348ff.), while Aegisthus revels in the power he has gained by killing Agamemnon and seizing his property (1638-9).[16] At the end of the *Agamemnon* Aegisthus and Clytemnestra are said to be joint rulers in Argos (1672-3). Although the chorus of old men considers revolt, they are appeased by Clytemnestra's persuasion and accept the pair as rulers (albeit reluctantly) rather than fighting (1654ff.). This ending is paralleled by Athena's persuasion of the Erinyes at the end of the *Eumenides*. The association of Athena with the ability to bring about compromise and prevent violent disputes in the community has been noted in Chapter 1.

In the third generation, Orestes returns from exile to kill Aegisthus and his mother.[17] According to Burnett's analysis, this tragic plot is an excellent example of traditional revenge where there is disguise, deception, divine aid and a female relative to rescue.[18] She also insists that a man should not advance himself by taking revenge and should not have other 'ignoble' motives.[19] However, it is not always clear that Orestes adheres to these lofty values. He does not tend to cite revenge for his father's death as his own primary motive, but as one motive among several. Here, as elsewhere, a man acts in revenge, but only in a case where other compelling motives exist, as Orestes himself makes clear in *Choephori* when he points out that he has several motives (299) and outlines his reasons for acting (300-5).[20]

Escaping from poverty and exile appears prominent in Orestes' motivations, and a key motive for him (just as for Aegisthus in the previous generation) is attaining the power and wealth of the house (Aeschylus *Cho.* 135, 250, 297-305, 479-80; *Eum.* 757-8; Euripides *El.* 610-13; 810; *Or.* 1600-7; Sophocles *El.* 67-72). Orestes' desire to regain his lost throne, wealth and homeland is so strong that even without the god's command, he would have acted to achieve a return to power (*Cho.* 297-305). For living as an exile he is without honour (295-6, 405-9; Euripides *El.* 233-6).[21] When Orestes is acquitted in *Eumenides* he says 'I was an exile, you have brought me home again'. He will return to his father's house where he will attain his power and wealth (755-62; cf. Euripides *Or.* 1643-65). From this point of view, the killing is just part of an ongoing family dispute about power and wealth: typical motivations for murder, as is discussed further below.

Orestes' murder of Aegisthus is also portrayed as the legitimate killing of an adulterer (*Cho.* 989-90). Notably, in Aeschylus' play Orestes goes into exile for his mother's murder, but not for the murder of Aegisthus (1034-43), which can be understood as an instance of lawful homicide.[22] When seen in this light, Orestes' revenge is indeed very closely related to the revenge of Odysseus against the suitors, and, therefore, as argued in Chapter 2 and as suggested by Burnett, it too can be seen as an archetypal example of Greek revenge, although not perhaps for the reasons cited by her. Instead, Orestes, like Odysseus, should be seen as an avenger who is interested in protecting the male bloodline in the household by annihilating the adulterer who is threatening his position by siring new offspring to replace Agamemnon's brood and keep them from the throne. Within Aeschylus' trilogy the association is made between the legitimate inheritance of property and power handed on from father to son and the continuation of the male line (*Cho.* 859-65). The survival of the bloodline of Agamemnon is much at issue in the *Oresteia* where the children appeal to their father not to allow the line to be blotted out, because through them he still lives (*Cho.* 500ff.; cf. Euripides *Or.* 664; Sophocles *El.* 764-5). These thoughts about the continuation of the man through his children offer further evidence of the Greek preoccupation with siring legitimate offspring, as discussed in Chapter 2. Simultaneously, both Orestes and Odysseus aim to re-establish themselves and their offspring in a position of power and to secure for themselves the other advantages of their paternal households.

Electra, on the other hand, tends to focus much more on the significance of blood revenge and on Orestes' role as avenger. Typical of the difference in the children's thinking is Orestes' wish that his father had died a hero's death at Troy. Electra, by contrast, does not wish this, but would prefer to see his killers suffering a similar fate to the one they inflicted on him (*Cho.* 345-53, 363-71). As I have argued elsewhere, Electra's insistence on revenge is typical of dramatic and literary portrayals of women's involvement in revenge plots.[23] As seen in Chapter 1, while men are often shown as willing to compromise in order to avoid a death, women are more closely associated with demands for blood revenge regardless of political or financial expediency.[24] Electra's role in avenging her father, Agamemnon, is largely restricted to praying for the return of her brother Orestes (*Cho.* 138-9; Euripides *El.* 137-9, 269; Sophocles *El.* 113, 209-12, 453-8) and then urging him on towards vengeance (Euripides *El.* 967-78; Sophocles *El.* 1487), although in Euripides' plays she does take a larger role. Euripides' *Electra* shows a particularly reticent Orestes urged on by a particularly keen Electra. While Orestes lingers and seems unsure of what to do, Electra pronounces her desire to slay her mother and Aegisthus with the

5. What Motivates Orestes?

same axe used to kill her father (276-9). Electra's appeals insist on the importance of avenging their father (970, 974 τιμωρῶν; 976 ἀμύνων; 978 τιμωρίαν) and it is she who convinces Orestes, when he doubts his ability to kill their mother, that Clytemnestra ought to die as she had killed (967-87). Notably she attempts to motivate Orestes by accusing him of cowardice (ἀνανδρίαν, 'lack of manliness', 982).[25] She helps Orestes in the deed by holding onto the sword (1224-6), claiming revenge (τιμωρούμενοι) from her mother for her father's death at her own hands and those of Orestes (1093-5). Only at the end of the play does Electra seem to realise the enormity of the deed (1224-6). She grieves as she is told by Castor as *deus ex machina* that she must live in exile and never return to Argos (1311-13). In *Orestes*, Electra also shares the blame for the murders (in particular the matricide) with her brother (32, 46-51).

In Sophocles' play, Electra, who is accused of rescuing Orestes to ensure revenge (601-4, 1133; cf. 12-14, 777-87), even decides to take revenge into her own hands when she believes that her brother is dead. For help in this plan she turns to her sister Chrysothemis (954-7). She feels that not only do the sisters have nothing to lose, but also their revenge will gain them a good marriage and praise (970-2).[26] However, when Orestes reveals that he is alive, Electra returns to praying and encouraging, leaving the actual killing to her brother (1487). In Aeschylus' *Choephori*, Electra, sanctioned by the chorus of women who say revenge (τὸν ἐχθρὸν ἀνταμείβεσθαι κακοῖς) is right (121-3), calls on the gods to send an avenger (τιμάορον), so that the slayers will be slain in just retribution (τοὺς κτανόντας ἀντικατθανεῖν δίκῃ) (142-4). The chorus agree that revenge is just in this case (306ff.), saying that each murderous stroke ought to be repaid with like (ἀντὶ δὲ πληγῆς φονίας φονίαν / πληγὴν τινέτω. δράσαντα παθεῖν) (312-13). For them, violent revenge of this nature is a *nomos* (400-2). Significantly, it is a female chorus that expresses all these well-known lines about revenge. The association of women with a great interest in blood revenge is manifested strongly in this play. The group of women also play a part in encouraging Orestes to act.[27] Nevertheless he is still doubtful about murdering his mother and must finally be convinced by Pylades who tells him briefly, but significantly, 'Count all men enemies rather than the gods', referring to the command of Apollo that Orestes must avenge his father (900-2; cf. Euripides *El.* 967-87).

As seen in these vital lines of Pylades, Apollo too is associated with urging Orestes to avenge his father's death. He says Orestes must slay Aegisthus and Clytemnestra as they slew (ἀνταποκτεῖναι) or suffer tortures brought on by his father's wrath (Aeschylus *Cho.* 269-94; 1030-3; *Eum.* 462-9; cf. Euripides *El.* 87-9; Sophocles *El.* 32-7). Like Electra, Apollo will not accept compensation or compromise, only blood. There is a question as to whether Orestes would have killed Clytemnestra without Apollo's directive. Although in the *Choephori* he earlier claims that he would act even without the god's oracle out of other motives (298-305), he balks at the prospect of killing his mother (899), and would perhaps have relented, but for the god's command. Similarly in Euripides' *Electra* he balks at murdering his mother while Electra remains resolute (967-70) and a doubtful Orestes finally agrees to act because of the god's command (986-7). In all the plays Orestes is portrayed as doubting the wisdom of the god's oracle. In Aeschylus' and Sophocles' versions his doubts are muted (*Cho.* 297; *El* 1425), but in Euripides' *Electra* he openly challenges Apollo's ruling, on the grounds that it is wrong to commit matricide (971-81).[28] In *Orestes* he further suggests that Agamemnon would not have wanted him to kill Clytemnestra because of the terrible consequences of matricide (288-92). He points out that he is still an exile and now is worse off than before because he is a matricide (Euripides *El.* 1190-7; cf. *Or.* 28-32, 160-5, 416-18). Once again these plays suggest that Orestes' principal concern was with killing the usurper Aegisthus and taking control of the throne and family wealth rather than with avenging his father by killing his mother. Orestes' decision to kill his mother is a difficult one and it is suggested in all the plays that the command of Apollo is instrumental in motivating him to do so.

Apollo's motivations in urging on Orestes to take revenge do not appear to be identical to those of Electra. While she is frequently represented as wholeheartedly supporting the cause of her father (to the point where she rejects marriage) and desiring blood revenge for his sake, Apollo is connected more closely to dominance over the female and to the importance of the continuation of the male bloodline. In Aeschylus' presentation Apollo (supported by Athena and Zeus) is clearly associated with the superiority of patriarchy. In *Eumenides,* Apollo defends Orestes by arguing that a child is not truly of its mother, but is entirely of its father (657-66; cf. 606; Euripides *Or.* 552-4). It is hard to assess to what extent this biological point would have been believed by the audience, but certainly this kind of thinking has prevailed into more recent times.[29] What is of primary significance is the sociological importance of the claim. By giving primacy to the claims of the father, Apollo places the patrilineal bloodline first.[30] The dispute is settled in favour of Orestes because Athena, who casts the deciding vote, favours the male bloodline and, hence, does not favour an adulterous, husband-slaughtering wife (734-40).[31] The decision is made by removing the problem of what it is to kill one's mother. Clytemnestra is no longer truly thought of as a mother, but as a woman who treacherously killed her husband, Orestes' father. Seen in this light, the problems associated with the matricide are obliterated. Orestes is said to have acted justly against an adulteress who harmed his father in his own household.[32]

Similar feelings underlie the plot of Euripides' *Orestes*, where Orestes and Electra are facing the death penalty in Argos for what is perceived by some of the community as a hideous crime against their mother (46-51). Those who speak in favour of acquittal at the assembly do not mention the mother / son relationship, but point out that Orestes has rid the world of an adulterous wife (923-9), a point which Orestes himself also feels should prove justification enough (565-78). It is emphasised that Agamemnon and Menelaus went to fight in Troy because of Paris' adultery, so this crime should be severely punished at home too. However, while no one disputes Orestes' right to kill Aegisthus as an adulterer in his home, his right to kill Clytemnestra in these circumstances is not made so clear. Her father Tyndareus is furious that Clytemnestra has been killed by Orestes and attempts to have Orestes and Electra put to death for their actions (526-39, 915-16). Other evidence clearly indicates that husbands or their relatives do not kill a treacherous wife themselves without the permission of her father or brothers.[33] Most frequently, the woman is returned home and killed by her own relatives (although co-operation is also a possibility). This is because men risk bad blood with the woman's relatives if they kill her, as happens here in the *Orestes*. This interpretation explains why Tyndareus condemns his daughter while at the same time appearing to support her (*Or.* 496-506; 538-9).[34]

It can be seen that Apollo's desire for revenge in its connection to the protection of patriarchy and the family bloodline is closely related to Orestes' desire to return to power and receive his rightful inheritance, although Orestes could have achieved a return to power without killing his mother. The murder of Clytemnestra in tragedy is symbolic of the dominance of the male over the female in power, inheritance and blood. It is clear that in the story of Orestes as it is presented in the various sources multiple motives for action are present and that different characters are represented prioritising different motives. I have suggested here that the theme of return to power is a prominent motive for Orestes and should not be seen as a less important motive than blood revenge for him. Rather it should be seen as a highly significant motive driving Orestes to attack rather than to agree on a settlement.[35] Certainly the dispute over power within the royal family is a vital component of this myth as it is told in tragedy. Orestes' motivations and reactions are closely comparable to those of Aegisthus in the previous generation. His story also features an adulterous wife (Aerope wife of Atreus) who colludes against her husband with one of his relatives (Aegisthus' father Thyestes) to achieve power. Atreus' terrible revenge against his brother for his adultery and his theft of the kingdom results in exile for Thyestes and Aegisthus. In tragedy Aegisthus' desire to regain the power lost by his father leads to him plotting with Clytemnestra to kill the son of Atreus and take the throne.

When viewed in this light, the conclusion of scholars that the killings in this myth are representative of vendetta in early Greek society can be seen to be dubious. Instead the tragic plot-lines suggest that autocrats are inclined to kill their own relatives in order to attain and retain power and wealth. Rather than seeing this myth as evidence of how Greek people behaved following a homicide until the institution of the law-court prevented bloodshed, I would prefer to read the myth as a saga of violence between elite rulers over power – the antithesis of desirable behaviour in democratic Athens.

Parallels to the Oresteia story

Support for this theory can be found in other myths, as well as in historical sources describing the tendency of ruling families to fight among themselves over power and to kill one another to seize control.[36] The tale of Cresphontes, about which Euripides composed a now fragmentary tragedy, shares many features with the tale of Orestes, although the matricide is absent.[37] In this myth Polyphontes murdered his brother and two of his nephews in order to seize the throne. However, a third nephew (whose name differs in the different sources) survived and was smuggled to safety by his mother Merope. Unlike Clytemnestra, Merope did not collude in the death of her husband and was supportive of her surviving son.[38] The sources suggest that Polyphontes married Merope, presumably because being married to the queen helped to legitimate his claims for power as suggested above.[39] Hyginus equates the acquisition of power with the acquisition of a wife in the opening sentence of his summary of the story (*Fab.* 137; cf. Apollodorus 2.8.5). In adulthood the surviving son, like Aegisthus and Orestes, returned from exile to kill his uncle Polyphontes and to take back his father's throne. There is an emphasis in one of the remaining fragments of Euripides' play on the fight over power within the family and on the importance of continuing the family bloodline (448a Kn). The fight over power is also central to Apollodorus' account where no mention of revenge is made (2.8.5). Hyginus' account, which does mention revenge, also focuses on the importance of the return to power in the closing line of his summary (*Fab.* 137). The similarity of the plot to the story of Orestes is pronounced in this myth, yet the emphasis on blood revenge is small in the extant accounts. Without the full version of Euripides' play it is impossible to speculate further on the extent to which blood revenge was emphasised as a motive by any of the characters. However, it is clear from all the sources that the story was based on a dispute over power within the family.

Stories referring to disputes over power between members of ruling families proliferate in the historical sources.[40] The story of Arcesilaus of Cyrene as it is told by Herodotus refers to a dispute over power which leads to murders within the family. Herodotus tells us that Arcesilaus quarrelled with his brothers over power and that the brothers went into exile where they built a new settlement (Barca). Later Arcesilaus' brother Learchus is said to have strangled him and to have been killed in turn by Archesilaus' wife Eryxo (4.160.4). Although Herodotus does not make it explicit in his rather cryptic account of the strangling and of Eryxo's response, it seems likely considering the earlier disagreement between the brothers that Herodotus meant the reader to connect this murder to the dispute over power. Following the death of Learchus, we are told that Arcesilaus' son Battus came to the throne, so it appears that Eryxo, like Merope, is shown acting in support of her son against her brother-in-law.[41] Similarly in the next generation, Pheretima wife of Battus is represented as highly supportive of her son Arcesilaus throughout his career and as desirous of revenge for his death.[42] In this story some resemblances to tragic plot-lines can readily be discerned. In particular the prominent role of women in instigating and carrying out murders is notable. This element casts some doubt upon the historicity of the tale, but Herodotus' account provides interesting evidence for the belief that brothers fought ruthlessly over power and that women might intervene to support male family members (both ideas which recur in tragic plot-lines).

The story of the family of Jason of Pherae also seems to borrow from tragic plot-lines and shares many elements with the tale of Cresphontes. The sources allege that members of this family indulged heavily in murdering one another over power. Following the death of Jason, his brothers Polydorus and Polyphron took office (in 370 BC). When Polydorus died in suspicious circumstances, Xenophon tells us that many people assumed that he had been murdered by his own brother (*Hell.* 6.4.33). The expectation that brothers fight and kill one another over power is apparent in the assumption that Xenophon describes here. The conclusion can also be drawn from his description of Polyphron behaving like a tyrant (i.e. a man who is not satisfied with sharing power with others, but who desires supreme power for himself). Polyphron was then killed in turn by Alexander who, according to Plutarch, was Polyphron's nephew (*Pel.* 29). Alexander then made himself tyrant in his uncle's place.[43] The description in Xenophon's account of a fratricide followed by counter-murder by a nephew closely parallels the myth of Cresphontes. That family members were prepared to kill one another in order to achieve more power is readily understood from this tale. Moreover, Xenophon provides clear evidence that Greek people expected despots to act in this way.[44] His account has an even more interesting element though, as he maintains that Alexander claimed to be the avenger of Polydorus and a tyrannicide (ὡς τιμωροῦντος τῷ Πολυδώρῳ καὶ τὴν τυραννίδα καταλύοντος, 6.4.35), apparently both motives which would have been viewed as just and appropriate. However, after making these claims, he went on to behave like a tyrant belying his stated motives and suggesting that his intent all along was to take power for himself. Once again here revenge appears as one of a number of motives, perhaps even as a 'moral motive' for action,[45] although it is clear that Xenophon did not believe this to be Alexander's prime motivation. Like Orestes, Alexander is represented as expressing more than one motive for his murder, but it also appears that he had ulterior motives – particularly the seizing of power for himself.

Xenophon goes on to claim that Alexander was slain in turn by his wife's brothers through the woman's instigation (*Hell.* 6.4.35-7). Xenophon does not state that this murder was an act of blood revenge. Instead he says that people mooted various reasons for the murder including her fears that her husband intended to take another wife (the widow of Jason) (*Hell.* 6.4.37). This fear is based on two notions: the first suggestion is that Alexander's wife was barren. The importance of fertility to a marriage has been established in Chapters 1 and 2. The second notion is that Alexander may have hoped to support his position of power by marriage to a former leader's wife.[46] Here the wife of Alexander is cast as a Medea-like figure who wanted to slaughter her husband because he desired to take a new wife to boost his claims to power and have children (like Jason in the *Medea*). However, since Xenophon tells us that her eldest brother took power after this incident, it is possible to see the murder of Alexander as a way for him to acquire leadership. Some similarity can perhaps be found here to the tale of Candaules' wife, in which a wife colludes with another man to kill her husband (Herodotus 1.10; cf. Plato *Rep.* 360b). Certainly Plutarch's version of the scene of Alexander's death in his bed at the urging of his wife is reminiscent of Herodotus' story (*Pel.* 35). We are told that after the death of Candaules, Gyges took the throne, but that the people of Lydia took up arms against the faction of Gyges suggesting that they perceived him as a usurper of the throne (1.13). Although Herodotus does not make it explicit, it seems possible that underlying his version is a more straight-forward case of regicide in the quest for power by Gyges.[47] Interestingly, Plutarch asserts that Thebe wife of Alexander was the daughter of Jason (and hence married to a relative). If true, this means that her brothers would have had a claim to power from their father Jason and their murder of Alexander is a continuation of the family dispute over power.

The story of the family of Jason of Pherae with its intrigues and murders is highly reminiscent of tragic plot-lines and it is not impossible that Xenophon was influenced by tragic and other forms of myth when writing his history. He certainly makes it clear that he is speculating about the participants' motives and, in places, about what actually happened. For this reason, his account is unhelpful in determining the real actions and motivations of the characters involved. However, his version does take into account the views and beliefs of the people of the day regarding what had occurred and why. The story of this family is a particularly interesting comparison piece for the tale of Orestes as it makes clear that family disputes over power were thought to lead to murder even within the classical age. However, the tale of Jason and his family is not usually perceived as an example of vendetta and blood revenge in ancient society, even though one participant supposedly claimed revenge for his actions. Instead, it is apparent from Xenophon's text that he at least saw this as an ongoing dispute over power within the family and as testament to the problems associated with tyranny.

The suggestion in Xenophon's account that Alexander publicised certain motives for killing his uncle, but was in fact privately motivated by other aims is noteworthy. That men are likely to put forward publicly acceptable motives for action has been noted by Ferguson in his account of the Yanomami warriors. He notes that while honour and revenge may be the stated reason for an attack, more material and self-interested motives are often in the background.[48] Ferguson suggests that a forgotten murder from many years before can be remembered and used as motivation for an attack.[49] He argues that this occurs because participants desire to frame their materially self-interested actions in moral terms.[50] Herman says of ancient Greece: 'In most cases this desire for revenge coincides admirably with calculations of expediency. In other words, it is by no means clear whether it is the reason for, or a justification of, an action.'[51]

A good example illustrating this is given by Herodotus in his discussion of the rise to power of Cyrus the Great. Although the historian couches the fairytale-style narrative in the language of revenge, there is a clear underlying story about the competition for power and resources which drives the action. The tale begins with Astyages' decision to expose his infant grandson to prevent the child from seizing his throne. Astyages' fear of passing power to his own descendant – an event which would naturally occur in a monarchy – is somewhat irrational, but emphasises the importance of the struggle for power in the story (cf. 1.120). Astyages entrusts the task of exposing the child to his steward and kinsman Harpagus (1.108). Harpagus' decision not to kill the child himself is driven in part by his blood relationship to him – a decision we might expect from a consideration of the importance of kin solidarity and the general lack of desire to kill kin.[52] He is also driven by self-interest, since he believes that the child's mother Mandane would seek revenge against him for the loss of her baby as soon as she ascended to the throne if he were to kill her son (1.109). Therefore he gives the child to a herdsman of Astyages who also decides not to kill him. When Astyages discovers that Cyrus is alive, he places the blame on Harpagus and devises a cruel revenge which he describes as 'a sacrifice to the gods' (1.118).[53] Harpagus is invited to dine with the king where he is fed a dish made of his only son's flesh. By this revenge Astyages intends to destroy Harpagus' life and future hopes by killing his only son.[54] Astyages' ruthlessness is explained as being the desire of a king to impose his absolute rule (1.119). Harpagus strongly desires vengeance (τίσασθαι) for the murder of his son, but Herodotus tells us that he did not feel able to achieve his revenge without the help of Cyrus (1.123).[55] His appeal to Cyrus is couched in terms of revenge; he urges him to take revenge on his would-be murderer (σύ νυν Ἀστυάγεα τὸν σεωυτοῦ φονέα τείσαι) reminding him that he saved his life as a baby (1.124), a clear demand for a reciprocal favour. However, there is a secondary-stated motive – the conquest of the lands of Astyages. For Cyrus, as for Astyages (and the other characters discussed above), the prominent motivating factor is the possession of the throne. Herodotus goes on to say that the men were motivated to revolt by the prospect of future plenty. Cyrus gives the Persians a choice between doing menial tasks (symbolic of their present servitude to the Medes) and eating feasts (symbolic of their future prosperity) (1.126). Although revenge is given as the primary motivation, it sits alongside the quest for power and the attainment of plentiful resources. Herodotus maintains that after he had seized the throne, Cyrus did not kill Astyages, but kept him safely at court until his death.[56] This suggests that despite the appeal of Harpagus, Cyrus' quest for power and resources outweighed his desire for revenge against his grandfather. Harpagus too is portrayed as being content with this revenge (turning the king into a slave), even though he does not achieve a life for a life.[57]

The folktale quality of the narrative here is important in interpreting how we should understand this revenge, as is the setting in the early history of Persia. The extreme thirst for power can readily be associated with autocratic rulers and the tendency towards kin-killing and cannibalism demonstrated in this tale is equally associated with tyrannical rulers and with exotic foreign peoples.[58] Nevertheless, the combination of motivations demonstrated here and the careful calculations of the characters before taking action can inform us of the subtleties of revenge tales, even when they are so clearly fictional. Throughout the story characters weigh up the risks and benefits of taking certain actions. Astyages takes advice on whether to kill his grandson as he fears the threat of his usurpation and decides to send him to his death. Harpagus elects not to kill Cyrus with his own hands as he feels that it will leave him in a risky position. The story also demonstrates the desire for kin to take revenge, even in situations where it is difficult for them to do so. In this case Harpagus achieves a kind of revenge with the help of Cyrus, although he does not succeed in killing Astyages or his offspring. In addition, although Harpagus first attempts to persuade Cyrus to help him by instructing him to take revenge against Astyages for attempted homicide, the narrative makes it clear that Cyrus and his Persians are motivated to a greater extent by the quest for power and resources.

Litigants in legal cases at Athens also argue that their opponents are acting out of ulterior motives.[59] There are several examples in the extant cases where someone allegedly filed false charges of homicide against an opponent in order to achieve some other end. The speaker of Antiphon 6 (*On the Chorister* – a case concerning a chorister who died after drinking a potion) maintains that his opponents charged him with 'planning' of unintentional homicide (*bouleusis*) because they were paid to do so by his political opponents (6.34-8, 48-50).[60] Such a charge had a twofold purpose: first a man who had been indicted for murder could not prosecute others and so his cases against them would not succeed. Second if a man were to be convicted, his political career would be severely damaged or even at an end – a great advantage to his political opponents. The speaker in this case makes it clear that he believes that his opponents are using a 'morally acceptable motive' in order to attack him for other less savoury reasons (monetary gain and political motivations). He says, 'They claim that they are bringing the action for motives of piety and justice, but the whole case for the prosecution has been marked by calumny and deceit' (6.7).[61] He asserts that although the boy's relatives claim to be taking just revenge against him for the death of the boy (δικαίως με βούλονται τιμωρεῖσθαι, 6.7), they are aware that the speaker is innocent. In these lines it is suggested that revenge for kin following a death might be used as a morally acceptable motive for attacking a man, even where the real underlying motive is political. Further it is suggested within the speech that the relatives of the dead boy raised the current case after a delay because it was convenient to do so for the political enemies of the speaker (6.49). Earlier, it is claimed, the relatives of the dead boy settled matters with the speaker at the temple of Athena and were friendly towards him in public (6.39-40).[62] Here, as in the cases cited by Ferguson, a death which occurred in the past and had been set aside is brought up again as a murder when it is convenient to use it as an excuse to attack someone. Although it is not possible to confirm the accuracy of all the speaker's claims, the case is interesting evidence that Athenian litigants might accuse one another of having more than one motive for prosecution and that men were thought to use the pretext of blood revenge to gain money and political advantages.[63]

Similar claims are made in *Against Neaera* where it is said that Stephanus tried to get Apollodorus sent into exile by having false charges of homicide brought against him at the Palladium ([Demosthenes] 59.9-10). This case too appears to have been politically motivated, since the two opponents had a history of politically motivated attacks on one another through the law courts.[64] In another case cited by Isocrates a similar ruse was attempted where Cratinus' opponents claimed that he had killed a woman, but Cratinus was able to find her where she had been hidden and prove their claims to be false (18.51-4).[65] This dispute was allegedly over property. In these cases the litigants appear to be interested in prosecuting a homicide to achieve justice and revenge, but when the murders are proved to be fake, it becomes apparent that they are driven by other motives.

These examples show that Athenians found revenge an acceptable motive for prosecution in cases of homicide, but they are not testament to the fact that revenge was the primary motivation of litigants or that Athens was a society built out of blood feuding. Instead they show that Athenians too were inclined to dispute over power and property. Just as in the case of Orestes, these Athenians depicted here are primarily interested in their own political and financial positions and their fights in court are apparently motivated by these causes even though they cite other motivations.

Concluding Remarks: Patterns of Revenge

Throughout this book my suggestion has been that men calculate the risks they are taking and do not fly to take revenge without consideration. Although it has frequently been assumed in the past that revenge was a duty or an obligation for Greeks in certain circumstances and that revenge was the norm following a homicide, instead the evidence suggests that there was much greater flexibility than this for individuals to decide for themselves what they were prepared to risk and what they stood to gain by acting. Although most of the examples discussed here are of a highly literary nature and many of the stories examined are invented by their authors, there is a striking correspondence of their representation of characters taking careful consideration with anthropological accounts of how men react when angered and insulted. This suggests to me that the authors reflect the ways in which men typically behaved in situations like this and that the representation of the characters in these tales is not wholly fantastic. In calculating like this, the evidence suggests that men acted largely in a self-interested way. Men who felt too weak to face their opponents might elect to make a compromise, or they might prefer the material gains which such a settlement proffered. Others were thought to take advantage of weak opponents to consolidate gains for themselves. Naturally enough, though, men were sometimes thought to miscalculate and to suffer harm from their actions. This emphasis on individual decision-making explains why victims sometimes elect not to retaliate (e.g. Demosthenes in *Against Meidias*) without recourse to suggestions that revenge was totally rejected in Athenian society.

At the same time, certain kinds of attack by certain kinds of enemy are portrayed as being more likely to prompt revenge than others and violence is evidently more readily tolerated in some situations than in others. The patterns for revenge suggested by this analysis are revealing, demonstrating that an analysis of revenge by motivation is an important step forward in this area of study. The sources suggest that men were much less likely to take revenge for a homicide or to perpetuate a blood feud based solely on previous deaths, than to fight others over women, property and power. Without any of these other compelling motivations, men were thought unlikely to want to risk their lives to take blood revenge. The sources, both mythical and historical, are surprisingly consistent in depicting this situation. Support for these findings can even be perceived in the difficult and idiosyncratic evidence of tragedy, where normal situations are twisted and

119

subverted to show atypical revenge attacks of *philos* against *philos*. Through wealth and status men gain advantages in life and with them they gain better access to women. The Homeric account of the dispute between Agamemnon and Achilles appears to reflect this thinking in mythic form. For this reason the evidence suggests that men will protect their women, their wealth and their status carefully and will react decisively to attacks upon them in order to keep them safe and deter others from attacking them. As can be seen in the key mythical examples of Odysseus and Orestes, the protection of female reproductive resources and the continuation of the male bloodline were of the greatest significance in driving revenge. Tales depicting the annihilation of a man's family and reproductive capabilities, such as the Herodotean tale of Panionius and Hermotimus, lend further support to this theory. It seems too that the priorities of the heroes of myth were valued highly in classical Athens and that popular thought about appropriate revenge drew inspiration from their exploits. Certainly the importance of avenging insults to women, a central theme in mythical stories, was carried through into Attic laws. It appears then that the biological imperatives of procreation reflected in the myths are supplemented by the cultural influence of earlier literature and myths to affect revenge behaviour at Athens.

The arguments of the anthropologists and evolutionary psychologists presented in this book were my starting point and influenced my thoughts on how to approach the Greek texts in order to draw conclusions about revenge. I am aware that this approach will be considered controversial, but it is my belief that the Greek evidence standing alone is sufficient to support the conclusions presented here even without these theoretical props. Certainly I hope to have convinced that there are difficulties with generalising about 'Greek revenge' without discrimination as to motive and that arguments that revenge as a whole is either acceptable or unacceptable are therefore insufficient. I am also hopeful that the arguments presented here will inspire further debates and discussions on this subject and will provide a stepping-stone to new research in this area. I look forward to developing my own research on this fascinating topic and to the new directions the study of ancient revenge will take in the future.

Notes

Introduction

1. See especially Allen (2000); Blundell (1989); Burnett (1998); Cohen (1995); W. Harris (1997), (2001); Herman (1993), (1994), (1995), (1996), (1998a), (1998b), (2000); D. Wilson (2002).

2. Dover (1974) 3, 14; cf. Herman (2000) 8-9; Mossman (1995) 169-70.

3. For the most part, attention is given to those ancient examples that have generated the most scholarly debate, since it is not possible within the scope of this study to examine every example of revenge in ancient Greek literature.

4. Herman (2000) 11.

5. Belfiore (1998), (2000); McHardy (2005).

6. Cf. Allen (2000) 76; Herman (2000) 14; Jacoby (1985) 19. Burnett (1998) tends to treat the representation of revenge in tragedy as unproblematic. See Gibert (1999) and Lloyd (1999) for criticism of this view.

7. See pp. 32-4, 53-6 on the inspiration provided by the central Homeric revenges of Achilles and Odysseus. Cf. also pp. 76-9. There are notorious difficulties with dating the Homeric epics and determining whether the ideas depicted in the poems correspond to any particular time period, or to a combination of periods or to no real period at all. Cf. pp. 21-2, 67. Here, my focus is on the links between the representation of revenge in Homer and in classical texts.

8. The focus of the book is mainly on the reactions of individuals, not cities.

9. Herman, in particular, associates vengeance with violence in his studies on revenge. See for example Herman (2000) 9.

10. Aristotle (*Rhet.* 1369b12); Plato (*Prt.* 323d-324b; cf. *Grg.* 525b, *Leg.* 934a). Cf. Allen (2000) 18-19; Blundell (1989) 54-5; Mackenzie (1981) 11-12; Oldenquist (1986) 76-7. This distinction is central to the arguments of Gabriel Herman.

11. Allen (2000) 18. Francis Bacon argued for the incompatibility of revenge and the law (*Essays – Of Revenge*). Cf. Bar-Elli and Heyd (1986) 77. Jacoby (1985) has argued against this view. Cf. Cohen (2005) 172.

12. See Adkins (1960b) 24; Jacoby (1985) 4. Cf. Oatley and Jenkins (1996) 293.

13. Allen (2000); cf. also Saunders (1991). Allen prefers to use the vocabulary of punishment in her book because she wants to emphasise that these acts were seen as proper in Greek eyes. I prefer to use vengeance or revenge on the grounds that the reactions discussed are vengeful in spirit. See p. 55.

14. Allen (2000) 21. Her account of the issues and difficulties (2001: 18-24) is excellent.

15. Allen (2000) 21-2; Cohen (1995); Hunter (1994) 120-53; Todd (1993) 79.

16. Cf. Christ (1998a) 227. Plato puts forward the view that vengeance does not achieve proper justice, but his texts also make it clear that his views are atypical and unrepresentative of what Athenians thought. (*Crito* 48b-d; *Rep.* 335c-e; *Leg.* 854d-e). Allen (2000) 135; Saunders (1991) 120; Vlastos (1991) 179. Cf. also Bar-Elli and Heyd (1986) 80; Blundell (1989) 56; Kitto (1951) 244.

17. A surprising amount of violence between litigants appears in the sources. See pp. 76-8.

18. Kurihara (2003) emphasises that litigants in public and private cases were supposed to be differently motivated, but notes that this did not always follow in reality.

19. McHardy (forthcoming); cf. Miller (2006) 149-50. Examples of this literary technique, which occur across a wide variety of genres are discussed on pp. 26, 29, 31-2, 43, 51, 55, 83.

20. Adkins (1960b), (1969); Allen (2000) 52; Cairns (2003) 49; Dover (1974) 46, 49; W. Harris (2001) 34-5; Herman (2000) 19. For a list of Greek revenge vocabulary and possible derivations of the words see Milani (1997).

21. Cf. Herzfeld (1980).

22. W. Harris (2001) 167; Herman (1998b) 614. G. Davies (1967: on *Exodus* 21:20) observes that the same Hebrew word is used to denote both revenge and punishment. In my opinion, the tendency to use traditional vocabulary associated with revenge in the law courts indicates that the laws and legal apparatus grew out of traditional practices and norms rather then being a break with them. See pp. 12, 18-19.

23. This case has been extensively discussed by commentators who draw divergent conclusions about what it can tell us about Athenian attitudes to revenge. See pp. 95-9.

24. Carey (1994: 184) observes that the Athenians blur distinctions which seem fundamental to us. Greek terms exist which refer exclusively to punishment – ζημία and κόλασις. See Allen (2000) 69; W. Harris (2001) 167.

25. See p. 10.

26. Cf. Allen (2000) 10, 69.

27. Cf. Mossman (1995) 171. Adkins (1960b) notes that 'honour' is not broad enough to cover τιμή. Cf. Cairns (2003) 49.

28. Saïd (1984) 48. Cf. Chantraine 1120. Adkins (1960b) saw the entire τιμωρία word group as a semantic network to do with 'transfers of τιμή'. Allen (2000: 61) defines τιμωρεῖν as 'to assess and distribute honor'.

29. Van Wees (1992) 67-9, 110; cf. Finley (1979) 113.

30. Allen (2000) 59ff.; Dover (1974) 230-1; Roisman (2005) 64-6; 72; cf. Adkins (1972) 15; Todd (1993) 162. Cf. also Aristotle *Rhet.* 1361a28ff.

31. Fisher (1976) 177, (1992) 1; cf. Blundell (1989) 37 n. 55. For the significance of honour in relation to *hybris* see Fisher (1976) 177; (1992) 1. Cf. Cairns (1996b); MacDowell (1990) for slightly different ideas about *hybris*. Aristotle links *hybris* and *oligoria* to dishonour (*Rhet.* 1378a-b). Note his use of Homeric examples to establish his argument.

32. On the importance of anger in driving revenge, both violent and legal, see Allen (2000). Cf. Burnett (1998) 7; Cairns (2003) 17-18; W. Harris (2001) 146.

33. Miller (2006) 17; cf. D. Wilson (2002) 14.

34. Allen (2000) 61; cf. Fisher (1976) 180. See Chapter 4 on insults and throughout on revenge as a response to attacks on honour.

35. Cf. Vlastos (1991) 181. Saïd (1984: 49-51) suggests that there is also a connection between τίσις and τιμή, meaning that τίσις is related both to a notion of honour and to a notion of exchange. Cf. Chantraine 1120-1.

36. D. Wilson (2002: 25) notes that the related term ποινή can signify both blood price and blood revenge.

37. D. Wilson (2002) 21.

38. See Miller (2006: 68-9) on the metaphor of payment. Cf. Cohen (2005) 173.

39. Jacoby (1985) 152. See pp. 9-10 on equivalence and balance in revenge.

40. Lloyd (1999) 349. Cf. pp. 43-4.

41. Miller (2006) 1-7, 24.

42. The definition of δίκη is by no means straightforward. See Gagarin (1973), (1974a) and (1976).

43. Allen (2000) 69. Words beginning with *anti* (eg. ἀνταποθανεῖν, Antiphon 5.10) also suggest the notion of equal exchange.

44. Miller (2006) 17-20, 67. See pp. 26-7, 31 for further examples.

45. Cf. Gagarin (1986) 66. Cf. also Diodorus Siculus (12.17.4-5).

46. See pp. 43-4 for further discussion of 'an eye for an eye' in Greek thought. See pp. 6-7 on individuals making decisions.

47. De Romilly (1971) explains revenge in Herodotus as a literary device used to link events.

48. This phenomenon has also been noted by Gould (1989) 44; cf. also 55. Cf. Pearson (1957: 22) on Thucydides.

49. Cf. pp. 103-17.

50. Christ (1998a) 133. See further pp. 116-17.

51. For examples and further discussion of this idea, see pp. 77, 96, 100.

52. Ferguson (1995) 58; cf. Herman (1987) 126; Lendon (2000) 16. See further on pp. 115-17.

53. See further in Chapter 2.

54. Daly and Wilson (1988a) 132; Oatley and Jenkins (1996) 294. See pp. 7, 73, 89 on the connection between holding high status and greater access to women.

55. Shylock's famous words in *Merchant of Venice* (3.1.45-66) suggest it is natural for a man to want revenge when wronged just as it is natural to bleed when pricked. Cf. Burnett (1998) 1; Miller (2006) ch. 6. See Burnett (1998) for discussion of English Renaissance revenge tragedies.

56. Cf. Herman (2000) 26.

57. Other examples suggest that men decide against a physical attack based in part upon the opinions of others around them (e.g. *Iliad* 1.188-216; Dem. 21.76). See pp. 87, 96-7.

58. It is unclear to what extent the tale reflects Spartan ideas and values. Certainly the case can find parallels in Attic oratory. Christ (1998a) 133; cf. Kurihara (2003); Mitchell and Rhodes (1996) 26.

59. Boehm (1984) 202ff., 212; Herzfeld (1985) 82; Peters (1967); S. Wilson (1988) 177; cf. Ferguson (2001: 101) on the Yanomami; Seremetakis (1991: 39) on Mani. Cf. also Saunders (1991: 12) on Homer.

60. Djilas (1958) 187-8.

61. Boehm (1984) 245; cf. Bourdieu (1977) 3-71.

62. In particular, there is a tendency to overemphasise the necessity and inevitability of revenge and violent reactions among Homeric heroes (e.g. Brooks (1977) 455, W. Harris (2001) 134; Mueller (1984) 33, Redfield (1975) 104; van Wees (1992) 66), although van Wees does note that friends do not react aggressively in Homer (1992: 114).

63. Oatley and Jenkins (1996) 13.

64. Miller (2006) 62; cf. Dover (1974) 3.

65. Cf. Dawkins (1989) 69.

66. Oatley and Jenkins (1996) 300.

67. Daly and Wilson (1988a) 128; cf. Cairns (2003) 20; Chagnon (1988); Miller (2006) 51; van Wees (1992) 88. See pp. 14, 48, 53, 55, 60, 65, 86, 88 for discussion of revenge as a deterrent.

68. Sigmund (1993) 203; cf. Axelrod (1984); Daly and Wilson (1988a) 234.

69. See in particular Blundell (1989) esp. ch. 2. Cf. Dover (1974) 180-4; Mossman (1995) ch. 6; Vlastos (1991) ch. 7. Herman (2000: 12) makes the point that we cannot rely on such maxims to understand how people behave. This notion of reciprocity is criticised by Plato (n. 16 above).

70. Cf. Cairns (2003).

71. Ferguson (1995), (2001). His arguments focus specifically on the Yanomami people of the Amazon rainforest who, he argues, fight mainly over Western tools and weapons. Ferguson rejects the highly controversial socio-biological explanations of Napoleon Chagnon (1988) regarding the Yanomami, mainly on the grounds that Chagnon's own evidence cannot support his claims. Chagnon's use of statistics has also been criticised as inaccurate by Albert (1989). Cf. Ferguson (1995) 359-60, (2001) 107-9.

72. Ferguson (1995: 359) says: 'I find nothing to argue about in the proposition that individuals tend to their material self-interest and that in evolutionary perspective, such self-interest has a generally favourable impact on reproductive success.' Cf. Rabben (1998) 39.

73. See pp. 50-3, 60-4, 103-12 for discussion of these stories.

1. A Life for a Life

1. Even in societies where central authorities monopolise the right to redress (Daly and Wilson (1988a) 257). In this chapter I use the term 'blood revenge' to refer to revenge for a homicide.

2. Black-Michaud (1975) 31; Boehm (1984) 218; Daly and Wilson (1988a) 257; Deliyanni (1985) *Prologue* 3; D. Hall (1994) 26; Hasluck (1954) 159; cf. Prevelakis (1989) 81.

3. Ginat (1987) 27.

4. See p. 109 on these lines. Cf. Burnett (1998) xvi.

5. This familiar term derives from the Roman Twelve Tables.

6. Sarna (1986: 160) believes that such laws developed naturally out of arbitration.

7. Cf. Mossman (1995) 171.

8. Sarna (1986) 186-9. Miller (2006: 50-1) argues that the threat of losing an eye causes the guilty party to reconsider the true value of his victim's eye when deciding on compensation.

9. Cf. MacDowell (1963) 148. Plato (*Leg.* 679e) is disturbed by the lack of emphasis on justice in the legal system.

10. See Sarna (1986: 186) on equivalence and Ashby (1998: on Exodus 21:22-7) on escalation. Cf. Daly and Wilson (1988a) 233. The Albanian *Kanun* – a vendetta code – also seems to insist on a life for a life in order to prevent escalation (Vickers and Pettifer 1997: 132).

11. See further in Chapter 4 on insults, punches and assaults.

12. Boehm (1984) 112; Deliyanni (1985) *Corsica* 66; Miller (2006) 178-9. See pp. 26-7 on the valuation of lives in Homeric warfare.

13. MacDowell (1963: 19-20) argues that this speech was probably delivered at the *euthynai* of Eratosthenes.

14. See Thucydides on the trial of the men at Plataea (3.65.5) where a similar argument is made.

15. See p. 3.

16. Cf. Adkins (1960a) 61-2; Finley (1979) 77; Lacey (1968) 48; Posner (1979) 31-2; Saunders (1991) 12.

17. Daly and Wilson (1988a) 221.

18. Daly and Wilson (1988a) 221ff., esp. 230.

19. See Daly and Wilson (1988b: 519) on the significance of nepotism in the family.

20. For this reason, in modern sources men are known as 'guns' or 'teeth'. Black-Michaud (1975) 180; Bourdieu (1977) 60-1; Deliyanni (1985) *Discussion and Comparison* 6, *Corsica* 69; S. Wilson (1988) 178.

21. Evidence from Persepolis, which shows rations given to female workers after childbirth, informs us that mothers of boys received twice as much as mothers of girls (Hallock 1969: 37f.).

22. Daly and Wilson (1999) 64; cf. Otterbein and Otterbein (1965) 1479.

23. Daly and Wilson (1988a) 10; (1999) 63.

24. Daly and Wilson (1988a) 18-20, 293; (1988b) 519; (1999) 67; cf. Dunbar et al. (1995) 233-4, 239, 242. Note the increased role of spouses in cross-sex killings (ESRC Violence Research Programme 2002: 30). Note too that agnatic and cognatic kin are not always properly distinguished in the statistics for 'family' (Daly and Wilson 1988a 19; 1988b: 519). Other than in cases of endogamy, cognatic kin are not related by blood.

25. For a detailed analysis of the subject see Belfiore (1998) and (2000), although note that her lists include all kinds of harm, not just homicide. She argues persuasively that harm to *philoi* is a defining feature of the genre (2000: 120). See also McHardy (2005) for similar arguments regarding infanticide in tragedy.

26. Black-Michaud (1975) 52, 229; Boehm (1984) 105; Hardy (1963) 92; Hasluck (1954) 211; Peters (1967) 263; Whitaker (1968) 268. However, kin do sometimes fight, especially over property and power. See pp. 70-1, 101-2, 111-15.

27. Black-Michaud (1975) 41; Campbell (1964) 54; Daly and Wilson (1988a) 222; Deliyanni (1985) *Mani* 49, *Corsica* 24, 74; Hasluck (1954) 220, Otterbein and Otterbein (1965) 1470; Whitaker (1968) 267; S. Wilson (1988) 191. Ferguson (1995: 353-4) finds that agnatic kin are much more likely to exact revenge for an attack than the village as a whole.

28. Glotz (1904) argues for the solidarity of kin, esp. in blood revenge. Finley (1979) 77; Lacey (1968) 48; Posner (1979: 31-2) and Saunders (1991: 12) suggest vengeance is a family matter in Homer. Cf. also Burnett (1998) 52; MacDowell (1963) 32; Lintott (1982) 23-7; Visser (1984) 194.

29. He makes the point that Orestes' case is problematic for while it is right for him to avenge his father, he ought not to kill his mother.

30. Clement of Alexandria *Stromateis* 7.2.19; Aristotle *Rhet.* 1376a6-7; Herodotus 1.155.1; cf. Homer *Od.* 22.221-2; Sophocles *El.* 964-5; Euripides *Andr.* 519-22, *El.* 19-42, *Hec.* 1138-44, *HF* 168-9, *Hcld.* 1006-8, *Supp.* 545-6, *Tro.* 723; Xenophon *Cyr.* 5.3.6. Cf. Wilkins (1993) on *Hcld.* 1006-8.

31. Durham (1928) 147; Whitaker (1976) 196. Cf. Boehm (1984) 51-2.

32. Lendon (2000) 13; MacDowell (1963) 16. Cf. Harpocration 1 πενεγκεῖν δόρυ, Pollux 8.65.

33. Cf. *IG* 1^2.115, 20-30 – a proclamation that relatives must pursue a killer. We are also told that failure of relatives to prosecute in such cases was deemed disgraceful (Demosthenes 58.28-9). Blundell (1989) 55; Glotz (1904) 68; Lacey (1968) 27; MacDowell (1963) 1, 18, 27, 124.

34. There is disagreement over whether anyone other than kin could prosecute in a murder case. Gagarin (1979) says that only kin would be expected to prosecute for homicide (cf. MacDowell (1963) 17-19; (1978) 111; Todd (1993) 272-3). Hansen

(1981) claims that only kin *could* prosecute in such cases (cf. Burnett (1998: 53 n. 61); Tulin (1996) passim). Plato makes kin responsible for prosecuting murder (*Leg.* 865a-74d).

35. MacDowell (1963) 1-2.

36. Cf. also Antiphon 1.29-30 (ἐπισκήπτουσι τιμωρῆσαι σφίσιν αὐτοῖς ἠδικημένοις).

37. See McHardy (2004) on this case.

38. Cf. Glotz (1904) 69.

39. Cf. Burnett (1998) xvii; Gagarin (1986) 115. See pp. 3, 18-19.

40. Bourdieu (1977) 3-71; Daly and Wilson (1999) 60; Ferguson (1995) 11 n. 3. Similar considerations also affect retaliation in state relations in ancient Greece. See further on p. 37.

41. Miller (2006: 96) notes that blood revenge can be scary, as the killer has already demonstrated his ability to kill.

42. Although this is not an instance of blood revenge, it exemplifies the importance of kin as allies in a dispute. See pp. 65-6.

43. Gagarin (1986) 15. Cf. Demosthenes 47.68-73.

44. See pp. 116-17 on cases where prosecutors apparently bring homicide charges for political reasons.

45. Cf. Burnett (1998) 143.

46. See McHardy (2004); cf. Allen (2000) 99.

47. Cf. Buxton (1982) 64.

48. Timoleon's mother curses him for killing his brother Timophranes (Plutarch *Timoleon* 5). Cf. Althaea who in the *Iliad* curses her son for killing her brothers (9.565-72). Glotz (1904: 65) interprets Erigone's suicide by hanging following her father's death as a suicide curse (Hyginus *Fab.* 130; cf. Apollodorus 3.14.7). See van Hooff (1990) 106-7 on suicide curses.

49. McHardy (2004).

50. See pp. 37-42.

51. See p. 18 on Hercules' murder of a guest in Homer.

52. Cf. Durham (1928) 169; Hasluck (1954) 225; Khalaf (1990) 232; Miller (2006) 133-4; Whitaker (1968) 270. Black-Michaud (1975: 117) equates kin-killing with guest killing. This is because in agreeing to be host and guest men form a quasi-kinship relationship. Cf. Rabinowitz (1993) 91.

53. Cf. Herman (1987: 124ff.) for an account of the horror felt about killing a guest-friend. Cf. also Mossman (1995) 168. See pp. 29, 40 on guests in battle and on Hecuba.

54. Cf. van Wees (1998) 13.

55. See also pp. 115-16 on Harpagus.

56. See pp. 92-3 for divine reactions to insults.

57. See Boehm (1984) 202ff., 212; Herzfeld (1985) 82; Peters (1967); Seremetakis (1991) 39; S. Wilson (1988) 177. See pp. 6-7.

58. Miller (2006) 96.

59. Ferguson (1995) 51.

60. See Chapter 5.

61. MacDowell (1963) 9-10. Todd (1993: 273) also argues against MacDowell's view. See Demosthenes 24.105 on particular rules governing maltreatment of parents. Cf. Blundell (1989) 41-2; Dover (1974) 274; A. Harrison (1968) 78; Parker (1983) 124.

62. Cf. Antiphon (5.95) where it is suggested that *philoi* will not be willing to avenge a man once he is dead (οὐδὲ γὰρ οἱ φίλοι ἔτι θελήσουσιν ὑπὲρ ἀπολωλότος τιμωρεῖν).

63. Lintott (1982) 16. On the choice of exile for kin-killers, see Black-Michaud (1975) 52, 229; Boehm (1984) 105; Hardy (1963) 92; Hasluck (1954) 211; Peters (1967) 263; Whitaker (1968) 268. Mythical examples of exile for kin-killing include: Amphitryon (Hesiod *Shield* 79-82); Tlepolemus (Homer *Il.* 2.661-70); Theseus (Euripides *Hipp.* 34-7); Peleus (see further below); Agaue (Euripides *Bacch.* 1350ff.); Hercules (Euripides *HF* 1358-9); Medea (Euripides *Med.* 166-7, cf. 1333-4); Tydeus (Euripides *Supp.* 148); Bellerophon (Euripides *Stheneboea* fr. 661 Kn); Ixion (Pindar *Pythian* 2.21-48); Oedipus (Sophocles *OC* 599-601; cf. *OT* 417-18); Daedalus (Sophocles fr. 323 R); Atreus (Thucydides 1.9.2); Alcmaeon (Thucydides 2.102.5).

64. Examples include: Lycophron (*Il.* 15.431-9); Patroclus (*Il.* 23.85-90); the guest of Eumaeus (*Od.* 14.380-1; cf. also Odysseus' story to Athena 13.259-75); Pylades (Euripides *Or.* 765-7); the Alcmeonids after the murder of the Cylonian conspirators (Thucydides 1.126-7; Plutarch *Sol.* 12.2-3; *Ath. Pol.* 1).

65. Cf. Allen (2000) 81.

66. See further on pp. 106-7.

67. Cf. Barrett (1964) 357-8; Ostwald (1986) 90-1.

68. For the sufferings of exile see Euripides *Med.* 645-53; cf. 359-63, 462-3, 510-15. Note also the joy of return from exile for Odysseus and Orestes. See further on pp. 107-8, 110.

69. Cf. van Wees (1992: 119) on the choice of exile as retainers.

70. Allen (2000) 201. Cf. Antiphon 6.4 on the connection between *atimia* and exile.

71. Van Wees (1992) 119. Cf. Schlunk (1976) 206. See Aristotle (*Rhet.* 1378b) for discussion of this line and further in Chapter 4 on insults to honour.

72. A similar risk is undertaken by Polynices when he returns to Thebes with an army in order to end his period of exile and reclaim his lost homeland and throne. See further on pp. 101-2.

73. Beye (1964) 358; Gagarin (1981) 5-18; Glotz (1904) 51; W. Harris (2001) 135; Parker (1983) 115-17; Seaford (1994) 25; Svenbro (1984) 48-52.

74. Beye (1964) 358.

75. See Schlunk (1976) and Heiden (1998) for detailed discussion of this simile.

76. Seaford (1994) 28.

77. See further on Phoenix on pp. 57, 133n.250.

78. No relationship between Peleus and Telamon is mentioned in the Homeric epics.

79. Diodorus Siculus (4.72.6) says that the killing was accidental. See Heiden (1998: 4 n. 12) on Peleus as killer-in-exile. See further on pp. 91-2 on violence associated with athletic competitions.

80. Heiden (1998) 6.

81. Schlunk (1976) 202.

82. See further on pp. 25-35 on revenge in battle.

83. Although this does happen in the case of Peleus. Cf. also Herodotus 1.44 where Croesus' son Atys is killed (albeit accidentally) by Adrastus, a killer-in-exile whom he had received in his house and purified.

84. See Seaford (1994) 27-8.

85. See Chapter 5 for detailed discussion of the story of Orestes.

86. Gagarin (1986) 14.

87. Gagarin (1986) 14 n. 43. See Parker (1983) 130-1.

88. See Garner (1987: 3, 106) on the use of traditional language in the law courts; cf. Burnett (1998) 54; Mossman (1995) 171. Plaintiffs are τιμωροῦντες. See p. 3.

89. MacDowell (1963) 141.

90. Cf. Allen (2000) 202.

91. Carey (1997) 61; Edwards and Usher (1985) 26, Gagarin (1997) 180, 183. Alternatively it is possible that the relatives felt unsure of getting a conviction at the Areopagus and preferred to try the case in front of ordinary jurors. In particular, the lack of a dead body might have undermined their case.

92. Gagarin (1986) 88.

93. Miller (2006) 105.

94. See p. 4 for the problems associated with making these valuations.

95. Much has been written on this passage. See e.g. Bonner and Smith (1930) 31-41; Gagarin (1986) 26-33; MacDowell (1978) 18-21; Thür (1970); van Wees (1992) 32-4; Wolff (1946) 34-49.

96. Gagarin (1986) 32-3; cf. Seaford (1994) 26.

97. Gagarin (1986) 11.

98. Cf. Allen (2000) 225; MacDowell (1963) 9, 30.

99. MacDowell (1963: 9) states that this should be conceived of as a bribe to prevent prosecution rather than as the payment of compensation. In either case though payment of money prevents revenge.

100. See p. 56 for similar problems relating to compensation for adultery.

101. See Ormand (1999: 14-15) on marriage as an exchange of property and the creation of a relationship between men. Cf. also Rabinowitz (1993).

102. Cf. Deliyanni (1985) *Discussion and Comparison* 7; Dunbar et al. (1995) 233; Durham (1928) 70; Herzfeld (1985) 79; Whitaker (1976) 198.

103. Black-Michaud (1975) 92 n. 1; Durham (1909) 30.

104. Cf. Demosthenes (27.5) where a man bequeaths his wife to his nephew in the hope that this will ensure a strong bond and a good future for his children. Cf. Visser (1986) 149.

105. Cf. Littman (1979: 16) for this and other Athenian marriage alliances.

106. See Nenci (1994) 177.

107. See p. 106.

108. Parker (1983) 125. Cf. Gagarin (1981) 18; W. Harris (2001) 135. Allen suggests exile was the norm.

109. Seaford (1994) 26-7.

110. Ferguson (1995: 46-7) notes that the cycle of revenge often spoken of by scholars is not as prominent in reality as has sometimes been suggested. Herman (1998b: 611) maintains, contra Cohen (1995), that there was no vendetta in Athens. Cf. W. Harris (2001) 135.

111. Seaford (1994) 92-9. The best textual evidence to support this theory is *Eumenides* 976-87, a passage referring generally to the problems of civil war in the *polis*. See Chapter 5 on the *Oresteia*.

112. Cf. Black-Michaud (1975); Miller (2006) 51-2.

113. Cf. de Ste. Croix (1972) 218-20; van Wees (1998).

114. Cf. p. 18.

115. Cf. Westbrook (1992: 69-70) who suggests that revenge and exile were only for heroes, while ordinary people had to rely on trials in cases of homicide.

116. Ferguson (1995) 46-7. On the 'eternal' cycle of revenge see e.g. Black-Michaud (1975) 16-17; Girard (1977) 14.

117. See pp. 113-17.

118. Boehm (1984) 106-8; Herzfeld (1985) 76, 78; Peters (1967) 265; S. Wilson (1988) 247. Cf. also Deliyanni (1985) *Mani* 69; Ginat (1987); Hasluck (1954) 10-11.

119. Miller (2006) 53.

120. Gagarin (1986). There are even efforts to settle the principal disputes in the Homeric poems although they are not successful (id. 38-9).

121. Daly and Wilson (1988b) 520. See p. 7.

122. Seaford (1994) 103.

123. Cf. Lintott (1982) 29; Mossman (1995) 170. Burnett (1998: 41) believes that the ending dates to the reign of Pisistratus and reflects the ideals of that time. Cf. West (1989). Seaford (1994: 40) believes that this ending shows a development towards the values of the *polis* in Homer. See also Svenbro (1984). For criticism of Svenbro, see Burnett (1998) 42 n. 23; Gagarin (1986) 106.

124. Aristotle fr. 507 Rose; Apollodorus *Ep.* 7.40; Plutarch *Mor.* 249c-d. Cf. Seaford (1994: 29) who believes that the exile of Odysseus at the end of the *Odyssey* would have been 'incompatible with the overall movement of the narrative'.

125. Loraux (1998: 94); cf. Allen (2000) 81, 170. See also below on Ares' need to forget his anger before peace can be assured among the Olympians.

126. See MacDowell (1963: 64-6) for discussion of how this was interpreted.

127. Cf. Lysias 10.31, where a speaker claims somewhat obliquely to have prosecuted the Thirty at the Areopagus. Cf. also Lysias 12; 13.56.

128. See pp. 67-70.

129. See pp. 14-15.

130. Deacy (2005: 47) sees this as a way of preventing a more terrible act than infanticide.

131. Burnett (1998) 34 n. 5. Lendon (2000: 6-7) and Cairns (2003: 27-9) have argued well that Burnett's definition of revenge is too narrow and that battlefield revenges should not be discounted. Cf. Lloyd-Jones (1971) 21.

132. Lendon (2000) 3; cf. Mylonas (1962) 480.

133. Shay (2000) 37.

134. See Lendon (2000) on this topic. He argues that citizens see their cities as Homeric heroes (22), and that like heroes, cities are ranked in honour (13).

135. Lendon (2000) 4-6, 11.

136. See p. 26.

137. Note the nexus of meanings connected to this term which incorporates ideas of honour and of payment. See p. 4.

138. See McHardy (forthcoming) on the use of speeches to indicate that a killing is an act of revenge and not random.

139. Such valuations and re-evaluations have been discussed on pp. 4, 10.

140. The Icelandic sagas also feature men making calculations of value while fighting (Miller 2006: 119). Although these poetic accounts do not seem wholly realistic to us, they testify to the importance placed on achieving a balance in reciprocity.

141. Cf. Kitts (2005) 69.

142. These difficulties will be further discussed on pp. 30-1, 36 with reference to Achilles and Odysseus.

143. Cf. Shay (1994) 90.

144. Shay (1994), (2002); cf. (2000) 42.

145. Shay (1994) 40. In Homer, Alcinous says that a good companion is like a brother (*Od.* 8.585-6).

146. Lendon (2000) 10.

147. Cf. Trypanis (1963) on brothers fighting together in the *Iliad*. Cf. also Stagakis (1975).

148. See p. 80.

149. See pp. 2-3.

150. Cf. Herman (1987) 128. See p. 14 on attitudes to guests in Athens.

151. Cf. the case of Croesus whose guest accidentally kills his son (Herodotus 1.44). See pp. 127n.83, 145n.56.

152. Kitts (2005) 93.

153. Contra Belfiore (2000: 189-91) who thinks the guest relationship is not heavily stressed in Homer.

154. See Mills (2000) for discussion of all the similes of parental care in Homer.

155. Cf. Shay (1994: 24) for expressions of paternal affection among Vietnam veterans.

156. Halperin (1990) 85; cf. Mills (2000) 16.

157. See further on Hecuba on pp. 37-44.

158. Shay (1994: xxi) sees Patroclus as a 'foster-brother'.

159. Cf. Shay (1994) 70.

160. Nagy (1979) 292. Cf. Arieti (1985) 199-200; Kitts (2005) 107; Muellner (1996) 136; Seaford (1994) 166; Shay (1994) 70. For the idea of a *philos* as a second self see Aristotle (*NE* 1170b6; *Magna Moralia* 1213a11-13) and Diogenes Laertius (*Life of Zeno*) 7.23: ἄλλος ἐγώ = alter ego

161. Arieti (1985) 198; Muellner (1996) 160; Seaford (1994) 166-7.

162. Shay (1994: 51) compares suicidal Achilles to Vietnam veterans who say they 'died' after losing a close comrade.

163. My interpretation differs slightly from that of Arieti (1985) who suggests that Achilles acts out of a new-found sense of guilt rather than a feeling of dishonour. I do not see Achilles as 'paving a new moral ground' (1985: 204) in the *Iliad*. See p. 144n.28.

164. See pp. 12-13, 65-6.

165. See Mills (2000) 14-15.

166. Gill (1996) 317 n. 303.

167. Cf. Arieti (1985: 202) who emphasises the fact that Hector dressed in Achilles' armour makes a second 'alter-ego' for Achilles. It appears that he is killing himself in his revenge against Hector.

168. Cf. Lloyd-Jones (1971) 21. See pp. 79-82 on the significance of armour.

169. Kitts (2005: 106-11) suggests that in his oath in Book 1 Achilles sacrifices Patroclus along with the other Greeks (1.239-44).

170. Scholars tend to see this as excessive (e.g. W. Harris (2001) 134).

171. The need to react strongly to present a credible threat of violence towards such potential attackers is further discussed in Chapters 2 and 4. See pp. 48, 85-6.

172. In my opinion, there is no good evidence in the Homeric texts themselves to support the classical Athenian tendency to see the relationship of Achilles and Patroclus as erotic.

173. Gill (1996) 318-19; cf. Michelakis (2002) 9 n. 39.

174. Hornblower (1996) 38-61; Michelakis (2002) 10-11.

175. Cf. Bryant (1996) 92.

176. Michelakis (2002) 15-18.

177. Michelakis (2002) 24.

178. See Flower and Marincola (2002) 11-14, 244-7.

179. For booty as a source of personal honour cf. e.g. Xenophon *Hell.* 4.1.26-7. See further on pp. 79-80.

180. Shay (2002) 237-8; cf. (1994) 24.

181. Shay (1994) ch. 2; (2002) 241.

182. Shay (2002) 236-7. He points out that Odysseus is better in the role of staff officer to Agamemnon (238) at individual fighting and at planning or intelligence tasks (241).

183. For discussion of the tricky topic of blame see Shay (2002) 272 n. 10.

184. Shay (2002) 44-5.

185. Burnett (1998) 74. By contrast, Burnett has argued that the Euripidean Odysseus in *Cyclops* takes simple vengeance. The difference is that Odysseus could escape in *Cyclops* (197), but he stays to avenge his eaten colleagues (τιμωρία, 441).

186. See further on pp. 51-3 on these women and on p. 97 on Melanthius.

187. The notion that gods take revenge through human agents appears also in the case of Protesilaus. See p. 75. See T. Harrison (2000) 105, 111.

188. See pp. 88-9.

189. See further on this subject in Chapter 5 in the discussion of Orestes' motivations.

190. Cf. Hudson-Williams (1951) 70; Vlastos (1991) 185; Wassermann (1956) 29, 38; Westlake (1968) 64; Winnington-Ingram (1965) 79.

191. Sir Thomas Browne (*Christian Morals* 3.12).

192. Foley (2001: 286-8) notes that men prefer political expediency and the common good whereas women prioritise the private arena of the family. Cf. also Durham (1928) 164; Deliyanni (1985) *Mani* 64-5; Holst-Warhaft (1992) 88; Knudson (1988); McHardy (2004) 93-6.

193. McHardy (2004). My account here aims to elaborate upon my earlier article through examination of different examples rather than to reiterate the arguments I have already expressed there.

194. See McHardy (2004) and pp. 37-42 below.

195. Daly and Wilson (1988a) 156. A recent study published in *Nature* argues that tests have shown that women are consistently less vengeful than men.

196. Cf. W. Harris (2001) 177 with his ch. 11; Lloyd (1999) 348. David Harvey suggests to me that their association with desiring revenge could have determined the gender of the Erinyes.

197. D. Wilson (2002) 32-3. Cf. W. Harris (2001: 266) on Hecuba's vengefulness. See pp. 39-42.

198. Although in the text she does not propose that Priam should attempt revenge and she shows fear for him going into Achilles' presence.

199. D. Wilson (2002) 32-3. See p. 30.

200. D. Wilson (2002) 33.

201. See p. 12.

202. See further examples of disputes over political power on pp. 111-17.

203. See further on pp. 115-16.

204. Cf. Mossman (1995) 174-5.

205. Cf. n. 234 on Tomyris.

206. See p. 13. Poison is also a favourite method for women (Euripides *Medea*). Elsewhere women are depicted poisoning men with 'love potions' (Antiphon 1 *On the Poisoning by the Step-Mother*, Aristotle *Magna Moralia* 1188b29-38, Sophocles *Trachiniae*).

207. Burnett (1998: 144) points out that female revenge in tragedy often attracts motifs such as cannibalism, infanticide and incest. Cf. Rabinowitz (1993) 103.

208. See Belfiore (2000); McHardy (2005).

209. Cf. McHardy (2004).

210. Burnett (1998) 144. Allen (2000: 116) notes that women who take revenge in tragedy are depicted as 'manlike', 'manic' and 'monstrous'.

211. See McHardy (2004) and further in Chapter 5.

212. See McHardy (2005) 145-8.

213. For tentative reconstructions of the plot see Collard, Cropp and Gibert (2004) 36-43; Jouan and van Looy (1998) 39-54; Webster (1967) 165-74. See Hyginus (*Fab.* 91) for a slightly different version of the story which does not mention Hecuba's attempted revenge.

214. A similar story pattern occurs in Herodotus' description of the boy Cyrus (1.108-17).

215. The plot of Sophocles' *Alexandros* is unknown, but a herdsman winning at the games is mentioned in the fragments (see Collard, Cropp and Gibert 2004: 44).

216. See pp. 91-2 on athletic competitions.

217. Reconciling the hypothesis with the fragments at this point is tricky. See frs 62b-d Kn, with Collard Cropp and Gibert (2004) 40.

218. A number of vase paintings depict Paris on the altar attacked by a man and woman, probably Deiphobus and Hecuba or Cassandra (Collard, Cropp and Gibert 2004: 45).

219. Cropp speculates that Hecuba was persuaded to kill Paris because she thought he was a bastard son of Priam who would pose a threat to her sons (Collard, Cropp and Gibert 2004: 40).

220. This plot motif also occurs in Euripides' *Ion* and fragmentary *Cresphontes*. See p. 112.

221. See p. 61.

222. Cf. Rabinowitz (1993) 111. See pp. 101-2 on Eteocles and Polynices.

223. See p. 14.

224. See p. 13.

225. As in the case of Pheretima who convinces the Persians to act for her because they have an ulterior motive.

226. Cf. Foley (2001) 284.

227. Burnett (1998) 163; Foley (2001) 284, 286.

228. See pp. 29, 61, 63.

229. Burnett (1998) 165; Foley (2001) 296.

230. Foley (2001) 286.

231. Foley (2001) 285.

232. Hogan (1972). Gregory (1991: 113) links the themes in *Hecuba* to Thucydides' Melian debate.

233. Winnington-Ingram (1965: 73) and Wassermann (1956: 35) have pointed out the similarity between the cases of Plataea and Mytilene. See p. 37 on the Mytilene debate.

234. Apollodorus records a version in which Alcmena gouges the eyes out Eurystheus' severed head (2.8.1). This brutal revenge act after the death of the man deemed responsible for the troubles of her son is paralleled in Herodotus' tale of Tomyris who maltreats the head of Cyrus whom she blames for the suicide of her son (Herodotus 1.212-14). In each case the brutal attack aims to satisfy the anger of the woman involved. Cf. Allen (2000: 86) who notes that revenge can serve to satisfy anger.

235. Burnett (1998) 145. Her notion that Alcmena should be seen as an unproblematic 'justice-bearing avenger' like her son (145), does not accord well with this thought concerning the opposition of female revenge with male legalism in the play. Cf. Lloyd (1999) 349.

236. Alcmena is depicted as desiring revenge for her relatives elsewhere too. She is said to have insisted that her prospective husband Amphitryon take revenge for the deaths of her brothers before she would consent to marry him (Apollodorus 2.4.6; Hesiod *Shield* 15-22; Euripides *HF* 1078-80).

237. Rabinowitz (1993: 105) also points out the contrast of compliant and praiseworthy Macaria with aggressive and blameworthy Alcmena. The same contrast can be made between Polyxena and Hecuba.

238. Whether this revenge is depraved or just is extensively debated, especially with reference to Hecuba's transformation into a dog. See Burnett (1998: 166 n. 90), Foley (2001: 295 n.72) and Meridor (1978: 28) for a large number of references. Cf. also Adkins (1966) 206; Allen (2000) 116; Mossman (1995) 165, 195ff. Meridor is right to maintain that the transformation of itself says nothing about the character of Hecuba or about her revenge, but is a typical Euripidean element (1978: 32).

239. See p. 13. Rabinowitz (1993: 121-2) and Foley (2001: 286) note that she uses her womanly skills to succeed. Agamemnon will be killed by similar methods as noted by Polymestor at the end of the play.

240. Cf. T. Harrison (2000) 58 n. 69.

241. Meridor (1978) 30-1. Cf. also Burnett (1998) 171.

242. Gregory (1991) 108.

243. The horror felt by Athenians at the killing of a guest-friend has been noted on p. 14.

244. A punishment associated with barbarians – see Collard (1991) 185; E. Hall (1989) 159. Contra Burnett (1998) 169.

245. Lloyd (1999) 349. Cf. Burnett (1998) 144.

246. Cf. Collard (1991) 26; Meridor (1978) 35 n. 24; Mossman (1995) 189.

247. Belfiore (2000) 148.

248. Foley (2001) 284-5; E. Hall (1989) 108.

249. See Mossman (1995) 190 n. 56; Rabinowitz (1993) 122; Segal (1990) 122 n. 41. Burnett (1998: 172) notes the symbolism, but does not find it significant.

250. When Euenion is blinded the land suffers infertility (Herodotus 9.93.3); Phoenix is made infertile in the *Iliad* (9.453ff.) and is blinded in other versions (Apollodorus 3.13.8). Polyphemus' blinding by Odysseus has been connected to Cronus' castration by Zeus (Glenn (1978) 147-50; Nieto Hernández (2000) 352-3). Freud saw Oedipus' blinding himself as a self-castration (Devereux 1973: 36-7). Buxton (1980) is right to argue that blinding has other meanings too (especially its association with prophecy as seen in many of these tales and at the end of *Hecuba*). Cf. Seaford (1990) 83.

251. Compare the story of Oroetes who allegedly lured Polycrates into a trap by lying to him and promising him material rewards and power (Herodotus 3.122).

252. Similarly, Periander takes revenge against the Corcyreans for killing his son by castrating 300 of their sons (Herodotus 3.50-3).

253. E. Hall (1989) 157.

254. Contra Braund (1998) 166-7.

255. Cf. pp. 26, 29, 31-2, 51, 55, 83.

256. T. Harrison (2000) 110, 113 n. 33.

257. Miller (2006: 65-6) suggests that revenge acts in folktales are often meant to be darkly humorous and clever. Cf. Mossman (1995: 170) who cites Archilochus fr. 23.14-15 West. See p. 58.

258. Lendon (2000) 18. Rabinowitz (1993: 121) makes the point that Hecuba inflicts on Polymestor the sufferings which the Greeks have inflicted upon her. However, this view does not take into account that Polymestor was aware that Polydorus was the last son of Priam and his hope for the future.

259. See p. 4.

260. Hornblower (2003) 43.

261. Hornblower (2003) 53-5.

262. Devereux (1973) 46.

263. Cf. Miller (2006) 152. Compare Jason's fate discussed on p. 63. Cf. McHardy (2005) 144.

264. Miller (2006) 127.

265. Dodds (1960) 233 on *Bacch.* 1308; Seaford (1996) 251 on *Bacch.* 1308; cf. Devereux (1973) 46.

2. Adultery, Rape and Seduction

1. Burnett (1998) 35.

2. See p. 124n.71. Cf. Jacoby (1985) 194-6.

3. Contrary to some claims (e.g. Mead 1931 now refuted by Freeman 1983) there is no society in which male sexual jealousy and the violence brought about by this jealousy is absent.

4. Daly and Wilson (1998) 291.

5. Daly and Wilson (1998) 295. Women's concerns are different, focusing on emotional fidelity and the ability of the man to supply her and her offspring with resources. Experiments have proved that there is a division along gender lines regarding sexual jealousy (296-7).

6. Translated by Yun Lee Too (Mirhady and Too 2000).

7. See Harvey (1985) for all the instances of enslaved women in Thucydides' account of the Peloponnesian War.

8. Foley (1981); Gardner (1989) 51-3; Just (1989) 213-14; Roisman (2005) 33-4.

9. See Gardner (1989) on the similar anxiety of Athenian men manifested in Aristophanes (*Thesm.* 339-40, 407-8, 502ff., 564-5; *Pax* 674-8) that a woman might substitute another woman's child for her own.

10. Veiling can be used as an indication of modesty (Abu-Lughod (1987) 161). On modesty and veiling in ancient Greece see Cairns (1996a), (1996c), (2002); Llewellyn-Jones (2003).

11. Deliyanni (1985) *Mani* 39. Porter (1986: 217) notes that rape is like property theft as a girl loses her economic value.

12. Glotz (1904) 81; A. Harrison (1968) 35; MacDowell (1978) 88, 125; Todd (1993: 279). In myth they sometimes kill their wives (Odysseus in one version kills Penelope for being seduced, Apollodorus *Epit.* 7.39), although contra Burnett (1998: 142) this is the exception rather than the rule. Notably in another version cited by Apollodorus Odysseus returns the seduced Penelope to her father (7.38).

13. See Euripides' *Orestes* for the anger of Tyndareus over the death of his daughter. He simultaneously condemns her actions saying she deserved death and criticises Orestes for killing her (*Or.* 496-506, 538-9). His words indicate clearly the potential for disagreement between natal and affinal kin in matters such as this.

14. Deliyanni (1985) *Mani* 42; Durham (1928) 69; Whitaker (1968) 270.

15. Hasluck (1954) 215, Seremetakis (1997) 144ff.

16. MacDowell (1978) 80; cf. Roy (1997) 13.

17. Although Todd (1993: 279) points out that no Greek law mentions anything like the Roman law allowing fathers to kill both an adulterer and his daughter when caught in the act (*Digest* 48.5.33), it is notable that Augustus' legislation specifies that a father may kill his daughter, but her husband cannot, an apparent codification of normal practice in Athens.

18. Cf. also Nicolaus Damascenus 90 F 49; Suida Παρίππον καὶ κόρη. For the symbolic significance of imprisonment as a punishment for unchaste women, see Seaford (1990).

19. Cf. Fisher (2001) 331-4.

20. See McHardy (2007) for fuller discussion of the punishment of unchaste women in tragic plot-lines.

21. See Ormand (1999) 21.

22. See pp. 43-4, 61-3. Cf. also pp. 40-1 where men's lines are doomed to extinction because they have displeased the gods. See Lateiner (1989: 142) and T. Harrison (2000: 58) for examples from Herodotus.

23. Cf. Carey (1989) 80.

24. Daly and Wilson (1988a: 187, 190) explain this in evolutionary terms. Because a man shares his fitness with his wife, his continued line is guaranteed only by her fidelity.

25. Daly and Wilson (1988b) 520-1.

26. See Christ (1998b) 524; Roy (1997) 12.

27. Carey (1989) ad loc.; Pomeroy (1975) 82; Todd (1993) 276.

28. Pomeroy (1975) 82-3. Cf. MacDowell (1978) 88; Todd (1993) 216. Roy (1997: 13-14) suggests that problems concerning the dowry could be sufficient to cause a man to ignore an instance of adultery.

29. Ormand (1999) 105-6. See McHardy (2007) on the story of Aerope.

30. Cf. Herodotus 6.69 on the aspersions cast against Demaratus' mother. See pp. 5, 46.

31. See pp. 65, 85-6.

32. Christ (1998b) 524; Cohen (1991) 45, 62-3, 82.

33. See Plutarch (*Alc.* 39.5) for the anecdote (one of several) about Alcibiades' death in which he is killed by the brothers of a girl he had seduced. See Carey (1989: 64-5) on laws elsewhere in Greece.

34. See further on Orestes in Chapter 5.

35. Cf. Cairns (1996c).

36. See p. 114.

37. In Plato's version Gyges sets out to seduce the queen and take the throne (*Rep.* 359d-360b).

38. See esp. the story of Joseph and Potiphar's wife (Genesis 39:7-19) with Yohannan (1968).

39. Further on Clytemnestra's and Aegisthus' motives in Chapter 5.

40. Telemachus speculates that the Ithacans are paying him back (ἀποτινύμενοι) for some bad deeds of Odysseus (2.71-4).

41. See pp. 13-14, 61-3 on Medea.

42. Compare also Melanthius and Melantho whose bad characters are shown through their treatment of the disguised Odysseus.

43. See further in Chapter 4 on insults driving revenge.

44. Eurytion the centaur got drunk at the wedding of Peirithous and Hippodameia and tried to rape the bride in Peirithous' home (cf. *Od.* 21.295-8; *Il.* 1.268, 2.743-4). The furious hosts dragged him outside where they sliced off his nose and ears.

45. See pp. 91-2.

46. His vengeance is expressed by a host of τίνω-related words (e.g. *Od.* 20.121 τίσασθαι; 23.57 ἐτίσατο; 24.324-6 τινύμενος; 24.478-80 ἀποτίσεται; 24.482-6 ἐτίσατο).

47. See Chapter 3 on possessions.

48. See McHardy (forthcoming) and p. 29.

49. Daly and Wilson (1998).

50. See pp. 35-6.

51. See G.P. Rose (1979) on this metaphor and simile.

52. G.P. Rose (1979) 227.

53. Cf. Burnett (1998) 40.

54. Christ (1998b) 525. Cf. also Cohen (1995) 162.

55. Cf. Burnett (1998) 53; Carey (1989) 59; Christ (1998b) 524; Glotz (1904) 50; E. Harris (2004) 62; A. Harrison (1968) 32; Hunter (1994) 137.

56. The protection of other female relatives can also be seen in this light, as a man could expect to enhance his social network through the successful marriage of his female relatives. The attack of a predatory male, if discovered, could bring an end to a woman's hopes for marriage

57. See Chapter 3 for discussion of revenge for property.

58. Further on pp. 95-6 on lethal responses to insults in Athens.

59. Laws often allow a greater degree of violence than usual if a wife commits adultery, as this is believed to be a provocation (Daly and Wilson 1998: 292).

60. Cf. Apollodorus *Lib.* 3.14.2; Pausanias 1.21.4-7, 1.28.5; Hellanicus *FGH* 323aF22 = schol. Euripides *Or.* 1648. In historical times such murders were not tried at the Areopagus, but the myth is designed to explain the name of the hill.

61. MacDowell (1963) 79-81; cf. A. Harrison (1968) 33. As Fisher (1992: 105) correctly notes, it is not likely that the Athenians themselves saw it in this way.

62. MacDowell (1963) 70-81.

63. Cf. Allen (2000) 38, 126-7; Carey (1989) 60; Cohen (1995) 71.

64. Cf. Isaeus (fr. 32 Thalheim): 'Men who take revenge on those who wrong them prevent others from being wronged'.

65. Herman (1993), (1994), (1995), (1996) and (1998a) maintains that this speech demonstrates the desire of speakers to show that they do not indulge in violence or revenge. Cf. W. Harris (1997: 365-6) for a curt but correct rebuttal of Herman's suggestions. Cf. also Christ (1998a) 161 n. 5, (1998b) 525.

66. See p. 3.

67. See pp. 26, 29, 31-2, 43, 51, 83. See McHardy (forthcoming) on the literary *topos* of the avenger speech.

68. W. Harris (1997: 365) suggests this could be seen as a 'desperate reserve plea, in case the jury rejected his claim to have killed Eratosthenes upon catching him *in flagrante*'. I do not think we need to see this as a 'desperate reserve plea', but instead as an integral part of his argument suggesting the legality of his killing. His opponents, as Harris points out, are clearly suggesting that the killing was not legal.

69. Issues concerning the partiality and honesty of witnesses further complicate this case. Cf. Cohen (1995) 110-11.

70. Allen (2000) 127.

71. Bateman (1958) 278; Carey (1989) 60-1, 75; Todd (1993) 276-7; cf. Cohen (1995) 162.

72. See Roy (1997: 13-14) for examples.

73. The list of possible motivations which might reasonably have been expected to generate such a killing is revealing: financial gains (1.4), previous lawsuits, secrets, financial gains (1.44), insults and drunken quarrels (1.45). That material goods are deemed significant in causing violence will be further discussed in the following chapter. Insults and drunken quarrels will be examined in Chapter 4.

74. Cf. E. Harris (2004) 57.

75. See pp. 85-6, 99.

76. See pp. 19-21 on the use of marriage alliance to settle a dispute.

77. See Devereux (1973) 43-4; Seaford (1990) 87. See pp. 43-4.

78. Cf. Strauss (1993: 167-8) on the father / son relationship in this play.

79. Seaford (1994) 340, 357-8, 368-9. Compare also Euripides' *Bacchae*, p. 93. See further below on Medea.

80. Cf. Cohen (1995) 148.

81. There is some suggestion of castration and blinding as punishments for adulterers and rapists (Burnett (1998) 169). Cf. Horace *Sat.* 1.2.44-5; Valerius Maximus 6.1.13.

82. See pp. 43-4.

83. Cohen (1985) is not sure about the value of the comic evidence, but Roy (1997) thinks it could indicate real practice. Cf. Dover (1968) ad loc.

84. Christopher Brown (1989).

85. See p. 62 on Medea's desire to quell the laughter of her enemies by exacting revenge. See also p. 133n.257.

86. See also Castellani (1980: 45) who notes that Odysseus' two enemies Sun and Poseidon co-operate in helping a wronged husband in Demodocus' song.

87. See p. 70.

88. Here the vocabulary frequently used to express a metaphor of payment (in blood) is used to express the payment of a fine.

89. See further on the *Hymn to Hermes* in Chapter 3.

90. See pp. 9-10.

91. Foxhall (1991: 299) notes that rape and adultery are crimes against a man and his power to control sexual activities in the household. Cf. E. Harris (2004) 60; Omitowoju (2002) 5; Ormand (1999) 15-16; Sommerstein (2006) 233.

92. See further below pp. 60-1 on wars over women.

93. See Fuchs (1993-4) who compares this quarrel to similar in-fighting between American gang members over women. Cf. Jankowski (1991) 79, 146.

94. Shay (1994: 6) likens Briseis to a modern medal of honour. He says that it is the violation of 'what is right' by a commander that truly makes Achilles angry.

95. Pomeroy (1975) 26.

96. See pp. 79-82 for the similar function of horses and weaponry in the *Iliad*.

97. See further on this episode on pp. 87-8.

98. Cf. Iole who is compelled to marry the son of the man who killed her relatives and took her captive (Sophocles *Trach.* 1233-8; cf. 351ff.).

99. Ormand (1999) 116.

100. Elsewhere we are told that Telamon exiled Teucer (Euripides *Hel.* 90-4), perhaps for failing to avenge his brother (Velleius 1.1.1).

101. Pomeroy (1975: 26) notes the records of children born to captured women in the Mycenaean tablets. Cf. Ventris and Chadwick (1956).

102. Cf. Fitton (1970) 62; Todd (1993) 177. See MacDowell (1978: 67) on Timotheus, who had a Thracian mother yet was an Athenian general in the first part of the fourth century. See Ormand (1999: ch. 4) for a discussion of Teucer's and Eurysaces' parentage in Sophocles' *Ajax* in light of the Periclean citizenship law. See Ogden (1996) on bastardy in Athens and elsewhere.

103. On the disputed authenticity of this oration see Edwards (1995) 131-6.

104. Van Wees (1992) 173.

105. Cf. Aeschylus *Ag.* 399-402, 412; Euripides *IA* 370-2, 1264-6 for the notion that all the Greeks had been dishonoured by Helen's abduction.

106. See Kitts (2005) esp. 175-6.

107. For example, in the introduction to his source book on *Warfare in Ancient Greece* (1996) Sage makes no mention of the importance of revenge in Greek representations of warfare.

108. A similar justification is offered for the outbreak of the Peloponnesian War in Aristophanes' *Acharnians* where it is jokingly said that reciprocal abductions of Megarian and Athenian prostitutes began the hostilities (523-9).

109. See pp. 45-6.

110. Bongie (1977) underestimates the importance of sexual jealousy as a male trait, although she does note the universality of this emotion (46).

111. Barlow (1989) 161; Bongie (1977); Burnett (1998) 194; Foley (1989, up-dated in 2001: 243-68); Knox (1977); Mueller (2001) 473; Rabinowitz (1993) 148. Bongie and Knox emphasise her likeness to Sophocles' Ajax (see pp. 82-4). Barlow finds further similarity to Hercules.

112. Cf. Bongie (1977) 27, 29, 38, 56; Knox (1977) 197, 201-2. Mueller (2001: 483) notes that Medea's rejection of Jason's offer of money and help resembles Achilles' rejection of Agamemnon's gifts. Cf. also (2001: 486).

113. Cf. Barlow (1989) 161-2; Bongie (1977) 41; Rabinowitz (1993) 151-2.

114. Cf. Odgen (1996).

115. Burnett (1998) 195.

116. Burnett (1998) 200.

117. See pp. 40-1, 61 on the oaths in the *Iliad* and in Euripides' *Hecuba*.

118. See pp. 43-4.

119. Gill (1996: 156 n. 216) notes that the childless state of Aegeus seems to inspire Medea's attack on Jason. However, the nurse recognises the murder of the children is a possibility from the outset (95, 116-18).

120. Burnett (1998) 207; cf. Bongie (1977: 41) who calls Medea's choice of revenge 'a slow and prolonged retribution more in accord with his insult to her honour'.

121. Rabinowitz (1993) 147.

122. Cf. Segal (1990) 122 n. 41. See p. 42 on Hecuba. Rabinowitz (1993: 142, 146) compares the revenge acts of Medea and Hecuba and find both excessive.

123. See Bongie (1977) 55; Rabinowitz (1993) 146, 150-1.

124. See pp. 57, 101, 106, 147n.116.

125. Foley (2001) 243; Rabinowitz (1993) 142-5. See pp. 13, 39.

126. See pp. 38-42.

127. See McHardy (2005) on infanticide in Greek tragedy. Cf. also Clytemnestra who is motivated to attack her husband and reject her children in part because of his relationship with Cassandra. See p. 106.

128. Cf. Graf (1997).

129. Rabinowitz (1993: 150) argues that her lack of control by a man (symbolised by the fact that she was not given in marriage by her father) makes her powerful and dangerous.

3. Raiding, Theft and Property Disputes

1. Because of lack of good pasturage larger animals are less common and gain more value (Lonsdale 1979: 147). Cf. Herodotus 4.23.4 on Scythia. Cattle are sometimes used as a measure of wealth in Homer (e.g. *Il.* 23.700-5). See Athanassakis (1992) 159; Miller (2006) 37; H. Rose (1954) 219; Seaford (1998) 119-20. See also Lincoln (1976) 62-3.

2. Adkins (1960b) 31-2; Donlan (1993) 160; van Wees (1992) 72; D. Wilson (2002) 18-20. Cf. Campbell (1964: 298) on the dual value of sheep to the Sarakatsani.

3. Other goods, such as tripods, confer status upon a man (in particular the many gifts which are given and received in the Homeric epics) and enhance his standing in society (cf. Aristotle *Rhet.* 1361a34ff.; Finley 1979: 120-3; Redfield 1975: 111-12). D. Wilson (2002: 18) lists these as 'prestige goods' as distinct from subsistence goods and cultural wealth (such as the sceptre of a king). Clearly (as Wilson herself acknowledges) there is some cross-over between these categories.

4. Daly and Wilson (1988a) 179; van Wees (1992) 107-8. Cf. *Il.* 1.181-7.

5. Cf. van Wees (1992) 105, (1998) 12.

6. Cf. Zanker (1992) 23.

7. See pp. 14-15, 93, 101-2.

8. The question of who started a dispute is important to the Greeks, although it is not always simple to establish the answer with certainty. See pp. 6, 77, 96.

9. The close blood relationship between Diogeiton and the orphans makes his behaviour all the more shocking (Lysias 32.12, 18).

10. Todd (1993: 203) argues that the woman's speech is most likely a literary construct, not evidence of what this woman actually said or did. Cf. Foxhall (1996) 149. Gagarin (2001: 167) emphasises that these are not the woman's actual words, although he believes that she did make a speech upon which Lysias based his own 'masculine' version.

11. A. Harrison (1971) 163-4; Todd (1993) 203.

12. See McHardy (2004) for further discussion of this case and on the particular interest of mothers in supporting their children's rights to property and citizenship. See also Walters (1993) 195-200; Gagarin (2001).

13. Lincoln (1976: 44) cites various examples. Cf. H. Rose (1954) 218. See also Herzfeld (1990) and Walcot (1979: 334, 336) for modern examples.

14. Hesiod (*Works and Days* 161-5) connects the race of heroes with fighting over flocks and women. Cf. Pausanias 4.36.3; H. Rose (1954) 224, Walcot (1979) 327.

15. See Campbell (1964); Herzfeld (1990).

16. Mycenaean dating: Walcot (1979: 327-8); Willcock (1978: 308, on lines 670-761); dark age dating: Jackson (1993: 67); archaic dating: Lintott (1982: 17-18).

17. See Herzfeld (1990: 307) on modern Crete; cf. H. Rose (1954) 218. Cf. also Jackson (1993) 67-8, 71.

18. See also Lysias 32.29, which mentions theft by pirates and Polybius 22.4, which refers to retaliatory cattle raiding *c.* 196 BC. Treaties from the classical period prohibit plundering between allies, e.g. SV no. 146; cf. Lintott (1982) 17 n. 13.

19. See further below on the value and significance of weapons.

20. Iles Johnston (2002) 112; cf. Shay (2002) 278 n. 2.

21. Iles Johnston (2002) 112; Walcot (1979) 339; cf. Lincoln (1976) 62. Iles Johnston makes the link between raiding and athletic competitions, in which youths also had the chance to demonstrate their ability at a range of warlike contests and where they could win weapons as prizes (2002: 118). Cf. *Iliad* 22.158-61. Walcot (1979: 339) connects raiding to the *ephebeia* at Athens after which a youth first received his weapons and was qualified to fight for the city (*Ath. Pol.* 42.4).

22. See Walcot (1979: 334ff.) for detailed discussion of this story. See Pedrick (1983) on how Nestor's speech inspires Patroclus to fight.

23. Cf. *Il.* 5.638-42 and 14.250-1 where Hercules is said to have sacked Troy because Laomedon did not give him the mares he had promised him, but insulted him instead.

24. See Plato *Gorg.* 484b where this story is used by Callicles as a paradigm to prove that 'might is right'.

25. Odysseus asserts that men must be willing to receive wounds in order to protect their property, specifically livestock (*Od.* 17.469-72).

26. See also Apollodorus (2.4.6) where the sons of Electryon and the sons of Pterelaus kill each other over cattle. Here too of the sons of Electryon only the youngest survives. One son of Pterelaus also survives the carnage.

27. See Herzfeld (1990) and Walcot (1979) on the tendency to raid by night. Night is preferred for secrecy. In Athens thieves who were caught stealing by night could be killed (Demosthenes 24.113). In the *Iliad* mist is said to be even better than night for thieves (3.10-11).

28. Cf. *Od.* 23.356-8, where Odysseus maintains that he will replenish his flocks by raiding and gifts from the people.

29. Note that it is usual to blame the other party for staring hostilities. See pp. 6, 43.

30. Walcot (1979) 336.

31. Escalation can also arise from other forms of insult. The hostilities between men and centaurs are said to have begun with drunken insults at a wedding (*Od.* 21.293-310). See p. 51.

32. Ferguson (1995) has stressed the significance of property in causing disputes among the Yanomami. See p. 8.

33. For other versions of this story see Alcaeus (fr. 7 = Pausanias 7.20.4-5); Apollodorus (3.10.2); Sophocles' *Ichneutae* and Ovid (*Met.* 2.68ff.). Ovid's version is very different, ending without payment or resolution (Castellani 1980).

34. Iles Johnston (2002) 112, 116; cf. Haft (1996-7). The initiation aspect is true of other myth thefts too e.g. Jason and the Golden Fleece. See H. Rose (1941) and Walcot (1979: 339) on ritual stealing as part of initiation.

35. Harrell (1991) 308.

36. On Autolycus see Apollodorus 2.6.2; Hyginus *Fab.* 201; cf. *Od.* 19.395-7; cf. *Il.* 10.261-7; Hesiod fr. 65.15. Further on Odysseus on p. 76.

37. Walcot (1979) 345.

38. See p. 75.

39. See *Il.* 8.13, 477-83 for similar threats from Zeus.

40. Harrell (1991) 317.

41. See Harrell (1991) 321ff.

42. Golden (1990) 118. Cf. Daly and Wilson (1988a) 30-1; Djilas (1958) 312; Herzfeld (1985) 77-8; S. Wilson (1988) 130-1, 133-4. Further on rivalry over property and power in Chapters 2 and 3.

43. To overcome this problem, Hesiod advises only one son (*Works and Days* 376-9).

44. Iles Johnston (2002) 121.

45. Cf. Gagarin (1974a) 189.

46. The desire for revenge in cases of violent incursions on the home also occurs at Athens, as discussed by Christ (1998b). See further on pp. 75-8 on this subject.

47. Iles Johnston (2002) 115.

48. See Herzfeld (1990) on Crete. Haft (1996-7) draws the comparison with the Homeric Hymn.

49. The story also indicates a belief in the existence of raiding practices in early Attica.

50. Hunter (1994) 55-8; cf. Allen (2000) 123. Christ (1998a: 168-9) claims that while suits within nuclear families were rare, suits with extended family were frequent. See p. 11.

51. Cf. Hesiod's *Works and Days* in which a fraternal dispute over property is at the heart the poem. See Gagarin (1974b).

52. Shelmerdine (1986) 51.

53. Shelmerdine (1986: 59) relates this to the story of Odysseus and the cattle of the sun.

54. Iles Johnston (2002) 125-6.

55. Examples include the men at Troy: *Il.* 1.125-9, 6.424, 20.91-2, Thucydides 1.11.1; Odysseus returning from Troy: *Od.* 9.39-42, 224-7, 464-70; Sataspes circumnavigating Africa: Herodotus 4.43.5; the Persians in Scythia: Herodotus 4.130.1.

56. Cf. van Wees (1992) 208-10.

57. See Shay (2002: 101) who argues that the episode is further evidence for Odysseus' failings as a leader and that Eurylochus should not take the blame for the death of the men.

58. Cf. p. 68 for the story of Neleus' sons in which Nestor is spared because he took no part in the raid.

59. See further on pp. 92-3 on divine responses to insults. Cf. p. 13 on seeking help from allies.

60. And seems to indicate that wealth was essential for a husband even under a dowry system (cf. Isaeus 11.40).

61. Daly and Wilson (1998) 295-7. See p. 8.

62. H. Rose (1954: 218-19) and Lonsdale (1979: 147) note the use of cow-related names for girls.

63. These tales demonstrate that it is not always easy to supply a distinct reason for revenge. Instead interconnected reasons are involved. See pp. 103-16.

64. Iles Johnston (2002) 127.

65. Donlan (1993: 165) argues that the offer of marriage is a standard motif of domination. D. Wilson (2002: 78-80, 93) notes that the marriage would reassert Agamemnon's superiority over Achilles as a father figure.

66. A slightly different version of the story appears at *Od.* 15.225-38.

67. Cf. O. Murray (1980) 202-3.

68. Van Wees (1992) 100.

69. See Osborne (1985: 43) who highlights other possible reasons that procedures might be chosen.

70. Allen (2000) 228-9. Compare Ares and Aphrodite (p. 58) and Ajax (p. 83). See Allen (2000: 226-9) for discussion of imprisonment at Athens. Cf. A. Harrison (1971) 177; MacDowell (1978) 256-7.

71. Cf. also Demosthenes 35.47; Isaeus 4.30; *Ath. Pol.* 52.1. See Cohen (1983: 93-114) on *hierosulia*. Old Testament laws did not penalise a man who killed a thief either (Exodus 22:2).

72. Flower and Marincola (2002: 308-9) note the culpability of Xanthippus and his 'barbaric' actions.

73. See pp. 92-3 on responses to dishonour. Divine revenge in such circumstances is usually fatal.

74. Plato groups temple robbery with treason and subversion. He maintains that these are the greatest crimes against the social order (Cohen 1983: 114).

75. Cf. van Wees (1992) 257.

76. Iles Johnston (2002) 115, cf. 126. See also Jackson (1993: 71) who suggests that heroic poetry could have had a significant impact on the behaviour of dark-age rulers.

77. See Christ (1998b). See pp. 53-6.

78. With no police force, Athenians had to look out for their own interests: Allen (2000) 4, 21; Christ (1998a) 26, (1998b) 521; Gagarin (1986) 74, 143; Herman (1993) 411; Hunter (1994) 122, 125, 149; Lacey (1968) 155-6; Rhodes (1998); Todd (1993) 79.

79. Cf. Cohen (1983) 75.

80. Christ (1998b) 524, 527; cf. Cohen (1991) 82.

81. Daly and Wilson (1988a) 179.

82. Christ (1998b) 523, 527. See p. 56.

83. Christ (1998b) 525-6, 531-2.

84. Christ (1998b) 541. Cf. pp. 96-7.

85. See pp. 6, 96.

86. Cf. Christ (1998b) 537-9.

87. Cf. MacDowell (1963: 12-19) on this case. See p. 13.

88. See pp. 116-17.

89. Cf. *Il.* 1.152-6, 5.480-4. See p. 69.

90. Cf. Christ (1998a) 176-7; Cohen (1995) 103.

91. Ferguson (1995) highlights the acquisition of tools and weapons in his study of Yanomami warfare, but it should be noted that men do not aim to acquire weapons just for their own sake, but for their practical use in work and warfare and for the advantages they give them in life. See p. 8.

92. The men aim to protect not just the armour, but also the body from attack. In several cases mention is made of decapitation of corpses (11.12-17, 13.202-5, 14.496-507, 17.34-40, 124-5). This appears to be linked to head-hunting practices which in general are not mentioned in Homer (cf. G. Murray 1960: 10; van Wees 1992: 129).

93. See pp. 25-34 for discussion of these and other battlefield revenges.

94. Aeneas Tacticus (16.4-8) advises allowing the enemy to plunder freely as they are more easily defeated this way.

95. Cf. Finley (1979: 119) who argues that Homeric heroes prefer to take spoils than to help win the war.

96. Van Wees (1992) 98.

97. The shield made entirely of gold is surely a fantastic item which calls attention to the need to treat the historicity of every element of the narrative with caution. Nevertheless, its depiction shows symbolically the status of Nestor who bears such a valuable and unique object.

98. Cf. also Euripides *El.* 319-22, where Aegisthus is said to use Agamemnon's chariot, although he did not defeat Agamemnon at war

99. Examples which mention the stripping of the dead and the setting up of a trophy include: Thucydides 3.112.8; 4.44.3; 4.72.4; 5.10.12. Plato objected to such displays in temples (*Rep.* 469e-70a).

100. See Virgil (*Aen.* 11.4-11) for a description of this type of trophy. See also the Attic red-figure pelike by the Trophy painter (Boston 20.187) on which Nike is depicted erecting a trophy from armour and weapons.

101. Although note that Ajax cannot beat Odysseus at wrestling (*Il.* 23.708-37) and in the *Little Iliad* Odysseus is awarded the prize because he fought to protect the body of Achilles, while Ajax merely carried it from the field.

102. See Burnett (1998) 83. Knox (1961) suggests that the presentation of honour in the play is derived from Homer.

103. Cf. Cohen (1995) 137-8; Fisher (1992) 88; E. Harris (2004) 46; Hunter (1994) 182; Saunders (1991) 108. Cf. also Aeschines 1.62-6, Herodotus 1.114-15.

104. See pp. 26, 29, 31-2, 43, 51, 55.

105. Cf. Zanker (1992) 22.

106. Elsewhere, men defect to the other side to achieve revenge. In two plays, men pretend to be enemies of the Atreidae who have gone over to the other side. Odysseus does this when disguised as a beggar to get information in Troy (*Rhesus* 717-19) and Neoptolemus does this in an attempt to get Philoctetes' bow (Sophocles *Phil.* 585-6). Cf. Sinon (Virgil *Aen.* 2.77-104).

107. The authenticity of these lines is sometimes doubted, but the sentiment is not inconsistent with what occurs in the play.

108. Burnett (1998) 86 n. 63, cf. 87. See pp. 13-14.

109. See p. 68.

110. Seaford (1989: 94 n. 37) calls the raid a 'grotesque hunt' (cf. *Ajax* 297) and a perverted sacrifice (cf. 219).

111. As for example in the Doloneia discussed on pp. 81-2. This theme of theft from and destruction of allies is paralleled in the *Rhesus* where the charioteer accuses Hector of stealing from his own allies and killing them (833-55).

112. Compare the portrayal of Achilles in *Myrmidons* discussed on pp. 33-4.

4. Insults, Status and Power

1. I do not intend to reiterate the copious arguments on this subject here, but merely to cover some basic points pertinent to the theme of this book.

2. See Chapter 2 on insults concerning women. See further below on insults relating to military, athletic and hunting ability, as well as insults to leadership ability.

3. Cf. Miller (2006) 10.

4. Cf. Alexakis (1999); Black-Michaud (1975) 26, 179, 181; Boehm (1984) 41, 92; Campbell (1964) 197; Deliyanni (1985) *Context and Literature* 20, 34; *Corsica* 29-30; Durham (1928) 163; Hasluck (1954) 229; Whitaker (1968) 264-5; S. Wilson (1988) 90.

5. Miller (2006) 51; cf. van Wees (1992: 88) who notes the importance of fear as a deterrent. Cf. also Sigmund (1993) 194, 203. See p. 48.

6. Cf. Cairns (2001: 210), who cites Diomedes' calm response to Agamemnon's insult of his fighting ability. Although Sthenelus reacts angrily, Diomedes realises that Agamemnon is attempting to encourage him to fight (*Il.* 4.370-418). See also Wissmann (1997) ch. 2.

7. Paris takes Hector's rebukes mildly because they are brothers (6.332-40). Agamemnon accepts Odysseus' criticism of his leadership without getting angry, because they are friends and Odysseus is speaking sensibly (14.82-106). Likewise Menelaus forgives Antilochus' lack of deference because Nestor's family have done him many favours (23.600-11). Cf. van Wees (1992) 114.

8. See especially Peristiany (1965). Scholars have criticised this volume's view of a general 'Mediterranean society' (e.g. Herman (1996) 5-6). Here, I am not interested in the purported existence of cultural similarities between the people of the Mediterranean, but in the correlation between revenge and honour which these anthropologists note.

9. Cf. Cohen (1995) 66.

10. Roisman (2005: 14-15) notes the connection of young men to fights over honour in ancient Greece. See pp. 46, 56, 99, 102.

11. Daly and Wilson (1988a) 124-5; cf. Jankowski (1991) 146; Oatley and Jenkins (1996) 91.

12. For similar arguments about the behaviour of the Homeric heroes, see van Wees (1992) 69, 110.

13. See Aristotle (1361a28ff.) for an account of how honour is gained through public recognition. Cf. Aeschylus *Ag.* 938.

14. Cf. Jankowski (1991) 146.

15. Cf. Allen (2000) 61; Fisher (1976) 180. See W. Harris (2001: 140) for the role of anger (which prompts revenge) in maintaining the social hierarchy.

16. Van Wees (1992) 155; cf. W. Harris (2001) 139.

17. Daly and Wilson (1988a) 176-7; Hardy (1963) 16-21; Whitaker (1968) 66-7. See McHardy (forthcoming).

18. Daly and Wilson (1988a) 128; cf. Miller (2006) 51; van Wees (1992) 88.

19. Roisman (2005) 72; van Wees (1992) 115. Cairns (2001: 215) argues that deliberately insulting someone in this way could be perceived as *hybris* and would therefore lead to dishonour for the attacker. However, hybristic acts can lead to a useful reputation for ferocity. See pp. 96-8 on Meidias. Moreover, hybristic acts can still humiliate victims (van Wees (1992) 107, 117-18). Cf. p. 122n.31 on *hybris*.

20. Van Wees (1992) 123.

21. Daly and Wilson (1988a) 132-3.

22. Daly and Wilson (1988a) 136-7. This reasoning goes some way to explain cross-cultural discrepancies in levels of male and female violence (id. 149).

23. See esp. van Wees (1992). Cf. also Cairns (2001), Fuchs (1993-4), D. Wilson (2002). See p. 59.

24. D. Wilson (2002) 18-20, 36.

25. Cf. van Wees (1992) 108.

26. E.g. 1.244 ἔτισας; 1.354 ἔτισεν; 1.356 ἠτίμησεν; 1.412 ἔτισεν; 1.507 ἠτίμησεν.

27. See W. Harris (2001) 141-3; cf. Morris (1986) 123-5.

28. Van Wees (1992) (133) argues against scholars who claim that Achilles is seeking a new morality or breaching Homeric norms. See esp. Parry (1956). Cf. D. Wilson (2002) ch. 4.

29. Athanassakis (1992) 161; Gill (1996) 144; Mueller (2001) 483; D. Wilson (2002) 5.

30. Although Odysseus blames the men for their own deaths, he is also implicated in their destruction through his ill-management of the men. See Shay (2002: 101) on the treatment of Eurylochus. See pp. 35-6, 72.

31. Cf. also Saul and David (1 Samuel 18:6-8).

32. Cf. Postlethwaite (1988).

33. See pp. 45-8.

34. Hesiod also associates the race of heroes with violent behaviour for the sake of honour (*Works and Days* 156-69). Cf. van Wees (1998) on the problems of the heroes' claims.

35. See further on p. 79 on this example.

36. See Gaskin (1990) 8-9.

37. Cf. Hooker (1987).

38. David Harvey points out to me that in art cowardly men could be painted white, the usual colour for women. See Robertson (1959: 77, 80) for the sixth-century Corinthian vase-painting of Tydeus killing Ismene, where her husband Periclymenus, who is painted white, is depicted running away.

39. Contra Munson (1988).

40. Aegisthus is insulted for being 'like a woman' compared to the warrior Agamemnon (Aeschylus *Ag.* 1625-7).

41. See McHardy (2004) for women's use of insults to spur men on to revenge. See also Wissmann (1997) ch. 8. See further in Chapter 5 on Orestes' revenge.

42. In an alternative version, not much credited by Herodotus, Polycrates insults Oroetes by ignoring his messenger.

43. See p. 25.

44. Cf. van Wees (1992) 93.

45. Cf. Arrian (5.8) where Alexander is said to kill Cleitus with a spear because he denigrated his power and insulted him.

46. Van Wees (1992) 93-4.

47. In *Rhesus*, though, the Muses are said to have blinded him (923-5). Cf. Buxton (1980: 27-8) on the tendency of gods to punish poets and prophets with blinding.

48. See pp. 82-3.

49. Other mythical examples include Artemis' attacks on Actaeon, Oeneus and Agamemnon, Hera's punishment of Pelias and Athena's anger at the Greeks following the rape of Cassandra in her shrine.

50. Madness leading to the slaying of one's own children is a common theme in examples of divine retaliation. See McHardy (2005).

51. Cf. Seaford (1996) on lines 1248-9 for the view that Dionysus prefers the cause of the *polis* over that of an autocratic family.

52. For example, Hippolytus laments that he cannot curse the gods in revenge for his demise (*Hipp.* 1415). This would be an appropriate course of revenge as he himself was killed by a curse.

53. See pp. 58, 71 for stories involving peaceful resolution of disputes among the gods.

54. Cf. Hesiod (*Works and Days* 202-12) for the suggestion that it is foolish to fight against someone stronger.

55. Cf. Roisman (2005) 64.

56. Cf. Roiman (2005) 67. Cf. Herodotus 1.37 for Croesus' anti-heroic stance towards his son, and the young man's distress at being dishonoured by the townsmen and his wife for abstaining from fighting. Konstan (1987: 64) notes that this story reveals Croesus' failure to see that a long life is not as valuable as a short life where death achieves honour (the choice of Achilles).

57. Cf. Fantham et al. (1994) 63-4; Pomeroy (2002) 58-62.

58. See Ducat (2006).

59. Compare Sophocles' *Ajax* where the protagonist feels that the only way to save his honour is through suicide.

60. MacDowell (1978) 160; cf. 74-5; Roisman (2005) 117; cf. 188-9; Todd (1993) 183; cf. 142-3. Conversely good military service was an important qualification for political leadership (Roisman 2005: 118-19).

61. On Cleonymus, see MacDowell (1995) 24-5; Sommerstein (1986); Storey (1989). Cf. also Archilochus fr. 5 West.

62. Aeschines 3.148, 151, 152, 155, 159, 175-6, 181, 187, 226, 244, 253. Cf. Plutarch *Dem.* 20. Demosthenes also insults Aeschines in manifold ways in *De Corona*.

63. Cohen (1995) 78-82; cf. Sommerstein (1986) 104.

64. Carey (1997) 238-9. See also MacDowell (1978: 126-7) and Todd (1993: 258-62) for differing interpretations of this law.

65. Christ (1998a) 35.

66. See esp. Fisher (1992) on *hybris*. Cf. also Cohen (1995) 87-142; MacDowell (1978) 109-32; Roisman (2005) 73, 92-4; Todd (1993) 268-79.

67. Notably in the extant texts there is a tendency towards dropping or minimising lawsuits in these circumstances. See Demosthenes 54.1 and further below p. 97 on Demosthenes 21 and Aeschines 1.62-4.

68. Van Wees (1992) 162; cf. also W. Harris (2001); Lintott (1982) 174-5; Seaford (1994) 6. Athanassakis (1992: 180) links the alleged drop in violence to the rise in agriculture.

69. See p. 72 for suggestions of a less violent Homeric undersociety.

70. See pp. 25, 143nn.6-7.

71. See Christ (1998a) 191-2; Cohen (1995) 135; Fisher (1998a) 59-60; (1998b) 75-7; W. Harris (2001) 189; Roisman (2005) 73. Herman (1998b: 613) claims honour and revenge were not viewed positively in Athens. However, it is important to stress that ideas are not black and white, but there is complexity about how they are viewed depending on the circumstances. Cf. pp. 6-7.

72. Euthynus is characterised as young. Cf. pp. 85-6 on the association of violence with youth. It is possible that this dispute was related to athletic ability. See pp. 91-2 on the angry responses by athletes to slights to their abilities.

73. Cf. Fisher (1992) 35, 94. See p. 144n.19.

74. See pp. 122n.31, 127n.71 on Aristotle (*Rhet.* 1378b). He adds that anger can be greater if the slight occurs in front of others. See Allen (2000: 59-60) and W. Harris (2001: 134) on the role of anger in slights.

75. Examples occur at Aeschines 1.61; Demosthenes 47.19; 54.3-5, 7; Lysias 3.6-8, 15-18; 4.8. See Christ (1998a) 192 n. 98; Cohen (1995) 136. See also Daly and Wilson (1988a) 126.

76. Carawan (1993) 259; P. Wilson (1991) 170. Christ (1998a: 161ff.) discusses in detail the tension felt by Athenians between the need to take adequate revenge for a slight and the danger of this response turning into excessive violence. Cf. Allen (2000) 124-5.

77. See p. 6.

78. MacDowell (1963) 75.

79. Cf. Cohen (1995) 95.

80. Cf. W. Harris (1997) 364, contra Herman (1995).

81. Cohen (1995) 86, 94, 100; cf. Roisman (2005) 75-9.

82. Cf. also Demosthenes 54.19 on the problems of escalation from insult to murder. Although he makes the point to illustrate why it is better to go to court, nevertheless, his model suggests that escalation of this type was thought to happen in brawls.

83. Herman (1993) 418; (1995) 48-50; (1996) 14-15; (1998a) 213; (2000).

84. See pp. 6-7. Cf. Cohen (1995: 85) on the need for individual participants to make decisions about how to proceed in any given circumstances.

85. Demosthenes repeatedly argues for the death of Meidias (21.12, 21, 49, 70, 92, 142, 152, 180-2, 201).

86. On this allegation see Fisher (1992) 38; E. Harris (1989) 132-6; MacDowell (1990) 23-8.

87. Cf. Lysias 10.13, 24.18; Allen (2000) 123-4; Christ (1998a) 33; Cohen (1995) 99.

88. Christ (1998b) 535. See examples on pp. 76-8.

89. See Fisher (2001) 190-1.

90. MacDowell (1990) on 21.112. Cf. Christ (1998a) 34; Fisher (1992) 102; Roisman (2005) 93.

91. Christ (1998a: 125-6) notes that Strato is caught in the cross-fire of a dispute between rich men and none of them comes to his aid.

92. Cf. Christ (1998a) 123.

93. See pp. 90-1.

94. Burnett (1998) 54.

95. Cf. Cohen (1995) 99.

96. Cf. Christ (1998b) 535.

97. Cohen (1995) 119; cf. Roisman (2005) 17-21. On the typical characteristics of young men in Attic orations, see Roisman (2005: 14), with references to other scholarship in his n. 10. See pp. 85-6.

98. Herman (2000) 16; cf. (1993), (1994), (1995).

99. Carey (1997) 84, 96-7.

100. Allen (2000) 60-1; cf. Adkins (1972) 15; Carey (1994) 182; Christ (1998a) 35; Cohen (1995) 112, 188; Dover (1974) 230-1, 238; Roisman (2005) 67; Todd (1993) 160-2. Carey (1994) and Christ (1998a: 36) express reservations about viewing litigation primarily as status competition.

101. Christ (1998a) 34-5.

102. See p. 115.

103. See p. 120.

104. Herman (2000) notes the possible comparison to the tale of Oedipus, but does not elaborate upon it because of his decision to ignore tragedy in favour of oratory in his discussion of Athenian revenge.

105. Cf. Herodotus 6.69 for slurs directed against Demaratus' concerning his paternity. See pp. 5, 46.

106. This choice of implement may well have added to the insult felt by Oedipus.

107. Cf. Demosthenes 54.19. See pp. 77-8, 95-6, 99.

108. See pp. 6, 77, 96. For comic treatment of the problems associated with hitting a father see Aristophanes' *Clouds*.

109. See pp. 104, 111, 114.

110. Strauss (1993) 13-17.

111. See Plutarch *On Brotherly Love* (*Mor.* 478a-92d) where brothers are said to fight most frequently over inheritance and women. See pp. 70, 105-6, 112-16, 149n.40. See also Daly and Wilson (1988a: 30-3) and Daly et al. (2001) on fratricide.

112. See p. 18.

113. According to the scholiast, in *Oedipus* the servants of Laius blind him, presumably as a punishment on discovering he is the murderer of Laius (Euripides fr. 541Kn; cf. Webster (1967) 241ff.).

114. Cf. pp. 88-9.

115. Cf. however Euripides *Phoe.* 374, where he says that kin strife is terrible. Cairns (1993: 244) makes a similar point.

116. Seaford (1994: 346-50) argues that the self-destruction of the ruling family in these plays is beneficial to the *polis*.

117. See further on pp. 103, 107.

5. What Motivates Orestes?

1. Scholars who note (and in some cases reject) this reading include: Allen (2000) 19-21; Burnett (1998) 105; Cohen (1995) 3, 16; Goldhill (1992) 29; Lloyd-Jones (1971) 94; Mossman (1995) 172; Thomson (1941) 272-3.

2. Burnett (1998) 144.

3. D'Arms and Hulley (1946) 211-12.

4. Mark Davies (1969) 238; cf. also Olson (1990) 68.

5. See Burnett (1998) 99-100; cf. Belfiore (2000) 132-9; Garvie (1986) ix-xv; Goldhill (1992) 31; McHardy (2005) 131. Aristotle (*Po.* 1453b19-22) notes that kin-killing is the best plot theme for tragedy.

6. Cropp (1988) xxx; Mossman (1995) 173.

7. Cf. the story of Gyges on p. 49.

8. Lloyd-Jones (1996) speculates on the contents of the three fragmentary plays about Thyestes by Sophocles. Webster is equally unsure about the content of Euripides' *Thyestes,* but assumes that it focuses on the feast (1967: 114). For an extant version of Thyestes' feast, see Seneca's *Thyestes* which is presumably derived from a Greek source.

9. Padel (1995) 208; cf. McHardy (2005) 145.

10. Women are often thought to turn to men for help in achieving revenge. See p. 13.

11. Cf. Hdt. 3.88, where Darius marries the wife of the former kings, along with other royal women presumably to consolidate his power and the claims of his sons to the throne.

12. Cf. Rabinowitz (1993) 107.

13. The chorus also talk of exile for her following the murder of Agamemnon. See pp. 15-19, 21 on the predominance of exile as a response to murder.

14. Cf. the discussion of Medea on p. 62.

15. The use of revenge as a more acceptable or 'moral' motive for a killing is discussed on p. 115 below.

16. See Seaford (1998: 125) on the connection between money and power in tragedy.

17. See e.g. Aeschylus *Ag.* 1280-3; *Cho.* 571-8; *Eum.* 462-4; Euripides *El.* 87-9; 848-51; *IT* 558; Sophocles *El.* 1495-6.

18. Burnett (1998) 113. See p. 45.

19. Burnett (1998) 138.

20. See pp. 15, 22.

21. Cf. p. 16.

22. See p. 54.

23. McHardy (2004).

24. See p. 37.

25. See pp. 89-90, 94-5.

26. Goldhill (2004: 439) thinks Electra sees herself and Chrysothemis as tyrannicides, but she is consistently less concerned with the political aspect than her brother and more concerned with blood revenge.

27. Foley (1993) 113; McHardy (2004) 109.

28. Castor (and silent Pollux) also maintain that Apollo's command was not wise (Euripides *El.* 1245-6).

29. Cf. Anaxagoras (fr. A107 DK) where it is said that while the male provides the sperm, the female provides the place for it to go. Aristotle comments on this passage (*Gen. An.* 763b30), but seems to prefer the view of Democritus who says that both parents provide semen (764a7ff.). Nevertheless, he later says that the female does not discharge semen, but instead provides the uterus (765b8ff.). Cf. Sommerstein (1989) on lines 657-66 for other later variants of the same belief. Cf. also Gagarin (1976) 102; Maclean (1980) 35-9.

30. Cf. Littman (1979) 28ff.; Luban (1987) 301. Aristotle (*EE* 1244a10) also places ties to father above ties to mother.

31. The position of wives is not disputed. Clytemnestra is not kin to Agamemnon, cf. *Eum.* 212, 605.

32. Cf. Aristotle (*Rhet.* 1401a38-b1) on the fallacy of this division in the *Orestes* of Theodectes.

33. See p. 46.

34. See p. 16.

35. See pp. 8-9.

36. See pp. 101-2 on Eteocles and Polynices.

37. On Euripides' play see Collard, Cropp and Lee (1995) 121-47; Webster (1967) 136ff. Cf. also Euripides' lost *Peliades* and *Oeneus*, where sons return from exile to reclaim their patrimony.

38. She almost kills him unwittingly, thinking him to be the murderer of her son, but is prevented. See pp. 39-40.

39. See pp. 104, 114

40. E.g. brothers Artaxerxes and Cyrus (Xenophon *Anab.* 1.1ff.; *Hell.* 3.1.2); Croesus and his brother (Herodotus 1.92); Polycrates of Samos and his brothers (3.39); Sesostris of Egypt and his brother (2.107-8); Xerxes and his brother Masistes (9.108-13 with Sancisi-Weerdenburg 1993: 28-30); Artaxerxes and his brother Darius (Diodorus Siculus 11.69). The story of Cambyses and Smerdis discussed on p. 14 is also an excellent example of fratricide because of fear of a brother taking power (Herodotus 3.30-2). Cf. pp. 101-2.

41. I have argued elsewhere that mothers can be extremely supportive of their sons and that they often seek to promote their political careers (McHardy 2004: 103-4). See pp. 38-9

42. See p. 38 on Pheretima.

43. See Sprawski (2006) on Alexander of Pherae.

44. Cf. *Hiero* 3.8, where Xenophon argues that private citizens love their families, but tyrants tend to kill family members and be killed by them. See also Isocrates 8.113. See Seaford (1994) 345.

45. See p. 99.

46. See pp. 104, 111.

47. In Plato's fairytale version (*Rep.* 359d-60b) Gyges with the help of a magic ring seduces Candaules' wife and with her aid slays her husband to seize power. Cf. Gould (1989) 31; Thomson (1941) 79.

48. Ferguson (1995) 353-4.

49. Cf. Lendon (2000) 16.

50. Ferguson (1995) 58.

51. Cf. Herman (1987) 126.

52. See p. 11.

53. See Seaford (1994: 369-70) on child-killings in tragedy as perverted sacrifices.

54. See pp. 43-4, 63, 106.

55. See p. 14.

56. Isocrates (9.38) says that Cyrus impiously killed his maternal grandfather.

57. Mossman (1995: 174) notes that through Harpagus' desire for personal revenge the Medes lose their independence. She postulates that the story reflects criticism of those who choose private revenge over the interests of the community at large. See pp. 23-5 on Athena.

58. See pp. 14, 131n.207.

59. See p. 76.

60. See MacDowell (1963: 60-2) on *bouleusis*.

61. Trans. by Carey (1997) 64.

62. The location of their meeting implies once again that Athena was thought to preside over the settlement of disputes and ensure community harmony. Cf. pp. 23-5.

63. Cf. Carey (1997) 74. On the contrast of sycophancy and revenge (e.g. Demosthenes 53.2), see Christ (1998a) 34-5; Cohen (1995) 102, 106, 171; Harvey (1990); Kurihara (2003) 468.

64. Carey (1992) 4-5; (1997) 180; Kurihara (2003) 473. Cf. Trevett (1992: ch. 5) on the political career of Apollodorus. See Rhodes (1998) on enmity in the Athenian law courts. Cf. Roisman (2005) 73.

65. See MacDowell (1963: 54) on this case.

Bibliography

Abu-Lughod, L. (1987) *Veiled Sentiments: Honor and Poetry in a Bedouin Society*, Berkeley: University of California Press.

Adkins, A. (1960a) *Merit and Responsibility. A Study in Greek Values*, Oxford: Clarendon Press.

—— (1960b) ' "Honour" and "Punishment" in the Homeric Poems', *Bulletin of the Institute of Classical Studies* 7, 23-32.

—— (1966) 'Basic Greek Values in Euripides' *Hecuba* and *Hercules Furens*', *Classical Quarterly* 16, 193-219.

—— (1969) 'Threatening, Abusing and Feeling Angry in the Homeric Poems', *Journal of the Hellenic Society* 89, 7-21.

—— (1972) 'Homeric Gods and the Values of Homeric Society', *Journal of the Hellenic Society* 92, 1-15.

Albert, B. (1989) 'Yanomami "Violence": Inclusive Fitness or Ethnographer's Representation?', *Current Anthropology* 30, 637-40.

Alexakis, E. (1999) 'Το έθιμο του γδικιωμού στη Μάνη', *Laconian Diary*.

Allen, D. (2000) *The World of Prometheus: the Politics of Punishing in Democratic Athens*, Princeton: Princeton University Press.

Arieti, J. (1985) 'Achilles' Guilt', *Classical Jouranal* 80, 193-203.

Arnott, P. (1970) 'Greek Drama as Education', *Educational Theatre Journal* 22.35-42.

Ashby, G. (1998) *A Commentary on the Book of Exodus*, Grand Rapids: Wm. B. Eerdmans.

Athanassakis, A.N. (1992) 'Cattle and Honour in Homer and Hesiod', *Ramus* 21, 156-86.

Axelrod, R. (1984) *The Evolution of Cooperation*, London: Penguin.

Bar-Elli, G. and Heyd, D. (1986) 'Can Revenge be Just or Otherwise be Justified?', *Theoria* 52, 68-86.

Barlow, S. (1989) 'Stereotype and Reversal in Euripides' *Medea*', *Greece & Rome* 36, 158-71.

Barrett, W. (1964) *Euripides' Hippolytus. A Commentary*, Oxford: Oxford University Press.

Bateman, J. (1958) 'Lysias and the Law', *Transactions of the American Philological Association* 89, 276-85.

Belfiore, E. (1998) 'Harming Friends: Problematic Reciprocity in Greek Tragedy', in C. Gill, N. Postlethwaite and R. Seaford (eds) *Reciprocity in Ancient Greece*, Oxford: Oxford University Press, 139-58.

—— (2000) *Murder Among Friends*, Oxford: Oxford University Press.

Beye, C. (1964) 'Homeric Battle Narrative and Catalogues', *Harvard Studies in Classical Philology* 68, 345-73.

Black-Michaud, J. (1975) *Cohesive Force: Feud in the Mediterranean and the Middle East*, Oxford: Blackwell.

Bibliography

Blundell, M. (1989) *Helping Friends and Harming Enemies: a Study in Sophocles and Greek Ethics*, Cambridge: Cambridge University Press.

Boehm, C. (1984) *Blood Revenge: the Anthropology of Feuding in Montenegro and Other Tribal Societies*, Lawrence, Kan.: University Press of Kansas.

Bongie, E.B. (1977) 'Heroic Elements in the *Medea* of Euripides', *Transactions of the American Philological Association* 107, 27-56.

Bonner, R. and Smith, G. (1930-8) *The Administration of Justice from Homer to Aristotle*, 2 vols, Chicago: University of Chicago Press.

Bourdieu, P. (1977) *Outline of a Theory of Practice*, Cambridge: Cambridge University Press.

Braund, D. (1998) 'Herodotos on the Problematics of Reciprocity', in C. Gill, N. Postlethwaite and R. Seaford (eds) *Reciprocity in Ancient Greece*, Oxford: Oxford University Press, 159-80.

Brooks, C. (1977) 'The Heroic Impulse of the *Odyssey*', *Classical World* 70, 455-6.

Brown, Calvin (1966) 'Odysseus and Polyphemus: the Name and the Curse', *Comparative Literature* 18, 193-202.

Brown, Christopher (1989) 'Ares, Aphrodite, and the Laughter of the Gods', *Phoenix* 43, 283-93.

——— (1996) 'In the Cyclops' Cave: Revenge and Justice in *Odyssey* 9', *Mnemosyne* 49, 1-29.

Bryant, J.M. (1996) *Moral Codes and Social Structure in Ancient Greece*, Albany, NY: State University of New York Press.

Burnett, A. (1971) *Catastrophe Survived: Euripides' Plays of Mixed Reversal*, Oxford: Oxford University Press.

——— (1973) 'Medea and the Tragedy of Revenge', *Classical Philology* 68, 1-24.

——— (1998) *Revenge in Attic and Later Tragedy*, Berkeley: University of California Press.

Buxton, R. (1980) 'Blindness and Limits: Sophokles and the Logic of Myth', *Journal of the Hellenic Society* 100, 22-37.

——— (1982) *Persuasion in Greek Tragedy – a study of Peitho*, Cambridge: Cambridge University Press.

Cairns, D.L. (1993) *Aidos. The Psychology and Ethics of Honour and Shame in Ancient Greek Literature*. Oxford: Oxford University Press.

——— (1996a) 'Veiling, αἰδώς and a Red-Figure Amphora by Phintias', *Journal of the Hellenic Society* 116, 152-8.

——— (1996b) '*Hybris*, Dishonour and Thinking Big', *Journal of the Hellenic Society* 116, 1-32.

——— (1996c) 'Off with Her ΑΙΔΩΣ: Herodotus 1.8.3-4', *Classical Quarterly* 46, 78-83.

——— (2001) 'Affronts and Quarrels in the *Iliad*', in D. Cairns (ed.) *Oxford Readings in Homer's Iliad*, Oxford: Oxford University Press, 203-19.

——— (2002) 'The Meaning of the Veil in Ancient Greek Culture', in L. Llewellyn-Jones (ed.) *Women's Dress in the Ancient Greek World*, London and Swansea: Duckworth with the Classical Press of Wales, 73-93.

——— (2003) 'Ethics, Ethology, Terminology: Iliadic Anger and the Cross-Cultural Study of Emotion', in S. Braund and G. Most (eds) *Ancient Anger, Yale Classical Studies* 32, Cambridge: Cambridge University Press, 11-49.

Campbell, J. (1964) *Honour, Family and Patronage*, Oxford: Clarendon Press.

Carawan, E. (1993) 'The Tetralogies and Athenian Homicide Trials', *American Journal of Philology* 114, 235-70.

Carey, C. (1994) 'Legal Space in Classical Athens', *Greece & Rome* 41, 1-15.

——— (1995) 'Rape and Adultery in Athenian Law' *Classical Quarterly* 45, 407-17.

——— (1997) *Trials from Classical Athens*, London and New York: Routledge.

——— (ed.) (1989) *Lysias: Selected Speeches*, Cambridge: Cambridge University Press.

——— (ed.) (1992) *Apollodoros, Against Neaira*, Warminster: Aris and Phillips.

Cartledge, P., Millett, P. and Todd, S. (eds) (1990) *Nomos: Essays in Athenian Law, Politics and Society*, Cambridge: Cambridge University Press.

Castellani, V. (1980) 'Two Divine Scandals: Ovid *Met.* 2.68ff. and 4.171ff. and his Sources', *Transactions of the American Philological Association* 110, 37-50.

Chagnon, N. (1988) 'Life Histories, Blood Revenge, and Warfare in a Tribal Population', *Science* 239, 985-92.

Christ, M. (1998a) *The Litigious Athenian*, Baltimore and London: John Hopkins University Press.

——— (1998b) 'Legal Self-Help on Private Property in Classical Athens', *American Journal of Philology* 119, 521-45.

Cohen, D. (1983) *Theft in Athenian Law*, München: Beck.

——— (1985) 'A Note on Aristophanes and the Punishment of Adultery in Athenian Law', *Zeitschrift der Savigny-Stiftung* 102, 385-7.

——— (1991) *Law, Sexuality and Society*, Cambridge: Cambridge University Press.

——— (1995) *Law, Violence and Community in Classical Athens*, Cambridge: Cambridge University Press.

——— (1998) 'Women, Property and Status in Demosthenes 41 and 57', *Dike* 1, 53-61.

——— (2005) 'Theories of Punishment', in M. Gagarin and D. Cohen (eds) *The Cambridge Companion to Ancient Greek Law*, Cambridge: Cambridge University Press, 170-90.

Collard, C. (ed.) (1991) *Euripides: Hecuba*, Warminster: Aris and Phillips.

———, Cropp, M. and Lee, K. (eds) (1995) *Euripides: Selected Fragmentary Plays*, vol. I, Warminster: Aris and Phillips.

———, Cropp, M. and Gibert, J. (eds) (2004) *Euripides: Selected Fragmentary Plays*, vol. II, Oxford: Aris and Phillips.

Cropp, M. (ed.) (1988) *Euripides: Electra*, Warminster: Aris and Phillips.

d'Arms, E. and Hulley, K. (1946) 'The Oresteia-Story in the *Odyssey*', *Transactions of the American Philological Association* 77, 207-13.

Daly, M. and Wilson, M. (1988a) *Homicide*, New York: Aldine de Gruyter.

——— and Wilson, M. (1988b) 'Evolutionary Social Psychology and Family Homicide', *Science* 242, 519-24.

——— and Wilson, M. (1998) 'Sexual Rivalry and Sexual Conflict', *Theoretical Criminology* 2, 291-310.

——— and Wilson, M. (1999) 'An Evolutionary Psychological Perspective on Homicide', in D. Smith and M. Zahn (eds) *Homicide Studies: a Sourcebook of Social Research,* 58-71.

——— Wilson, M., Salmon, C., Hiraiwa-Hasegawa, M. and Hasegawa, T. (2001) 'Siblicide and Seniority', *Homicide Studies* 5: 30-45.

Davies, G. (1967) *Exodus. An Introduction and Commentary*, London: SCM Press.

Davies, Malcolm (1987) 'Aeschylus' Clytemnestra: Sword or Axe?', *Classical Quarterly* 37, 65-75.

——— (1989) *The Epic Cycle*, Bristol: Bristol Classical Press.

Davies, Mark (1969) 'Thoughts on the *Oresteia* before Aeschylus', *Bulletin de Correspondence Héllenique* 93, 214-60.

Dawkins, R. (1989) *The Selfish Gene*, Oxford: Oxford University Press.

de Romilly, J. (1971) 'Le vengeance comme explication historique dans l'oeuvre d'Herodote', *Revue des Etudes Grecques* 84, 314-37.

de Ste. Croix (1972) *Origins of the Peloponnesian War*, London: Duckworth.

Deacy, S. (2005) 'Herakles and his "Girl": Athena, Heroism and Beyond', in L. Rawlings and H. Bowden (eds) *Herakles and Hercules*, Swansea: Classical Press of Wales, 37-50.

Deliyanni, H. (1985) 'Blood Vengeance Attitudes in Mani and Corsica', unpub. typescript held by the Department of Sociology, University of Exeter.

Devereux, G. (1973) 'The Self-Blinding of Oidipous in Sophocles' *Oidipous Tyrannos*', *Journal of the Hellenic Society* 93, 36-49.

Diamond, A. (1971) *Primitive Law, Past and Present*, London: Methuen.

Djilas, M. (1958) *Land Without Justice*, New York: Harcourt Brace.

Dodds, E.R. (1951) *The Greeks and the Irrational*, Berkeley: University of California Press.

—— (ed.) (1960) *Euripides' Bacchae*, Oxford: Oxford University Press.

Donlan, W. (1993) 'Duelling with Gifts in the *Iliad*', *Colby Quarterly* 29, 155-72.

Dover, K. (1968) *Aristophanes: Clouds*, Oxford: Clarendon Press.

—— (1974) *Greek Popular Morality in the Time of Plato and Aristotle*, Oxford: Oxford University Press.

—— (1983) 'The Portrayal of Moral Evaluation in Greek Poetry', *Journal of the Hellenic Society* 103, 35-48.

Ducat, J. (2006) 'The Spartan "Tremblers"', in S. Hodkinson and A. Powell (eds) *Sparta and War*, Swansea: Classical Press of Wales, 1-56.

Dunbar, R., Clark, A. and Hurst, N. (1995) 'Conflict and Co-operation Among the Vikings: Contingent Behavioural Decisions', *Ethnology and Sociobiology* 16.3, 233-46.

Durham, M. (1909) *High Albania*. London: E. Arnold.

—— (1928) *Some Tribal Origins, Laws and Customs of the Balkans*, London: George Allen and Unwin.

Easterling, P. (1977) 'The Infanticide in Euripides' *Medea*', *Yale Classical Studies* 25, 177-91.

Edwards, M. (ed.) (1995) *Greek Orators IV: Andocides*, Warminster: Aris and Phillips.

—— and Usher, S. (eds) (1985) *Greek Orators I – Antiphon and Lysias*, Warminster: Aris and Phillips.

ESRC Violence Research Programme (2002) *Taking Stock: What Do We Know about Interpersonal Violence?* London: Economic and Social Research Council.

Fantham, E., Foley, H., Kampen, N., Pomeroy, S. and Shapiro, H. (1994) *Women in the Classical World*, Oxford: Oxford University Press.

Ferguson, R.B. (1995) *Yanomami Warfare*, Sante Fe, NM: School of American Research Press.

—— (2001) 'Materialist, Cultural and Biological Theories on Why Yanomami make War', *Anthropological Theory* 1, 99-116.

Finley, M.I. (1979) *The World of Odysseus*, Harmondsworth: Penguin.

Fisher, N. (1976) 'Hybris and Dishonour 1', *Greece & Rome* 23, 177-93.

—— (1979) 'Hybris and Dishonour 2', *Greece & Rome* 26, 32-47.

—— (1992) *Hybris. A Study in the Values of Honour and Shame in Ancient Greece*, Warminster: Aris and Phillips.

—— (1998a) 'Workshops of Villains', in K. Hopwood (ed.) *Organized Crime in Antiquity*, London: Duckworth with the Classical Press of Wales, 53-96.

—— (1998b) 'Masculinity, Violence and the Law in Classical Athens', in L. Foxhall and J. Salmon (eds) *When Men were Men*, London: Routledge, 68-97.

—— (2001) *Aeschines: Against Timarchos*, Oxford: Clarendon Press.

Fitton, J. (1970) 'That Was No Lady, That Was', *Classical Quarterly* 20, 56-66.

Flower, M. and Marincola, J. (2002) *Herodotus: Histories Book IX*, Cambridge: Cambridge University Press.

Foley, H.P. (1981) 'The Concept of Women in Athenian Drama', in H.P. Foley (ed.) *Reflections of Women in Antiquity*, New York: Gordon and Breach Science Publishers.

—— (1989) 'Medea's Divided Self', *Classical Antiquity* 8, 61-85.

—— (1993) 'The Politics of Tragic Lamentation', in A. Sommerstein, S. Halliwell, J. Henderson and B. Zimmerman (eds) *Tragedy, Comedy and the Polis*, Bari: Levante Editori, 101-43.

—— (2001) *Female Acts in Greek Tragedy*, Princeton: Princeton University Press.

Foxhall, L. (1991) 'Response to Eva Cantarella', in M. Gagarin (ed.) *Symposion 1990*, Köln: Bölhau, 297-304.

—— (1996) 'The Law and the Lady: Women and Legal Proceedings in Classical Athens', in L. Foxhall and A. Lewis (eds) *Greek Law in its Political Setting*, Oxford: Clarendon Press, 133-52.

Freeman, D. (1983) *Margaret Mead and Samoa: the Making and Unmaking of an Anthropological Myth*, Cambridge Mass, Harvard University Press.

Fuchs, J. (1993-4) 'The Greek Gang at Troy', *Classical World* 87, 62-4.

Gagarin, M. (1987) 'Morality in Homer', *Classical Philology* 82, 285-306.

—— (1973) '*Dike* in the *Works and Days*', *Classical Philology* 68, 81-94.

—— (1974a) '*Dike* in Greek Thought', *Classical Philology* 69, 186-97.

—— (1974b) 'Hesiod's Dispute with Perses', *Transactions of the American Philological Association* 104, 103-11.

—— (1976) *Aeschylean Drama*, Berkeley: University of California Press.

—— (1979) 'The Prosecution of Homicide in Athens', *Greek, Roman and Byzantine Studies* 20, 301-24.

—— (1981) *Drakon and Early Athenian Homicide Law*, New Haven: Yale University Press.

—— (1986) *Early Greek Law*, Berkeley: University of California Press.

—— (2001) 'Women's Voices in Attic Oratory', in A. Lardinois and L. McClure (eds) *Making Silence Speak*, Princeton: Princeton University Press, 161-76.

—— (ed.) (1997) *Antiphon: the Speeches*, Cambridge: Cambridge University Press.

Gager, J. (ed.) (1992) *Curse Tablets and Binding Spells from the Ancient World*, Oxford: Oxford University Press.

Gardner J.F. (1989) 'Aristophanes and Male Anxiety – the Defense of the Oikos', *Greece & Rome* 36, 51-62.

Garner, R. (1987) *Law and Society in Classical Athens*, Wolfboro, NH: Croom Helm.

Garvie, A. (ed.) (1986) *Choephori*, Oxford: Oxford University Press.

Gaskin, R. (1990) 'Do Homeric Heroes make Real Decisions?', *Classical Quarterly* 40, 1-15.

Gibert, J. (1999) 'Review of Burnett, *Revenge in Attic and Later Tragedy*', *Bryn Mawr Classical Review* 9.2, 1-6.

Gill, C. (1996) *Personality in Greek Epic, Tragedy and Philosophy*, Oxford: Oxford University Press.

Bibliography

Ginat, J. (1987) *Blood Disputes among Bedouin and Rural Arabs in Israel – Revenge, Mediation, Outcasting and Family Honor*, Pittsburgh: University of Pittsburgh Press.

Girard, R. (1977) *Violence and the Sacred*, London: Johns Hopkins University Press.

Glenn, J. (1978) 'The Polyphemus Myth: its Origin and Interpretation', *Greece & Rome* 25, 141-55.

Glotz, G. (1904) *La solidarité de la famille dans le droit criminel en Grèce*, Paris: Fontemoing.

Golden, M. (1990) *Children and Childhood in Classical Athens*, Baltimore: John Hopkins University Press.

Goldhill, S. (1992) *Aeschylus: Oresteia*, Cambridge: Cambridge University Press.

——— (2004) Review of Rosen and Luiter (eds) *Andreia*, in *Classical Review* 54 437-39.

Gould, J. (1989) *Herodotus*, London: Weidenfeld and Nicolson.

Graf, F. (1997) 'Medea, the Enchantress from Afar: Remarks on a Well Known Myth', in J. Clauss and S. Iles Johnston (eds) *Medea: Essays on Medea in Myth, Literature, Philosophy and Art*, Princeton: Princeton University Press, 21-43.

Gregory, J. (1991) *Euripides and the Instruction of the Athenians*, Ann Arbor: University of Michigan Press.

Haft, A. (1996-7) 'The Mercurial Significance of Raiding: Baby Hermes and Animal Theft in Contemporary Crete', *Arion* 4, 27-48.

Hall, D. (1994) *Albania and the Albanians*, London and New York: Pinter.

Hall, E. (1989) *Inventing the Barbarian: Greek Self-Definition through Tragedy*, Oxford: Oxford University Press.

Hallock, R. (1969) *Persepolis Fortification Tablets*, Chicago: University of Chicago Press.

Halperin, D (1990) *One Hundred Years of Homosexuality*, New York: Routledge.

Hansen, M. (1981) 'The Prosecution of Homicide in Athens: a Reply', *Greek, Roman and Byzantine Studies* 22, 11-30.

——— (1983) *'Graphe* or *Dike Traumatos?'*, *Greek, Roman and Byzantine Studies* 24, 307-20.

Hardy, M. (1963) *Blood Feuds and the Payment of Blood Money in the Middle East*, Leiden: Brill.

Harrell, S. (1991) 'Apollo's Fraternal Threats: Language of Succession and Domination in the *Homeric Hymn to Hermes'*, *Greek, Roman and Byzantine Studies* 32, 307-29.

Harris, E. (1989) 'Demosthenes' Speech against Meidias', *Harvard Studies in Classical Philology* 92, 117-36.

——— (1990) 'Did the Athenians Regard Seduction as a Worse Crime than Rape?', *Classical Quarterly* 40, 370-7.

——— (2004) 'Did Rape Exist in Classical Athens?', *Dike* 7, 41-83.

Harris, W. (1997) 'Lysias III and Athenian Beliefs about Revenge', *Classical Quarterly* 47, 363-6.

——— (2001) *Restraining Rage: the Ideology of Anger Control in Classical Antiquity*, Cambridge, Mass: Harvard University Press.

Harrison, A. (1968) *The Law of Athens*, vol. 1, Oxford: Oxford University Press.

——— (1971) *The Law of Athens*, vol. 2, Oxford: Oxford University Press.

Harrison, T. (2000) *Divinity and History*, Oxford: Clarendon Press.

Harvey, D. (1985) 'Women in Thucydides', *Arethusa* 18, 67-90.

——— (1990) 'The Sykophant and Sykophancy: Vexatious Redefinition', in P.

Cartledge, P. Millet and S. Todd (eds) *Nomos*, Cambridge: Cambridge University Press.

Hasluck, M. (1954) *The Unwritten Law in Albania*, Cambridge: Cambridge University Press.

Heiden, B. (1998) 'The Simile of the Fugitive Homicide, *Iliad* 24.480-84: Analogy, Foiling and Allusion', *American Journal of Philology* 119, 1-10.

Herman, G. (1987) *Ritualised Friendship and the Greek City*, Cambridge: Cambridge University Press.

―――― (1993) 'Tribal and Civic Codes of Behaviour in Lysias I', *Classical Quarterly* 43, 406-19.

―――― (1994) 'How Violent was Athenian Society?', in S. Hornblower and R. Osborne (eds) *Ritual, Finance, Politics: Athenian Democratic Accounts Presented to David Lewis*, Oxford: Oxford University Press, 99-117.

―――― (1995) 'Honour, Revenge and the State in Fourth Century Athens', in W. Eder (ed.) *Die athenische Demokratie im 4. Jahrhundert v. Chr.*, Stuttgart: Franz Steiner Verlag, 43-66.

―――― (1996) 'Ancient Athens and the Values of Mediterranean Society', *Mediterranean Historical Review* 2.1, 5-36.

―――― (1998a) 'Reciprocity, Altruism and the Prisoner's Dilemma', in C. Gill, N. Postlethwaite and R. Seaford, (eds) *Reciprocity in Ancient Greece*, Oxford: Oxford University Press, 199-225.

―――― (1998b) Review of Cohen, *Law, Violence, and Community*, in *Gnomon* 70, 605-15.

―――― (2000) 'Athenian Beliefs about Revenge: Problems and Methods', *Proceedings of the Cambridge Philological Society* 46, 7-27.

Herzfeld, M. (1980) 'Honour and Shame: Problems in the Comparative Analysis of Moral Systems', *Man* 15, 339-51.

―――― (1985) *The Poetics of Manhood: Contest and Identity in a Cretan Village*, Princeton: Princeton University Press.

―――― (1990) 'Pride and Perjury: Time and the Oath in the Mountain Villages of Crete', *Man* 25, 305-22.

Hogan, J.C. (1972) 'Thucydides 3.52-68 and Euripides' *Hecuba*', *Phoenix* 26, 241-57.

Holst-Warhaft, G. (1992) *Dangerous Voices: Women's Laments and Greek Literature*, London and New York: Routledge.

Hooker, J. (1987) 'Homeric Society: a Shame Culture?', *Greece & Rome* 34, 121-5.

Hornblower, S. (1996) *A Commentary on Thucydides*, vol. 2, *Books IV-V.24*, Oxford: Oxford University Press.

―――― (2003) 'Panionios of Chios and Hermotimos of Pedaia Hdt. 8.104-6', in P. Derow and R. Parker (eds) *Herodotus and his World*, Oxford: Oxford University Press, 37-57.

Hudson-Williams, H. (1951) 'Political Speeches in Athens', *Classical Quarterly* 1, 68-73.

Hunter, V. (1994) *Policing Athens*, Princeton: Princeton University Press.

Iles Johnston, S. (2002) 'Myth, Festival, and Poet: the "Homeric Hymn to Hermes" and its Performative Context', *Classical Philology* 97, 109-32.

Jackson, A. (1993) 'Wars and Raids for Booty in the World of Odysseus', in J. Rich and G. Shipley (eds) *War and Society in the Greek World*, London and New York: Routledge, 64-76.

Jacoby, S. (1985) *Wild Justice: the Evolution of Revenge*, London: Collins.

Bibliography

Jankowski, M. (1991) *Islands in the Street*, Berkeley: University of California Press.

Jones, F. (1941) 'The Formulation of the Revenge Motif in the *Odyssey*', *Transactions of the American Philological Association* 72, 195-202.

Jouan, F. and van Looy, H. (1998) *Euripide, Fragments*, vol. 1, Paris: Les Belles Lettres.

Just, R. (1989) *Women in Athenian Law and Life*, London and New York: Routledge.

Keiser, R. (1986) 'Death Enmity in Thull: Organised Vengeance and Social Change in a Kohistani Community', *American Ethnologist* 13.3, 489-505.

Khalaf, S. (1990) 'Settlement of Violence in Bedouin Society', *Ethnology* 29.3, 225-42.

Kitto, H. (1951) *The Greeks*, Harmondsworth: Penguin.

Kitts, M. (2005) *Sanctified Violence in Homeric Society*, Cambridge: Cambridge University Press.

Knox, B. (1961) 'The Ajax of Sophocles', *Harvard Studies in Classical Philology* 65, 1-37.

―――― (1977) 'The *Medea* of Euripides', *Yale Classical Studies* 25, 193-225.

Knudson, A. (1988) 'Men Killed for Women's Songs', *Culture and History* 3, 79-97.

Konstan, D. (1987) 'Persians, Greeks and Empire', *Arethusa* 20, 59-73.

Kubo, M. (1966) 'The Norm of Myth: Euripides' *Elektra*', *Harvard Studies in Classical Philology* 71, 15-31.

Kurihara, A. (2003) 'Personal Enmity as a Motivation in Forensic Speeches', *Classical Quarterly* 53, 464-77.

Lacey, W. (1968) *The Family in Classical Greece*, Ithaca, NY: Cornell University Press.

Lateiner, D. (1980) 'A Note on ΔΙΚΑΣ ΔΙΔΟΝΑΙ in Herodotus', *Classical Quarterly* 30, 30-2.

―――― (1989) *The Historical Method of Herodotus*, Toronto: University of Toronto Press.

Lendon, J. (2000) 'Homeric Vengeance and the Outbreak of Greek Wars', in H. van Wees (ed.) *War and Violence in Ancient Greece*, London: Duckworth, 1-30.

Lesky, A. (1961) *Göttliche und menschliche Motivation im homerischen Epos*, Heidelberg: Winter.

Lincoln, B. (1976) 'The Indo-European Cattle-Raiding Myth', *History of Religions* 16, 42-65.

Lintott, A. (1982) *Violence, Civil Strife and Revolution in the Classical City 750-330 BC*, London, New York and Sydney: Croom Helm.

Littman, R. (1979) 'Kinship in Athens', *Ancient Society* 10, 5-31.

Lizot, J. (1985) *Tales of the Yanomami*, Cambridge: Cambridge University Press.

Llewellyn-Jones, L. (2003) *Aphrodite's Tortoise: the Veiled Woman of Ancient Greece*, Swansea: Classical Press of Wales.

Lloyd, M. (1999) Review of Burnett, *Revenge in Attic and Later Tragedy*, in *Classical Review* 49, 348-9.

Lloyd-Jones, H. (1971) *The Justice of Zeus*, Berkeley: University of California Press.

―――― (ed.) (1996) *Sophocles' Fragments*, Cambridge, Mass: Loeb Classical Library.

Long, A. (1970) 'Morals and Values in Homer', *Journal of the Hellenic Society* 90, 121-39.

158

Lonsdale, S. (1979) 'Attitudes towards Animals in Ancient Greece', *Greece & Rome* 26, 146-59.

Loraux, N. (1998) *Mothers in Mourning with the essay Of Amnesty and its Opposite*, transl. C. Pache, Ithaca and London: Cornell University Press.

Luban, D. (1987) 'Some Greek Trials: Order and Justice in Homer, Aeschylus and Plato', *Tennessee Law Review* 54, 279-325.

MacDowell, D. (1963) *Athenian Homicide Law in the Age of the Orators*, Manchester: Manchester University Press.

―――― (1978) *The Law in Classical Athens*, Ithaca: Cornell University Press.

―――― (1990) *Demosthenes' Against Meidias*, Oxford: Oxford University Press.

―――― (1995) *Aristophanes and Athens: an Introduction to the Plays,* Oxford: Oxford University Press.

Mackenzie, M. (1981) *Plato on Punishment*, Berkeley: University of California Press.

Maclean, I. (1980) *The Renaissance Notion of Woman*, Cambridge: Cambridge University Press.

McHardy, F. (2004) 'Women's Influence on Revenge in Ancient Greece', in F. McHardy and E. Marshall (eds) *Women's Influence on Classical Civilization*, London and New York: Routledge, 92-114.

―――― (2005) 'From Treacherous Wives to Murderous Mothers: Filicide in Tragic Fragments', in F. McHardy, J. Robson and D. Harvey (eds) *Lost Dramas of Classical Athens*, Exeter: Exeter University Press, 129-50.

―――― (2008) 'The Trial by Water in Greek Myth and Literature', *Leeds International Classical Studies* 7.1.

―――― (forthcoming) 'The Language of Avengers in Greek Texts', in D. Cairns and F. McHardy (eds) *The Vocabulary of Vengeance in Ancient Greece*, Swansea: Classical Press of Wales.

Mead, M. (1931) 'Jealousy: Primitive and Civilized', in S.D. Schmalhausen and V.E. Calverton (eds) *Woman's Coming of Age*, New York: Liveright, 35-48.

Meridor, R. (1978) 'Hecuba's Revenge: Some Observations on Euripides' *Hecuba*', *American Journal of Philology* 99, 28-35.

Michelakis, P. (2002) *Achilles in Greek Tragedy*, Cambridge: Cambridge University Press.

Milani, C. (1997) 'Il lessico della vendetta e del perdono nel mundo classico', in M. Sordi (ed.) *Amnestia, Perdono e Vendetta nel Mundo Antico*, Milan: Vita e Pensiero, 3-18.

Miller, W.I. (2006) *An Eye for an Eye*, Cambridge: Cambridge University Press.

Millet, P. (1998) 'Encounters in the Agora', in P. Cartledge, P. Millett and S. von Reden (eds) *Kosmos*, Cambridge: Cambridge University Press, 203-28.

Mills, S. (2000) 'Achilles, Patroclus and Parental Care in Some Homeric Similes', *Greece & Rome* 47, 3-18.

Mirhady, D.C. and Too, Y.L. (2000) *Isocrates I*, Austin: University of Texas Press.

Mitchell, L. and Rhodes, P. (1996) 'Friends and Enemies in Athenian Politics', *Greece & Rome* 43, 11-30.

Morris, I. (1986) 'The Use and Abuse of Homer', *Classical Antiquity* 5, 81-138.

Mossman, J. (1995) *Wild Justice: a Study of Euripides' Hecuba*, Oxford: Oxford University Press.

Mueller, M. (1984) *The Iliad*, London and Boston: G. Allen and Unwin.

―――― (2001) 'The Language of Reciprocity in Euripides' *Medea*', *American Journal of Philology* 122, 471-504.

Bibliography

Muellner, L. (1996) *The Anger of Achilles*, Ithaca and London: Cornell University Press.

Munson, R. (1988) 'Artemisia in Herodotos', *Classical Antiquity* 7, 91-106.

Murray, G. (1960) *The Rise of the Greek Epic*, Oxford: Oxford University Press.

Murray, O. (1980) *Early Greece*, London: Fontana.

Mylonas, G. (1962) 'Burial Customs', in A.J.B. Wace and F.H. Stubbings (eds) *A Companion to Homer*, London: Macmillan.

Nagy, G. (1979) *The Best of the Achaeans*, Baltimore: John Hopkins University Press.

Nenci, G. (ed.) (1994) *Erodoto. Le Storie: Libro V, la rivolta della Ionia*, Milan: Arnoldo Mondadori editore.

Nieto Hernández, P. (2000) 'Back in the Cave of the Cyclops', *American Journal of Philology* 121, 345-66.

Oakley, J. and Sinos, R. (1993) *The Wedding in Ancient Athens*, Madison: University of Wisconsin Press.

Oatley, K. and Jenkins, J. (1996) *Understanding Emotions*, Cambridge, Mass.: Blackwell.

Ogden, D. (1996) *Greek Bastardy in the Classical and Hellenistic Periods*, Oxford: Clarendon Press.

——— (1997) 'Rape, Adultery and Protection of Bloodline in Classical Athens', in S. Deacy and K. Pierce (eds) *Rape in Antiquity*, London and Swansea: Duckworth with the Classical Press of Wales, 25-41.

Oldenquist, A. (1986) 'The Case for Revenge', *Public Interest* 82, 72-80.

Olson, S. (1990) 'The Stories of Agamemnon in Homer's *Odyssey*', *Transactions of the American Philological Association* 120, 57-72.

Omitowoju, R. (2002) *Rape and the Politics of Consent in Classical Athens*, Cambridge: Cambridge University Press.

Ormand, K. (1999) *Exchange and the Maiden: Marriage in Sophoclean Tragedy*, Austin: University of Texas Press.

Osborne, R. (1985) 'Law in Action in Classical Athens', *Journal of the Hellenic Society* 105, 40-58.

Ostwald, M. (1986) *From Popular Sovereignty to the Sovereignty of Law*, Berkeley: University of California Press.

Otterbein, K. and Otterbein, C. (1965) 'An Eye for an Eye, a Tooth for a Tooth: a Cross-Cultural Study of Feuding', *American Anthropologist* 67.2, 1470-82.

Padel, R. (1995) *Whom Gods Destroy: Elements of Greek and Tragic Madness*, Princeton: Princeton University Press.

Parker, R. (1983) *Miasma. Pollution and Purification in Early Greek Religion*, Oxford: Oxford University Press.

Parry, A. (1956) 'The Language of Achilles', *Transactions of the American Philological Association* 87, 1-7.

Pearson, L. (1957) 'Popular Ethics in the World of Thucydides', *Classical Philology* 52, 228-44.

Pedrick, V. (1983) 'The Paradigmatic Nature of Nestor's Speech in *Iliad* 11', *Transactions of the American Philological Association* 113, 55-68.

Peristiany, J. (ed.) (1965) *Honour and Shame: The Values of Mediterranean Society*, London: Weidenfeld and Nicolson.

Peters, E. (1967) 'Some Structural Aspects of the Feud Among the Camel-Herding Bedouin of Cyrenaica', *Africa* 37.3, 261-82.

Pomeroy, S. (1975) *Goddesses, Whores, Wives, and Slaves: Women in Classical Antiquity*, New York: Schocken Books.

—— (2002) *Spartan Women*, Oxford: Oxford University Press.

Porter, R. (1986) 'Rape – Does it have a Historical Meaning?' in S. Tomaselli and R. Porter (eds) *Rape*, Oxford: Blackwell.

Posner, R. (1979) 'The Homeric Version of the Minimal State', *Ethics* 90, 27-46.

Postlethwaite N. (1988) 'Thersites in the *Iliad*', *Greece & Rome* 35, 123-36.

Prevelakis, P. (1989) *Ο ήλιος του θανάτου*, 6th edn, Athens: Estias.

Rabben, L. (1998) *Unnatural Selection*, London: Pluto Press.

Rabinowitz, N. (1993) *Anxiety Veiled: Euripides and the Traffic in Women*, Ithaca: Cornell University Press.

Radin, M. (1927) 'Freedom of Speech in Ancient Athens', *American Journal of Philology* 48, 215-30.

Redfield, J. (1975) *Nature and Culture in the Iliad*, Chicago: University of Chicago Press.

Rhodes, P. (1998) 'Enmity in Fourth Century Athens', in P. Cartledge, P. Millett and S. von Reden (eds) *Kosmos*, Cambridge: Cambridge University Press, 94-161.

Robertson, M. (1959) *Greek Painting*, Geneva: Skira.

Roisman, J. (2005) *The Rhetoric of Manhood*, Berkeley: University of California Press.

Rose, G.P. (1979) 'Odysseus' Barking Heart', *Transactions of the American Philological Association* 109, 215-30.

Rose, H. (1941) 'Greek Rites of Stealing', *Harvard Theological Review* 34, 1-5.

—— (1954) 'Chthonian Cattle', *Numen* 1, 213-27.

Roy, J. (1997) 'An Alternative Sexual Morality for Athens', *Greece & Rome* 44, 11-22.

Sage, M. (1996) *Warfare in Ancient Greece. A Sourcebook*, London and New York: Routledge.

Saïd, S. (1984) 'La tragédie de la vengeance', in R. Verdier and J. Poly (eds) *La vengeance, études d'ethnologie, d'histoire et de philosophie,* vol. 4, Paris: Cujas, 47-90.

Sancisi-Weerdenburg, H. (1993) 'Exit Atossa: Images of Women in Greek Historiography on Persia', in A. Cameron and A. Kuhrt (eds) *Images of Women in Antiquity*, London and New York: Routledge, 20-33.

Sarna, N. (1986) *Exploring Exodus: the Heritage of Biblical Israel*, New York: Schocken Books.

Saunders, T. (1991) *Plato's Penal Code*, Oxford: Oxford University Press.

Schlunk, R. (1976) 'The Theme of the Suppliant-Exile in the *Iliad*', *American Journal of Philology* 97, 199-209.

Seaford, R. (1984) 'The Last Bath of Agamemnon', *Classical Quarterly* 34, 247-54.

—— (1989) 'Homeric and Tragic Sacrifice', *Transactions of the American Philological Association* 119, 87-95.

—— (1990) 'The Imprisonment of Women in Greek Tragedy', *Journal of the Hellenic Society* 110, 76-90.

—— (1994) *Reciprocity and Ritual: Homer and Tragedy in the Developing City-State*, Oxford: Oxford University Press.

—— (1998) 'Tragic Money', *Journal of the Hellenic Society* 118, 119-39.

—— (ed.) (1996) *Euripides: Bacchae*, Warminster: Aris and Phillips.

Segal, C. (1990) 'Violence and the Other: Greek, Female and Barbarian in Euripides' *Hecuba*', *Transactions of the American Philological Association* 120, 109-31.

161

Bibliography

———— (1994) *Singers, Heroes, and Gods in the Odyssey*, Ithaca and London: Cornell University Press.

Seremetakis, C.N. (1991) *'The Last Word' – Women, Death and Divination in Inner Mani*, Chicago: University of Chicago Press.

Shay, J. (1994) *Achilles in Vietnam*, New York, London, Toronto, Sydney: Scribner.

———— (2000) 'Killing Rage: *Physis* or *Nomos* – or Both?', in H. van Wees (ed.) *War and Violence in Ancient Greece*, London: Duckworth, 31-56.

———— (2002) *Odysseus in America*, New York, London, Toronto, Sydney: Scribner.

Shelmerdine S. (1986) 'Odyssean Allusions in the Fourth Homeric Hymn', *Transactions of the American Philological Association* 116, 49-63.

Sigmund, K. (1993) *Games of Life*, Oxford: Oxford University Press.

Snell, B. (1966) *Gesammelte Schriften*, Göttingen: Vandenhoeck und. Ruprecht.

Sommerstein, A. (1986) 'The Decree of Syrakosios', *Classical Quarterly* 36, 101-8.

———— (2006) 'Rape and Consent in Athenian Tragedy', in D. Cairns and V. Liapis (eds) *Dionysalexandros*, Swansea: Classical Press of Wales, 233-51.

———— (ed.) (1989) *Aeschylus' Eumenides: a Commentary*, Cambridge: Cambridge University Press.

Sprawski, S. (2006) 'Alexander of Pherae', in S. Lewis (ed.) *Ancient Tyranny*, Edinburgh: Edinburgh University Press, 135-50.

Stagakis, G. (1975) 'A Study in the Homeric Family: Brothers in the *Iliad* and the *Hetairos* Association', *Historia* 26, 65-93.

Storey, I. (1989) 'The "Blameless" Shield of Kleonymos', *Rheinisches Museum* 132, 247-61.

Strauss, B. (1993) *Fathers and Sons in Athens*, London and New York: Routledge.

Stroud, R. (1968) *Drakon's Law on Homicide*, Berkeley: University of California Press.

Svenbro, J. (1984) 'Vengeance et société en Grèce archaïque. A propos de la fin de l'Odyssée', in R. Verdier and J. Poly (eds) *La vengeance, études d'ethnologie, d'histoire et de philosophie,* vol. 3, Paris: Cujas, 47-64.

Thomson, G. (1941) *Aeschylus and Athens*, London: Lawrence and Wishart.

Thür, G. (1970) 'Zum *dikazein* bei Homer', *Zeitschrift der Savigny-Stiftung zür Rechtsgesichte* 87, 426-44.

Todd, S. (1993) *The Shape of Athenian Law*, Oxford: Oxford University Press.

———— (1998) 'The Rhetoric of Enmity in the Attic Orators', in P. Cartledge, P. Millett and S. von Reden (eds) *Kosmos*, Cambridge: Cambridge University Press, 162-9.

Treston, H. (1923) *Poine: a Study in Ancient Greek Blood-Vengeance*, London: Longmans, Green and Co.

Trevett, J. (1992) *Apollodoros Son of Pasion*, Oxford: Clarendon Press.

Trypanis, C. (1963) 'Brothers Fighting Together in the *Iliad*', *Rheinisches Museum* 106, 291-7.

Tulin, A. (1996) *Dike Phonou: the Right of Prosecution and Attic Homicide Procedure*, Stuttgart: B.G. Teubner.

Van de Mieroop, M. (2005) *King Hammurabi*, Oxford: Blackwell.

Van Hooff, A. (1990) *From Autothanasia to Suicide: Self-Killing in Antiquity*, London and New York: Routledge.

Van Wees (1992) *Status Warriors: War, Violence and Society in Homer and History*, Amsterdam: J.C. Gieben.

———— (1998) 'The Mafia of Early Greece', in K. Hopwood (ed.) *Organized Crime in Antiquity*, London: Duckworth with the Classical Press of Wales, 1-51.

Bibliography

Ventris, M. and Chadwick, J. (1956) *Documents in Mycenaean Greek*, London: Cambridge University Press.

Vickers, M. and Pettifer, J. (1997) *Albania: From Anarchy to a Balkan Identity*. Washington Square, NY: New York University Press.

Visser, M. (1984) 'Vengeance and Pollution in Classical Athens', *Journal of the History of Ideas* 45, 193-206.

—— (1986) 'Medea: Daughter, Sister, Wife and Mother', in M. Cropp, E. Fantham and S. Scully (eds) *Greek Tragedy and its Legacy*, Calgary: University of Calgary Press, 149-65.

Vlastos, G. (1991) *Socrates: Ironist and Moral Philosopher*, Cambridge: Cambridge University Press.

Walcot, P. (1979) 'Cattle Raiding, Heroic Tradition, and Ritual: the Greek Evidence', *History of Religions* 18, 326-51.

Walters, K. (1993) 'Women and Power in Classical Athens', in M. DeForest (ed.) *Woman's Power, Man's Game*, Wanconda, Ill.: Bolchazy-Carducci, 194-214.

Wassermann, F. (1956) 'Post-Periclean Democracy in Action: the Mytilenean Debate (Thuc. 3.37-48)', *Transactions of the American Philological Association* 87, 27-41

Webster, T. (1967) *The Tragedies of Euripides*, London: Methuen.

West, S. (1989) 'Laertes Revisited', *Proceedings of the Cambridge Philological Society* 35, 113-43.

Westbrook, R. (1992) 'The Trial Scene in the *Iliad*', *Harvard Studies in Classical Philology* 94, 53-76.

Westlake, H. (1968) *Individuals in Thucydides*, Cambridge: Cambridge University Press.

Whitaker, I. (1968) 'Tribal Structure and National Politics in Albania, 1910-1950', in I. Lewis (ed.) *History and Social Anthropology*, London: Tavistock Publications, 253-93.

—— (1976) 'Familial Roles in the Extended Patrilineal Kin-Group in Northern Albania', in J. Peristiany (ed.) *Mediterranean Family Structures*, Cambridge: Cambridge University Press, 195-204.

Wilkins, J. (ed.) (1993) *Euripides' Heraklidae*, Oxford: Oxford University Press.

Willcock, M. (1978) *The Iliad of Homer, Books I-XII*, Basingstoke: Macmillan Education Ltd.

Wilson, D. (2002) *Ransom, Revenge and Heroic Identity in the Iliad*, Cambridge: Cambridge University Press.

Wilson, P. (1991) 'Demosthenes 21 (*Against Meidias*): Democratic Abuse', *Proceedings of the Cambridge Philological Society* 37, 164-95.

Wilson, S. (1988) *Feuding, Conflict and Banditry in Nineteenth Century Corsica*, Cambridge: Cambridge University Press.

Winnington-Ingram, R. (1965) '*Ta deonta eipein*. Cleon's Speech in the Mytilene Debate. A Study of Thucydides 3.37-48', *Bulletin of the Institute of Classical Studies* 12, 70-82.

Wissmann, J. (1997) *Motivation und Schmähung: Feigheit in der Ilias und in der griechischen Tragödie*, Stuttgart: M&P Verlag für Wissenschaft und Forschung.

Wolff, H. (1946) 'The Origin of Judicial Litigation among the Greeks', *Traditio* 4, 31-87.

Wolfgang, M.E. (1958) *Patterns in Criminal Homicide*, Philadelphia, PA: University of Pennsylvania Press.

Bibliography

Yohannan, J.D. (1968) *Joseph and Potiphar's Wife in World Literature*, New York: New Directions Pub. Corp.

Zanker, G. (1992) 'Sophocles' *Ajax* and the Heroic Values of the *Iliad*', *Classical Quarterly* 42, 20-5.

Index Locorum

Index Locorum

94; 7.220: **94**; 7.231-2: **94**; 7.238:
34; 8.27.4-5: **81**; 8.88: **90**; 8.104-6:
43-4; 8.106.3: **43**; 8.121.1: **81**;
9.17.4: **94**; 9.64: **34**; 9.78: **34**; 9.79:
34; 9.80: **34**; 9.93.3: **133n.250**;
9.107: **91**; 9.108-13: **149n.40**;
9.120: **75**

HESIOD

Catalogus feminarum Fr. 212a
M-W: **30**

Scutum Herculis 15-22: **132-3n.236**;
79-82: **127n.63**

Theogonia 287-94: **68**; 603-7: **13**;
979-83: **68**

Opera et Dies 156-69: **144n.34**;
161-5: **139n.14**; 202-12: **145n.54**;
238-9: **4**; 376-9: **140n.43**

HOMER

Iliad 1.31: **59**; 1.112-15: **59**; 1.125-9:
141n.55; 1.152-6: **69**, **142n.89**;
1.174-8: **87**; 1.181-7: **139n.4**;
1.184-7: **87**; 1.188-92: **87**;
1.188-216: **123n.57**; 1.190: **35**;
1.193-218: **25**; 1.205: **87**;
1.213-14: **87**; 1.216-18: **25**;
1.225-32: **89**; 1.239-44: **130n.169**;
1.241-4: **88**; 1.244: **144n.26**;
1.268: **135n.44**; 1.300-3: **87**;
1.354: **144n.26**; 1.356: **144n.26**;
1.412: **144n.26**; 1.507: **144n.26**;
2.239-40: **89**; 2.354-6: **61**; 2.360-8:
28; 2.590: **60**; 2.594-600: **92**;
2.661-70: **18**, **127n.63**; 2.743-4:
135n.44; 3.10-11: **140n.27**;
3.298-301: **61**; 3.351-4: **60**;
4.25-54: **37-8**; 4.31-6: **38**;
4.370-418: **143n.6**; 4.387-98: **91**;
4.463-9: **79**; 4.532-5: **79**; 5.159-65:
82; 5.181-3: **82**; 5.260-73: **82**;
5.273: **80**, **82**; 5.297-8: **79**;
5.319-27: **82**; 5.385-91: **70**;
5.434-5: **80**; 5.480-5: **69**, **142n.89**;
5.485-6: **46**; 5.621-6: **79**; 5.638-42:
140n.23; 5.668-9: **79**; 5.842: **79**;
6.68-71: **79-80**; 6.119ff.: **29**;
6.157ff.: **49**; 6.332-40: **143n.7**;
6.424: **141n.55**; 7.81-90: **81**;
7.233-43: **90**; 8.13: **140n.39**;
8.105-8: **82**; 8.146-50: **90**; 8.163:
90; 8.191-7: **80-1**; 8.281-5: **60**;
9.286-9: **74**; 8.296ff.: **70**; 8.477-83:

140n.39; 9.110: **88**; 9.158-61: **89**;
9.323-5: **31**; 9.337-43: **59**;
9.369-72: **88**; 9.378-87: **88**;
9.410-16: **89**; 9.448-63: **57**;
9.453ff.: **133n.250**; 9.458-61: **17**;
9.464-77: **17**; 9.565-72: **126n.48**;
9.632-6: **19**; 9.648: **16**; 10.261-7:
140n.36; 10.321-7: **81**; 10.391-9:
81; 10.401: **81-2**; 10.420-2: **46**;
10.436-7: **81**; 10.438-41: **81**;
10.503-11: **81**; 10.544-52: **81**;
11.12-17: **142n.92**; 11.99-100: **79**;
11.110-11: **79**; 11.244-5: **73**;
11.246-7: **79**; 11.248-50: **28**;
11.257-8: **79**; 11.333-5: **80**;
11.373-8: **79**; 11.403-10: **90**;
11.426-45: **28**; 11.672-6: **68**;
11.674-6: **68**; 11.677-81: **68**;
11.685-705: **68**; 11.688-9: **68**;
11.690-3: **68**; 11.694-5: **68**;
11.698-700: **68**; 11.707-9: **68-9**;
11.714-17: **69**; 11.714-21: **24**;
11.717-21: **69**; 11.737-44: **69**, **81**;
11.758: **24**; 12.195: **80**; 12.310ff.:
89; 13.182-3: **80**; 13.188-94: **79**;
13.195-6: **79**; 13.197-202: **79**;
13.202-5: **142n.92**; 13.206-9: **28**;
13.255-65: **80**; 13.363-673: **25**;
13.363ff.: **74**; 13.394-401: **28**;
13.414-16: **26**; 13.445-9: **26**;
13.463-6: **28**, **29**; 13.509-11: **79**;
13.520ff.: **26**; 13.533-9: **28**;
13.560-3: **28**; 13.653-9: **28**;
13.660-72: **29**; 14.82-106: **143n.7**;
14.250-1: **140n.23**; 14.440-505:
25; 14.470-4: **26-7**; 14.479-83: **27**;
14.482-4: **28**; 14.496-507:
142n.92; 14.500-5: **27**; 15.64-8:
32; 15.113-18: **26**; 15.115-18: **24**;
15.121-4: **24**; 15.138: **24-5**;
15.431-9: **17**, **127n.64**; 15.439: **29**;
15.553-8: **28**; 15.560ff.: **89**;
16.317-29: **28**; 16.570-92: **27**;
16.571-4: **17**; 16.866-7: **81**; 17.1-8:
79; 17.12-17: **80**; 17.34-40: **80**,
142n.92; 17.34-50: **28**; 17.75-8:
81; 17.82-105: **79**; 17.90-105: **90**;
17.124-5: **142n.92**; 17.131: **80**;
17.198-208: **81**; 17.207: **32**;
17.538-9: **31**; 17.575-92: **29**;
17.710-11: **80**; 18.23-34: **30**, **62**;

168

General Index

abduction: 48, 59, 60-1, 62, 137n.105, 138n.108
accidents: 7, 10, 17, 29, 127n.79, 127n.83, 130n.151
Achilles: 16-19, 22, 25, 28, 29-35, 37, 38, 59-60, 62, 65, 69, 74, 80-2, 87-91, 97, 120, 130nn.162-3, 130n.167, 130n.169, 130n.172, 131n.198, 137n.94, 138n.112, 141n.65, 142n.101, 143n.112, 144n.28, 145n.56
acquisitiveness: 72
adultery: 45, 47n9, 54-6, 57-8, 60, 62-4, 103-7, 111, 128n.100, 135n.28, 136n.59, 137n.91
Aegisthus: 1, 4, 18, 48, 49-50, 103-11, 112, 135n.39, 142n.98, 145n.40
Aeneas: 28-30, 80, 82
Agamemnon: 4, 16, 18, 19, 21, 25, 28, 33-4, 35, 40-2, 48, 49-50, 59, 74, 87-9, 91, 103-8, 110-11, 120, 130-1n.182, 133n.239, 138n.112, 141n.65, 142n.98, 143nn.6-7, 145n.40, 145n.49, 148n.13, 148n.31
Agauë: 93, 127n.63
aggression: 7, 8, 68, 79, 92, 95, 99, 123n.62, 133n.237
agnatic kin: 11, 29-30, 71-2, 125n.24, 125n.27
Agoratus: 10, 12-13, 48
agriculture: 67, 146n.68
Ajax (son of Telamon): 17, 19, 26-7, 28, 29, 30, 60, 66, 79, 81, 82-4, 89, 92, 138n.111, 141n.70, 142n.101
Alcibiades: 60, 135n.33
Alcmena: 39, 41-2, 132-3nn.234-7
alcohol: *see* drunken brawls and insults
Alexander (I of Macedon, son of Amyntas): 20-1, 56-7
Alexander (of Pherae): 113-15, 149n.43
Alexandros: *see* Paris

Althaea: 39, 126n.48
amnesty against prosecution: 24
ancestors: 46, 61
ancestry: 26
Andromache: 28, 44, 60, 66
anger: 2-7, 11, 13, 22, 24-5, 28, 30, 32, 36, 46, 48, 51-2, 56, 59, 62, 71, 72, 82, 87-8, 91, 92, 95-6, 100, 106, 119, 122n.32, 129n.125, 132n.234, 134n.13, 144n.15, 145n.49, 146n.74; *see also* rage, wrath
anthropologists: 2, 6-7, 9, 11, 45, 46, 85, 120, 143n.8
Antigone: 101
Antilochus (son of Nestor): 28, 30, 143n.7
Antinous: 23, 50-2, 104-5, 106; *see also* suitors
Aphrodite: 49, 57, 58, 92-3, 141n.70
Apollo: 15, 22, 70-2, 81, 92, 93, 109-11, 148n.28
Apollodorus (orator): 78, 117, 150n.64
arbitrations: 72, 98, 124n.6
Areopagus: 54, 128n.91, 129n.127, 136n.60
Ares: 24-5, 26, 54, 58, 79, 129n.125, 141n.70
armour: 28, 30, 31, 34, 65, 79-82, 130n.167-8, 142n.92, 142n.100
Artemis: 92-3, 145n.49
Artemisia: 90
assault: 77-8, 96, 97, 124n.11
Astyages: 115-16
Astyanax: 28, 66
Athena: 22-5, 35-6, 69, 83, 87, 91, 92, 104, 107, 110, 117, 127n.64, 145n.49, 149n.57, 149-50n.62
athletics: 17, 70, 74, 85, 91-2, 127n.79, 132n.216, 139n.21, 143n.2, 146n.72
atimia: 94, 98, 127n.70; *see also* dishonour
Atreus: 30, 105-6, 111, 127n.63

174